THE PRIESTHOOD OF ALL BELIEVERS

THE PRIESTHOOD
OF ALL BELIEVERS

An Examination of the Doctrine
from the Reformation to the Present Day

by

CYRIL EASTWOOD

WIPF & STOCK · Eugene, Oregon

Wipf and Stock Publishers
199 W 8th Ave, Suite 3
Eugene, OR 97401

The Priesthood of All Believers
An Examination of the Doctrine from the Reformation to the Present Day
By Eastwood, Cyril
Copyright©1960 Epworth Press
ISBN 13: 978-1-60608-730-5
Publication date 5/7/2009
Previously published by Epworth Press, 1960

Copyright © Epworth Press 1962
First English edition1962 by Epworth Press
This edition published by arrangement with Epworth Press

To

VINCENT TAYLOR
HAROLD ROBERTS
NORMAN H. SNAITH
and the late
HOWARD WATKIN-JONES

Contents

	INTRODUCTION	ix
1	MARTIN LUTHER	1

The doctrine of the Priesthood of all Believers is the basic doctrine which underlies Luther's teaching on the seven outward 'marks' of the true Church.—(1) The Preaching of the Word. (2) The Sacrament of Baptism. (3) The Sacrament of the Lord's Supper. (4) The Keys of Christian Discipline and Forgiveness. (5) A called and consecrated Christian Ministry. (6) Public worship, with prayer, praise, and thanksgiving. (7) The Holy Cross.

2	JOHN CALVIN	66

(1) The Threefold Office of Christ. (2) The Priesthood of Christ and Dependent Universal Priesthood. (3) Priesthood and Vocation. (4) The Power of the Keys. (5) Priesthood and Ministry. (6) Ministry and Succession. (7) Ministry and Ordination. (8) Priesthood and Spiritual Sacrifices.

3	ANGLICANISM	91

(1) Justification by Faith: Rome; Bucer; Cranmer. (2) The English Bible. (3) The Book of Common Prayer. (4) Cranmer's Interpretation of The Eucharist. (5) The mediation of Christ's justifying activity. (6) Cranmer's Interpretation of Ordination. (7) Hooker's Interpretation of Gospel Priesthood. (8) The Church as a succession of believers. (9) The Anglican Evangelicals (Theology). (10) The Anglican Evangelicals (Ecclesiology).

4	THE PURITAN TRADITION	130

(1) Beginnings. (2) Thomas Cartwright: (i) Spiritual Priesthood; (ii) Spiritual Priesthood based on the Priesthood of Christ; (iii) The Meaning of Sacerdos; (iv) Priesthood and Election; (v) Priesthood and the Marks of the True Church; (vi) Universal Priesthood as the basis of Cartwright's propositions for Reform. (3) Robert Browne. (4) John Owen. (5) Puritan Principles. (6) Developments in the Baptist Church. (7) Developments in the Congregational Church. (8) Developments in the Society of Friends.

5	METHODISM	183

(a) The Theology of Experience. (b) The Priesthood of all Believers: (1) Faith as the Christian's Priestly Office. (2) Christ as the great High Priest. (3) Succession as the Christian's Priestly Heritage. (4) Prayer as the Christian's Priestly Privilege. (5) Ministry as the Christian's Priestly Service. (6) Mission as the Christian's Priestly Obligation. (7) Praise as the Christian's Priestly Offering. (8) Experience as the Christian's Priestly Authority. (c) Servants of Mankind: In the Service of the Word; In the Service of the Church; In the Service of the World.

6	CONCLUSIONS AND REINTERPRETATION	238

(1) No single Church has been able to express in its worship, work, and witness, the full richness of this doctrine. (2) It has been a living

issue in each century since the Reformation. (3) It is a unitive, positive, and comprehensive principle which springs directly from the Evangelical concept of 'free grace'. (4) The doctrine affirms that the divine Revelation is more important than the means which God uses to mediate it. (5) It is an assertion that God's justifying activity is proclaimed in the lives of all believers. (6) It is intrinsically related to the High Priesthood of Christ. (7) The doctrine is significant for an understanding of the word 'ministry'. (8) It is significant for current Ecumenical studies. (9) The truths inherent in the doctrine should be incorporated in the worshipping life of the Church. (10) It anticipates the full participation of all Christians in the evangelistic action of the Church. (11) It leads to a fuller understanding of the doctrine of divine vocation. (12) The Eschatological significance of the doctrine.

BIBLIOGRAPHY	259
INDEX OF SUBJECTS	264
INDEX OF NAMES	266

Introduction

THERE IS both need and room for a thorough examination of the basis, meaning and development of the doctrine of the Priesthood of all Believers. It is time that the doctrine was taken out of the slogan category and set in its true context as an essential and determinative element in the theology of the Church.

The Old Testament presents us with three important patterns of thought: the People of God, the Servant of the Lord, and a Kingdom of Priests. The People of God are called and chosen by God Himself, and they are called to a priesthood of which sacrificial service is the characteristic feature. In the final consummation they, together with all peoples, will be presented before God as a Kingdom of Priests. Biblical evidence, therefore, shows that the doctrine of the universal priesthood is closely related to Election, Christology, and Eschatology, and that it can be properly interpreted only in the light of these doctrines. The three patterns of thought mentioned above reappear in the New Testament under new names and in more clearly defined terms: the People of God become the New Israel, the Servant of the Lord is the High Priest of our Confession, and the Kingdom of Priests comprises all believers who, through the mediation of Christ, are now kings and priests unto God.

The revelation to Israel was a revelation of grace. This revelation was made to Israel as a people and was sealed by the Covenant. There were perils in these privileges. There was the danger of confusing the means of revelation with the Revelation itself. There was also the danger of interpreting their election as an exclusive privilege, and of seeking to seal the Covenant by means which God would not own. Israel succumbed to all three dangers. Too soon they forgot that God had created a people out of no people, that their election was of grace and not through any merit of their own, and that this election involved them in a universal mission.

This mission and the nature of its fulfilment were steadily held before their eyes in the figure of the Servant of the Lord whose character and vocation are clearly bound up with his covenant responsibility. He bears the sins of many, for his mission is as wide as the world. All the idealistic, corporate and individual ideas concerning the Servant converge in the Lord Jesus who is the elect, lowly, suffering Servant, committed to an awful task, out of which He brings, as only He can bring, victory and hope to all mankind.

All this might have been fully understood by the Jews had they grasped the significance of three aspects of Old Testament teaching: the vital connexion between the Servant and the Covenant, the meaning of Jeremiah's inward Covenant, and the importance of the true function of the priesthood. Originally the priests were servants of the Word of God (Ex 4^{15-16}); servants of the Law of God (Mic 3^{11}); and servants of the Will of God (Deut 33^8). Their work was connected solely with proclamation, interpretation, and discernment. The transition from the didactic to the sacerdotal work of the priest was due to various reasons. Permanent shrines which did not exist in nomadic days were established in Canaan, and shrines require priests. Further, with the rise of the written tradition the work of teaching and interpretation was undertaken by the scribes and the work of the priest became more and more connected with sacrifice.

A loftier conception of the holiness of God together with a deeper consciousness of their sin resulted in the conception of the priest as an intermediary between men and God. His function had completely changed; he had become the mediator between the people and their God.

All such notions are abolished by the Incarnation. The word 'priest' and 'priesthood' are never applied in the New Testament to the office of the Ministry. Even in the extensive list of Church officers and activities in 1 Cor 12^{28-30} and Eph 4^{11-12} there is no mention of priests. In fact, there are but two forms of priesthood in the New Testament—the Priesthood of Christ (Heb 6^{20} and 7^{26-7}) and the Priesthood of all Believers (1 Pet 2^9 and Rev 5^{10}).

The New Testament takes up the ideal attributes of the People of God and applies them to the Church (Gal 6^{16}, Rev 1^6, Rom 9^{27-8}, 1 Cor 1^2, and 2 Cor 1^{20}). From these passages some important truths emerge: An entirely new relationship, based on the New Covenant, is claimed for the Church of God. Further, the Church as a whole undergoes a corporate experience whereby she emerges as a kingdom of priests—a new and redeemed community. Consequently the Church can no longer be regarded as an exclusive body, but as truly 'Catholic', for it is precisely the idea of the Church as a universal priesthood which distinguishes it from the priesthood of the People of God in the old dispensation. The corporate and universal significance of the Church is only fully appreciated in the person of the High Priest of the new dispensation.

Universal Priesthood is inseparable from the idea of sacrifice (Rev 5^{9-10}, 1 Pet 2^5, Rom 11^{30-3}, 12^1, Heb 7^{27}, 9^{14}, 13^{15}). The Sacrifice of Christ and the Priesthood of all Believers are combined for ever in the mystery of Holy Communion. At the same time there must be a time of initiation into the priestly community, and the teaching of the New Testament is that Baptism which symbolizes the death of sin and the life-dedication of the believer, inaugurates for believers the priestly office (Heb 10^{22}, Tit 3^{4-7}, John 3^5, Eph 5^{26-7}). Closely linked with the idea of sacrifice it follows that the universal priesthood can only be understood in terms of sacrificial service. The character, service and mission of the Church are only properly seen in the light of her Lord's. Christ is God's chosen Servant (Isa 42^{1-3}, Matt 12^{17-19}, Luke 22^{27}), who humbled Himself (Phil 2^{6-8}), and was made like unto His brethren (Heb 2^{16-17}). He is the Suffering Servant (Heb 5^8) and the High Priest of our Confession (Heb 3^1). Yet victory is the ultimate outcome of His work for men (Heb 1^8, 4^{14}), and in this victory all believers share (Eph 4^7), as indeed they receive His power and reign with Him as priests (Rev 20^6). Thus our Lord creates a New Community, becomes the High Priest of a new priesthood which is born of the Spirit, bound by an eternal Covenant, and committed to a universal task. Its task knows no end; only the Church victorious can be the Church at rest. By consecration and worship, service and mission, their priesthood is revealed. For in their lives they show forth His death, in their words they show forth His Gospel, and in their death they show forth His victory. In so far as they participate through faith in His Sacrifice and Service and Sovereignty they share the priesthood which is His and theirs till the end of time.

In the writings of the Early Fathers the doctrine of the universal priesthood has a central place. It is directly connected with the High Priesthood of Christ (Polycarp and Origen); with the layman's ordinances (Clement of Rome); with the Eucharist

(Clement of Rome and Justin Martyr); with the unity of the Church (Clement of Alexandria); with questions of Church discipline (Tertullian); with free access to the presence of the Father (Origen); with the Church's missionary task (Polycarp and Origen); with the conception of the Church as a High Priestly Race, and with the offering of spiritual sacrifices. The last two are mentioned in the writings of all the Fathers. The significance of this lies in the fact that the transition which took place under Cyprian was directly connected with these two ideas. As a difference in the idea of priesthood emerged, so also a difference in the idea of sacrifice followed. A new note was sounded by Cyprian, it was the authority of the priest. So the High Priestly Race gave place to a High Priestly Class, and the spiritual sacrifices gave place to a priestly sacrifice offered to God in the Eucharist. All authority was given unto the Bishop who unquestionably controlled the Church's teaching, worship, discipline, and ministry, and in an ill-defined and mystical sense he controlled also that most sacred treasure of Gospel—the offer of divine grace. This sort of teaching persisted in the Church without any serious and decisive opposition until the appearance of Martin Luther in the sixteenth century. It is of the Reformation under Luther and his contemporaries and of those who succeeded them in the Evangelical Tradition that the following pages will tell.

I

Martin Luther

LUTHER'S CONCEPTION OF THE CHURCH

LUTHER states that there are seven outward marks by which the true Church may be known. These are:

(1) The Preaching of the Word.
(2) The Sacrament of Baptism.
(3) The Sacrament of the Lord's Supper.
(4) The Keys of Christian Discipline and Forgiveness.
(5) A called and consecrated Christian Ministry.
(6) Public Worship, with prayer, praise and thanksgiving.
(7) The Holy Cross: i.e. suffering in many forms through which the Church must inevitably pass.

In considering Luther's doctrine of the Church we shall adopt the headings which he himself suggested. We begin with the important question: Is there any single basic truth which underlies Luther's teaching on the outward marks of the true Church?

1. THE PREACHING OF THE WORD

Article VII of the Augsburg Confession of 1530 contains a definition of the Church the substance of which was adopted by most of the Protestant Confessions of the sixteenth and seventeenth centuries, including the Articles of the Church of England and the Confessions of the Free Churches: 'The Church is the congregation of the saints, in which the Gospel is rightly taught and the Sacraments rightly administered. And for the true unity of the Church it is sufficient to agree about the teaching of the Gospel and the administration of the Sacraments, nor is it necessary to have everywhere like human traditions, whether rites or ceremonies instituted by man.'[1]

Luther proclaimed it 'for certain, and firmly established that

[1] Kidd, *Documents of the Continental Reformation*, p. 264.

the soul can do without everything except the Word of God'. This implies that the Church is inextricably related to the Gospel and the Sacraments and cannot exist without them. It means that the Word is constitutive of the Church. In what sense does the Word create the Church? Bishop Newbigin considers that this view has been accepted too easily in Protestantism and that some of its implications have been overlooked. He points out, for instance, that in the Amsterdam volume on the doctrine of the Church, Karl Barth commences every key paragraph with the phrase: 'The congregation (*ecclesia*) is an event (*Ereignis*)', and the Bishop makes the following comment upon it: 'The immediate relation of the Church in every moment of its being to its living Lord could not be more powerfully expressed. But there seems to be no place in the picture for a continuing historical institution, nor for any organic relation between congregations in different places and times. In so far as the Church possesses the character of a continuing institution it seems, on this view, to have fallen away from its proper centre. The eschatological has completely pushed out the historical.'[2] What does the phrase 'the Church is an event' mean? Professor Schlink elucidates Dr Barth's point: 'Thus the Church is constituted by the event (*Ereignis*), of the preaching of the Gospel and the administering of the Sacraments, and so by Christ Himself acting through and present in Gospel and Sacraments.'[3] Bishop Newbigin maintains that this view has led to two distortions in Protestant teaching, namely, to an over-intellectualizing of the content of the word 'faith', which in turn has resulted in the setting of Word and Sacraments in isolation over against the continuing life of the fellowship; and secondly, it has led to the virtual disappearance of the idea of the Church as a visible fellowship. The proclamation of correct doctrine does not of itself constitute the Church. Such proclamation presupposes a believing congregation, and if a response in faith is lacking, the Church does not exist. But the response of a believing people is impossible apart from the working of the Holy Spirit. It follows that at least two other factors are required in order to constitute a congregation, in addition to the proclaimed Word; these are—the working of the Holy Spirit and the awakening of faith in the believer. All three factors have been operative in many places and in many generations.

[2] Newbigin, *The Household of God*, p. 50.
[3] *The Nature of the Church*, p. 61, ed. R. N. Flew.

These truths are not absent in Luther's teaching. We shall inquire then what Luther says on the content of the word 'faith' and on the idea of the Church as a visible unity. We shall observe, in the first place, that the clauses in Article VII leave no doubt that the Reformers believed that the Gospel and Sacraments were operative *in* the congregation of believers and not apart from it.

(*a*) Gospel and Sacraments are *in* the congregation of believers the means by which the Holy Spirit arouses faith, effects the assembling of believers.[4]

(*b*) Gospel and Sacraments are *in* the congregation of believers the service imposed upon it and discharged by it. The Church is 'the mother who conceives and bears individual Christians through the Word of God'.[5]

It is the mission of the Christian ministry, in its administration of the Word and Sacraments, to convey this Gospel to every soul, and to arouse a corresponding faith. If this faith is not aroused, we cannot be incorporated in Christ and we can have no part in the congregation of believers. The Church is being created by the preaching of the Gospel, but even this presupposes the response of faith. In fact, the Church equals justification by faith in action. Faith does not exist in itself. It means listening to a Gospel which is preached and receiving Sacraments which are given. In Luther's view faith never exists alone. The exterior Word must always be there and the Holy Spirit is active through the proclamation of the Gospel. Not only is the fellowship of believers dependent upon the proclaimed Word; it is the result of it. Since the fellowship of believers cannot exist without the exterior Word, it follows that it does not exist apart from the Ministry. The Ministry is not placed, however, above the Church, but *in* the Church. According to the Episcopal view the Ministry is placed above the Church. In Luther's view the Ministry is placed in the congregation. This involves a different conception of grace from that which is held by those who accept the Episcopal view. For Luther, grace is God's favour expressed in the Gospel. Where there is faith in the Gospel, there is a listening congregation. Faith and Gospel are like two hands being shaken. The Church suffers whenever they are separated.

According to the Roman view, however, grace is not the favour of God expressed in the Gospel, but supernatural power in the

[4] Ibid. p. 59.   [5] *Greater Catechism*, II.42.

Sacraments and this has no relation to faith. Such supernatural power does not require faith to make it effective, it operates by the intrinsic authority which it is supposed to possess. Now when grace is thought of as a supernatural transforming power, it is necessary to believe in a hierarchy which possesses this authority and power. The reason for this is not difficult to find. Authority cannot be mediated through the congregation because the congregation has not got it. The Roman view is that it was given to St Peter only. We are faced, then, with two widely divergent views:

1. The Roman view which places the Hierarchy *above* the congregation and regards it as a special state or caste.

2. The Lutheran view which sets the Ministry *in* the congregation and maintains that it may adequately fulfil its function there.

The Gospel is the gracious will of God in relation to man. It is the task of the Ministry to make that gracious will known by proclaiming it. It does this not outside the congregation but within it, and in this way the Gospel is mediated through the congregation. So the Ministry becomes a function of the priesthood of all believers and not a hierarchical caste.

If this is true, the statement that the Reformers' doctrine of the Church 'resulted in the virtual disappearance of the Church as a visible unity' needs some modification.

'Invisible Church'

The problem centres on the interpretation of the term 'invisible'.[6] 'Yet by substituting at this crucial point for the true and biblical dialectic of holy and sinful, a false and unbiblical dialectic of outward and inward, visible and invisible, Luther himself helped profoundly to confuse the issue at the Reformation.' Again, in the American Theological Committee's Report on the Nature of the Church (1945), it is explained that the Anglicans regard the Church as 'a visible society with institutionalized officers, regulations and powers'. The report goes on to say: 'It is for this reason that among Anglicans, the term invisible Church seems quite meaningless.' The New Testament injunction to 'tell it to the Church' seemed void of meaning if the Church were invisible.

This problem dates back to the time of Augustine whose double interpretation of the Church resulted in complete confusion. Augustine held that the Church as the sphere of salvation and

---

[6] Newbigin, *The Household of God*, pp. 54, 56.

authority was the sole agent of grace. Alongside this view he also held that the Church is the elect who have not obtained their election through the Church but directly by grace, and these may not be identified with the visible society. Augustine was faced with a titanic problem in dealing with the Donatists who had been baptized by heretics, but to effect a congenial arrangement by expelling the Donatists from the visible Church and then to create an invisible Church to include them again was a high price to pay, and Augustine's solution created a much bigger problem than the one he sought to solve. The Church was left to make the best of this complicated issue and the result was that Rome has since held the view that there are many members who are not of the 'body' of the Church because of various impediments, but they may still be of the 'soul' of the Church on the ground of election.

Professor Henderson thinks that the Calvinistic solution is the right and final one: 'All that is meant by the Church "invisible" is "God's Elect", and that is sufficiently scriptural, and neither abstract nor imaginary.'[7] This solution, however, will not suffice because it is no more than a reassertion of Augustine's second interpretation, which, if taken alone, leaves no room for the idea of a visible community.

Luther was not happy about the term 'invisible'. 'When I have called the Church a spiritual assembly, you have insultingly taken me to mean that I would build a Church as Plato builds a state that never was.'[8] An *ecclesia abscondita* cannot be demonstrated. The fact that the saints are invisible does not mean that they are not in the world but that their holiness is not to be seen in themselves. The moment their holiness is attributed to themselves they are the false Church. This does not mean that they cannot visibly be called to serve or to suffer. The Church is visible in its functions—in its ministry and sacraments; it is invisible in the sense that the essence of the Church (holiness) is never contemplated in believers but in Christ. It is not something to be seen, but to be heard in the Word proclaimed to faith. While the Fellowship of believers is real, it is none the less hidden in the world. The Church that is hidden (*abscondita*) is not the same as the Church 'invisible'. It means a real presence with a

---

[7] G. D. Henderson, *The Church and Ministry*, p. 76.
[8] Quoted in Gordon Rupp, *The Righteousness of God*, p. 317.

veil surrounding it. The true Church is present and active in the world, but a veil surrounds it, and this veil is pierced only through faith. Faith recognizes the Church as the fellowship of true believers. It will be seen that Luther's emphasis upon the hidden Church in no way precludes the belief in a visible fellowship of believers. Luther's words on this point are emphatic: 'I believe that here below and throughout the world, there is only one Christian Church, the Church universal, and that this Church is identical with the universal fellowship of the saints, i.e. the devout believers everywhere on earth. This Church is gathered, sustained and ruled by the Holy Spirit . . . and strengthened day by day through the sacraments and the Word of God.'[9] Professor Skydsgaard is speaking for the Lutheran Church when he says: 'The predominating concept is that of the Congregation or People (*congregatio sanctorum seu fidelium*). Here the chief stress falls. It is therefore consistent with this that our Churches attach great significance to the priesthood of all believers; and the practical consequence of this is that the laity play a very real part in our Church life.'[10]

It is essential to understand the way in which Luther relates the ministry of the Word to the priesthood of all believers, since this will show us how firmly Luther believed in the visible community of Christians—the Congregation of the Faithful. 'Therefore everyone who knows that he is a Christian should be fully assured that all of us alike are priests, and that we all have the same authority in regard to the Word and the Sacraments, although no one has the right to administer them without the consent of the members of his Church, and the call of the majority.'[11] Immediately after this Luther says: 'The priesthood is simply the ministry of the Word.' This being the case, all possess the same authority though all are not called to exercise it. The fact that this was a common authority rather than a specially endowed authority helped to bring about the unity of believers.

To speak of unity in connexion with a man whose name is associated with the most conspicuous disruption in the history of the Church may seem ironical, but it must be made clear that Luther's main concern was the strengthening not the weakening

---

[9] Lee Woolf, *Reformation Writings of Martin Luther*, I.87.
[10] *The Nature of the Church*, ed. R. N. Flew, p. 83.
[11] *Reformation Writings*, I.318.

of the fellowship of believers. He was opposed to those who weakened its message and challenged the authority of Christ. Rome was not ready to face the possibility of drastic reform. Even so, the fact that Rome could not afford to delay the day of reckoning much longer is proved by the reforms which took place at Trent in 1546. Luther proclaimed the *una sancta* and he believed that to this one Church belonged the saints of all ages. Not only through the Church, but *principally* through it, God was governing the world. The proclamation of the Gospel was always an assertion of this fact. It is in this sense that the *Regnum Christi* is set forth and extended upon earth till the end of time. This was not something to be established by man; it was a fact, a divine fact. To this extent the conception of the preaching of the Gospel as an 'event' is appropriate, since it is not a hope or an aspiration but something which is taking place every moment. The Gospel rightly preached and the sacraments rightly administered effect a twofold unity. They unite the believer with his Lord, and they unite priesthood and laity.

(a) *The Unity of the Believer with his Lord*
Such a possibility of unity at the personal level had been seriously assailed in the process of ecclesiastical development. Professor Brunner points to the impasse which has been reached by the Church's misunderstanding of its task: 'Now it is the person of the priest-bishop, who, as authoritative vicar of Jesus Christ Himself, can distribute the salvation of Christ and claim for himself the obedience which believers owe to their Lord. The episcopal administration of a sacramental grace places the Christian community in the position of a receiving laity; episcopal apostolic authority makes of them subjects who owe obedience. Only through this twofold dependence upon the Church ruled by bishops and priests can the individual attain salvation. Out of the "mystical" brotherhood rooted in the Word and the Spirit, out of the Body of Christ whose Head is Christ Himself above, and whose members, therefore, are of equal status, out of the royal priesthood and holy nation has grown the Church—a totality composed of individual communities, each of which comes under the ecclesiastical jurisdiction of a bishop, who as administering priest stands opposed to the receiving laity because he controls the Sacrament, the food of salvation, the sacral thing

which holds together the individual components and makes them into a solidary collective.'[12]

This impressive statement by Brunner spotlights the problem: in the light of the conception of the Church as an institution, what is the believer's relationship with Christ?

This relationship is firmly based on faith. This is the believer's standing ground before God. How is God presented to our faith? The answer is: in Jesus Christ. But how is it possible to be sure of His living presence today? The Christian affirms that He is present with us in the Word and Sacraments of the Gospel. In the Word of the Gospel, Christ Himself is present in His saving power, to evoke faith, to reconcile sinful man with the holy God, and to build up the Church which is His Body by drawing all men to Himself. 'Wherever', says Luther, 'you see this Word preached, believed, confessed, and acted on, there do not doubt that there must be a true *ecclesia sancta catholica* . . . , for God's Word does not go empty away.'[13]

By these words Luther brought into question the whole structure of institutionalism. It does not matter who preaches and who gives the Sacraments, nor do they require the authority of the Pope, for the Word and the Sacraments are God's, not man's. By these God does His work. But it must not be thought that it is merely the formal proclamation of the Word or the enactment of the sacramental ritual which effects the salvation of the soul, for these are empty and void unless they are vehicles of the Holy Spirit. It is for this reason that Luther held the view that the authority of the Word, and the testimony of witnesses, are *in vacuo* until and unless they are accepted in faith and confirmed in experience by the Holy Spirit. The common notion[14] that Luther failed to hold the proper balance between the Word and the Spirit becomes strange in the light of his teaching. Indeed, it is only when Word and Sacraments are accepted in faith and become operative and effective in the life of the individual through the Spirit, that salvation is possible. It is also equally true that the Word of God is not operative unto salvation until accepted in faith and experience.

Perhaps we shall understand this more clearly if it is seen

---

[12] *The Misunderstanding of the Church*, p. 83.
[13] *On the Council and the Churches*, ed. Holman, V.271.
[14] See G. D. Henderson, *The Church and Ministry*, p. 40.

against the background of the Roman position at the Council of Trent. Justification is there regarded as a translation from the *standing* of sinful Adam into the standing of grace and adoption, and is effected by Baptism or the will to receive it. But later, the thought of translation becomes uncertain. It is claimed that the beginning of justification is wrought by prevenient grace (by which adults are called in the absence of any merit of their own). But its contemplated end is 'that those who have been alienated from God by their sins, *may be disposed* by His *inciting* and *aiding* grace, to convert themselves in order to gain their own justification, by their freely assenting to and co-operating with, the same grace'. The extent to which the Tridentine theologians completely misunderstood the Lutheran position is shown not only by the above Pelagian phrases, but by the fact that they were able to explain justification without any reference either to faith or the Holy Spirit.

Romanism and Lutheranism are agreed that the believer may be united with his Lord, but they are not agreed upon the manner in which this is brought about. Luther's position is that the unity of the believer with Christ is not the outcome of knowledge or learning or good works or religious ceremonial, but only through the faith which throws itself entirely upon the mercy of God. It seemed to Luther that a massive barrier made up of Church, Priesthood and Sacraments, had been raised up between the believer and Christ. This was bewildering to Luther who thought that the Priest should ensure the freedom of the believer and not his bondage. He describes this unity in moving words: 'Faith not only gives the soul enough for her to become, like the divine Word, gracious, free, and blessed. It also unites the soul with Christ, like a bride with the bridegroom, and, from this marriage, Christ and the soul become one Body, as St Paul says (Eph 5^{30}). Then the possessions of both are in common, whether fortune, misfortune, or anything else; so that what Christ has, also belongs to the believing soul, and what the soul has, will belong to Christ.'[15] Faith receives all. Christ gives everything for everything. 'All things are yours' takes on a new meaning. Luther returns to the idea that Christ shares all He possesses with all Christians: 'Since Christ has the primogeniture with all appropriate honour and worth, He shares it with all Christians who are His, that, through

---

[15] *Reformation Writings*, I.363.

faith, all may be kings and priests with Christ, as St Peter says in 1 Peter 2: "You are a priestly kingdom and a royal priesthood." The result is that a Christian is lifted up by faith so high above all things that he becomes the spiritual lord of all, for nothing can hinder his salvation.'[16] Luther longed for a relationship with Christ which could not be assailed by many hindrances. He thus proclaims with great vigour that every circumstance is made to serve God's end in the life of the Christian. Even death and suffering may be of service to salvation. 'Nothing is so good or so evil but that it must serve me for good, if I have faith. Indeed I need none of these (material) things. My faith is sufficient for me. How precious then is the freedom and potency which Christians possess!'[17]

This was no mere academic conclusion; it was a judgement of faith; moreover, it was Luther's personal history. Luther did not commence his work by searching the Scriptures to find a suitable weapon which he might wield against the Roman hierarchy. The Word came to his heart, and he believed. Restlessly, he searched for an answer to his problem. The answer was revealed to him: 'The just shall live by faith.' Instantly he saw the implication of this—God is a *gracious* God. With this overwhelming, comprehensive truth, Luther shook the whole religious system of his day.

Pope, priest, penance, indulgences, and good works had failed to help Luther in his attempts to find access into the immediate presence of the forgiving God. External aids having failed, Luther had to rely solely upon personal faith in a loving God. Thus the Reformation took its rise not primarily from criticism of the Roman system but from the enlightenment in the soul of a seeker. Luther had used *every* means provided by the penitential system of his Church. In all things he had submitted to the orders of his superiors. In obedience to the demands of his Church he was well-nigh without fault. He underwent every part of the complex system of expiations, and made full use of the Sacraments. At the Erfurt Convent which he entered in 1505, he was advised not to read the Bible: 'Brother Martin, leave the Bible alone and study the old teachers.' In addition, he was told that every man must work out his own salvation by strict asceticism, fastings and scourgings. Despite all this well-meant advice,

---

[16] *Reformation Writings*, I.365.   [17] Ibid. p. 366.

Luther knew that, as far as he was concerned, the appointed systems were of no avail. 'Though I listened to this glowing language about myself and allowed myself to be described as a wonder-worker who could make himself holy in such an easy way, yet I found neither Baptism nor monkery could assist me.' The attempt to live a consistently good life by human resources alone made such heavy demands upon him that the attempt could not possibly be sustained. 'When an awakened soul seeks to find rest in works-righteousness, it stands on a foundation of loose sand which it feels running and travelling beneath it, and it must go on from one good work to another, and so on without end.'[18]

The Monastery did not solve Luther's problem, neither did his pilgrimage to Rome. What tortured the great African, Augustine, tortured Luther also—the unbearable thought of permanent alienation from the God of love. In the case of Luther, however, Staupitz saw the real difficulty. He pointed out to Luther that he had been right enough in contrasting man's sin and God's holiness, but he had been wrong when he had kept these two thoughts permanently in opposition. Staupitz explained that God's righteousness might become man's in and through Christ. This brought Luther to the verge of his great discovery. He had sought help from others. He had been obedient to his superiors. He had tried by every means to help himself. But since *no* help was to be found in man, his soul was forced to find all in God.

Out of this experience arises his definition of the Christian religion. 'The Christian Religion is the living assurance of the living God who has revealed Himself and opened His heart in Christ—nothing more.'[19] This, in fact, was all Luther needed to know. Before, he was not permitted to come too near; now he could not get near enough. His new conception of the character of God has altered his whole conception of religion.

Unfortunately for his Mother Church, and fortunately for the whole of Protestantism, he began to ask some important questions. Whose responsibility was it to show him the way of salvation? Whose duty was it to unfold the true meaning of Scripture to a seeker? Whose duty was it to point another to the only Source of all grace and love? The logical answer was that these were the duties of the priests. If in this they had failed him, where had they

---

[18] T. M. Lindsay, *History of the Reformation*, I.201.
[19] A. Harnack, *The History of Dogma*, VII.183.

succeeded? Yet they were the chosen custodians of divine authority. They were the appointed channels of divine grace. The disturbing thought now occurred to Luther that it was because authority and Scripture and grace were securely enshrined in the very office of the priesthood and jealously guarded by the priests that Luther for so long had been deprived of personal and eternal salvation. Could it be that the ecclesiastical system especially appointed to offer grace to men had become the very means whereby they were deprived of it? To this crucial question there was but one answer, and it was inescapable. His answer to it is no less than a statement upon the meaning of priesthood in relation to all believers.

(b) The unity of priesthood and laity
1. All believers share a common dignity. It cannot be said that some Christians belong to a religious class and others do not. The honour and dignity conferred by Christ upon one are also conferred upon all. 'For all Christians whatsoever really and truly belong to the religious class, and there is no difference among them except in so far as they do different work. That is St Paul's meaning in 1 Corinthians 12, when he says, "We are all one body, yet each member hath his own work for serving others". This applies to us all, because we have one Baptism, one Gospel, one faith, and are all equally Christian. For Baptism, Gospel, and faith alone make men religious, and create a Christian people. . . . The fact is that our Baptism consecrates us all without exception, and makes us all priests.'[20] All believers share this high dignity whatever their daily calling might be: 'A shoemaker, a smith, a farmer, each has his manual occupation and work; and yet, at the same time, all are eligible to act as priests and bishops. Every one of them in his occupation or handicraft ought to be useful to his fellows, and serve them in such a way that the various trades are all directed to the best advantage of the community, and promote the well-being of body and soul, just as the organs of the body serve each other.'[21] The fellowship of believers implies that all men are essentially equal in the sense that they have received the treasures which God has given. God's grace is offered to all, and no vocation is too mean or poor to be the vehicle through which He may do His work.

[20] *Reformation Writings*, I.113.   [21] Ibid. p. 116.

2. All believers share a common calling. The Christian's dignity is a dignity of service, for all Christians are called *to serve*. 'Should you ask "What is the difference between the priests and the laity in Christian standing, if all are priests?" the answer is that spiritual mischief and other wrongs have been done to the little words "priest" or "pastor". These words have been taken away from the community in general and handed over to those little communities which we now call "the clergy". The Holy Scriptures make no distinction beyond calling the instructed or the consecrated, *ministros, servos, oeconomos*, i.e. helpers, servants, stewards, whose duty is to preach Christ, and faith, and Christian freedom to others. For although we are all equally priests, still not all of us can serve and minister and preach. Thus St Paul says in 1 Corinthians 4: "We do not desire to be held by the people to be other than servants of Christ and stewards of the Gospel." But there has now grown out of the stewardship such a worldly, outer, gorgeous and awe-inspiring lordship and authority that the worldly powers proper cannot compare with them. Indeed, it is as if the laity were something other than Christian people. The whole meaning of Christian grace and liberty and faith is taken away, together with everything we have in Christ, and, indeed, we are robbed of Christ Himself.'[22] The Christian's calling and not his status, is the all-important fact. This calling is characterized in two distinct ways: it is characterized by the possession of the grace of Christ, and by the Christian's acceptance of the role of 'servant'. The principal and only concern is not lest Christians should be robbed of privileges, status, powers and rights, for these are of the earth earthy, but lest they should be robbed of Christ. The Christian does not ask 'What is due to me?' but 'What is due to Christ?' He cannot claim anything on the ground that he is good, but he may claim everything on the ground of his calling. It is interesting to notice that when he speaks of the marks of the Church Luther never points to visible holiness in believers. The holiness of believers is never a holiness which is demonstrated but a holiness which is hidden. It is the holiness of Christ in which the believer participates. They contemplate their righteousness not in themselves but in Him. Their holiness is found in Him alone. The marks of the Church are not in them but in Christ. The fact that they are believers is seen in

[22] *Reformation Writings*, I.367.

the recognition of their calling and in their response to the Gospel which is proclaimed to them. They have no holiness apart from Christ, and if they are robbed of Christ they are robbed of everything. They are being most true to their calling when they sing:

> *Look, Father, look on His anointed face,*
> *And only look on us as found in Him.*

3. All believers share a common privilege. If all believers are called upon to become true servants of Christ, it follows that laymen as well as priests are called to be servants. The two passionate concerns of the Christian are to contemplate and receive the righteousness of Christ in the service of Holy Communion, and to intercede for all who seek that righteousness. To deny either of these is to strike at the very roots of his religion. Both were denied to the Christian in the Church as it then existed. Concerning the first, Luther says: 'To deny both kinds to the laity is impious and oppressive; and it is not in the power of any angel, nor of any Pope or council whatever to deny them.' Luther claims that to deny the Cup to the laity really means that the Sacrament is not for *all*. 'It is sin', he says, 'to refuse to give both kinds to those who wish to exercise freedom of choice; and it is the priests and not the laity, who must bear the guilt. The Sacrament does not pertain to priests alone, but to all; the priests are not lords but servants, and it is their duty to administer both kinds to those who so desire, and as often as they desire.'[23] In this instance, therefore, Luther is not pleading on the grounds of equality between priests and laymen, but on the grounds of the universal significance of the sacrament. There is strong support in the words of Jesus, 'Drink ye *all* of this', and if, as Hort suggests, 'the Twelve sat that night as representatives of the ecclesia at large', we may assume that the Supper was instituted for the benefit of all believers. The other reason which Luther gives for asserting that sharing in the Communion Service is a common privilege is the individual liberty of the Christian. He puts this briefly in the following words: 'Each man should be allowed his free choice in seeking and using the sacrament, just as in the case of Baptism and penance.'[24]

The other privilege which belongs to the Christian is that of

---

[23] *Reformation Writings*, I.223.   [24] Ibid. p. 224.

exercising the ministry of intercession, and Luther states this in noble terms: 'In addition, we are priests, and thus greater than mere kings, the reason being that priesthood makes us worthy to stand before God, and pray for others. For to stand before God's face is the prerogative of none except priests. Christ redeemed us that we might be able spiritually to act and pray on behalf of one another just as, in fact, a priest acts and prays on behalf of the people. . . . By virtue of his kingship he (the Christian) exercises authority over all things, and by virtue of his priesthood he exercises power with God, for God does what he asks and desires.'[25]

To sum up—the preaching of the Word effects this twofold purpose: first, it brings the believer into a true relationship with Christ through faith; and it unites all believers in a common dignity, a common calling, and a common privilege. The beginning, and the sign, and the seal of this relationship is the Sacrament of Baptism.

II. THE SACRAMENT OF BAPTISM

Jesus took a little child and blessed it; He alone has the power to bless it by imparting to it His grace. We cannot create faith; faith is given by God. The child of believing parents is born into the society of true believers. Even a little child may believe even though it may not be able to do anything more. To believe is not a human quality. Indeed, in many ways, a child stands in the ideal relationship to God. It only receives from God; it can do nothing more. This is the proper attitude of all believers. In complete trust, they receive at the hands of God, for, like the child, they can do nothing more. Two conditions are indispensable:

(i) We must receive the gift of faith.

(ii) We must permit God to work out His salvation in us. We cannot engender faith, it must be given. Faith is never the result of our effort; if it is, it becomes our work. The whole situation into which we are born is the creation of God. Church, State, family, are there before us; they are God's creation. It is sheer pride, blindness, and presumption to imagine that we who are born into a God-created world, can create the faith whereby we believe in God. All creation is God's act. God is always making man just. This process begins at Baptism. A little child is made just by

[25] *Reformation Writings*, I.366.

God. Baptism is the beginning of God's work in all believers.

This sort of teaching had been lost. Rome had succeeded in equating clergy and Church, and this was inevitable since there was a special spiritual estate (*ordo*) of the clergy in distinction from the laity. In contrast to this Luther, who criticizes in principle the Roman Catholic argument for the institution and sacramental nature of the spiritual estate of the priesthood, holds that the ministerial office as *office* (*ministerium*) is instituted by God. It is based upon the universal priesthood of the faithful which takes rise with Baptism, and at the same time it points back to the apostolic model and apostolic instruction to appoint office-bearers, by orderly calling through the congregation, for the ministerial office becomes real and efficacious through vocation.

(*a*) 'Therefore the Holy Ghost in the New Testament has diligently prevented that the name sacerdos, priest or parson, is given to any apostle nor other office, but is solely the name of the baptized or Christian as a congenital hereditary name from Baptism.'[26] In this passage we cannot evade the conclusion that Luther quite definitely regarded the terms Christian and priest as synonymous, and this is because he believed that all believers are initiated into a relationship of grace through the sacrament of Baptism.

(*b*) Why was Baptism easily forgotten? Because many people were preoccupied in securing remission of sins in other ways which had no sanction in the New Testament. Moreover, the result of this neglect and misunderstanding of Baptism had brought upon the Church an intolerable burden known as the 'system of vows'. This was strange indeed because Baptism was the one vow which was made under the seal of a holy Sacrament. What could be the use of other vows in the light of this? Luther writes: 'There is scarcely anyone now who recalls that he is baptized—to say nothing of glorying in his baptism—since so many other ways have been devised for securing remission of sins and entrance into the kingdom of heaven. The occasion for such opinions was given by that dangerous remark of St Jerome (whether the mistake lay in its utterance or in its interpretation), in which he calls repentance the "second plank after shipwreck", as if Baptism were not repentance. For hence those who have fallen into sin despair of their first plank, or ship, as if it were lost,

---

[26] *The Ministry and the Sacraments*, ed. R. Dunkerley, p. 438.

and begin to rely on the second alone, that is on repentance. Hence have arisen those endless burdens of vows, professions, works, satisfactions, pilgrimages, indulgences, sects ... so that the Church of God is now under a tyranny incomparably worse than that of any synagogue or any nation whatsoever.'[27]

(1) Here again, another artificial distinction had crept into the Church. Some were under 'spiritual vows', and others were not. The barriers between clergy and laity were scarcely more dangerous than the barriers between those under vow and those who were not. Because of this, Christians were placed in different 'spiritual categories'. 'There are some', says Luther, 'who assert and argue that a work done within the ambit of a vow is more valuable than a work outside, and takes precedence over it; and in heaven will be preferred to the others, and receive no one knows what reward. Oh! blind Pharisees who measure righteousness and sanctity by size, or number, or some such standard; although in God's sight, it is measured solely by faith.'[28]

(2) More serious still was the fact that with the multiplication of vows there came an increase in laws and good works, and faith was pushed out. But the fact that glory was diverted from God to the individual who took the vow was a grave offence which Luther could not tolerate. Even to take a vow was in some sense regarded as meritorious, and it crowned with glory the individual so consecrated. 'These votaries', says Luther, 'must take credit to themselves alone for their righteousness, holiness and glory.'[29] If faith is the measuring-line, there is no difference between what is done by those under vow and the common labour of any believer: 'However numerous, sacred, and arduous they may be, these works, in God's sight, are in no way whatever superior to the works of a farmer labouring in the field, or a woman looking after her home.' Then he carries this thought even farther: 'Indeed, it occurs quite frequently that the common work of a serving man or a maid is more acceptable than all the fastings and other works of monks and priests where faith is lacking.'[30]

The votive life is denounced as a mere human tradition, which is not commended in Scripture and which does not effect salvation. Far from accomplishing the latter, 'pretentious lives lived

---

[27] *Documents of the Christian Church*, ed. H. Bettenson, p. 278.
[28] *Reformation Writings*, I.273.
[29] Ibid.   [30] Ibid. p. 276.

under vows are more hostile to faith than anything else can be'.

(3) What, then, does Baptism mean?

We shall consider this in three respects: Concerning the one who administers Baptism; concerning the relation of faith to Baptism; and concerning Luther's statement that all Christians are priests in virtue of their Baptism.

(a) The one who administers Baptism

It is easy to misunderstand the real point of Baptism. Put simply, it is an assertion that everything depends upon the free grace of God and not upon human comprehension. It is Christ, and Christ alone, who is at work behind Baptism. We do not know how food is turned into flesh and blood but we eat it. The plant receives soil and rain and bears fruit—we do not know how. God has placed the child in the world and there is enough for its spiritual life if it takes what it needs and grows. In one sense every child of God has to say: 'I believe in the Holy Ghost.' For none of us is drawn to God by our works or intellect, or inclinations or desires, or even by our own faith; it is the Holy Ghost who has graciously worked within us and drawn us to God. Baptism asserts that God has made a beginning in our lives; the initiative is His, and all that follows is His also. It is not our works which bring us near to God. On the contrary, it is because we are brought near to God that loving service ensues. 'If you desire to be saved, you must start from faith in the sacraments—anterior to any works. The works will follow the faith. . . . You would be sustained by it alone, if you were prevented from doing any others. For faith is the work, not of man, but of God alone, as Paul teaches. God does the other works through us and by us; in the case of faith, He works in us and without our co-operation.'[31]

God is the one who is active in Baptism and it is false to attribute authority to any other. 'For the man baptizes, and yet does not baptize. He baptizes in as far as he performs the rite: he submerges the candidate. Yet, in one sense, he does not baptize, but only acts on God's behalf, and not on his own responsibility. Hence we ought to understand Baptism at human hands just as if Christ Himself, nay God Himself, baptized us with His own hands. The Baptism which we receive through human hands is Christ's and God's, just as everything else that we

[31] *Reformation Writings*, I.259.

receive through human hands is God's.'[32] The very fact that God has chosen to fulfil His purposes through human hands has often led to abuses. God, not man, controls the sacraments. If the sacraments become a means which man uses and controls, God is denied the right to use them. This is what happened in the Church of Rome. God was denied the use of the sacraments he had ordained. In this way Rome had changed the whole motion of the sacraments. Instead of coming from God to man, they were interpreted as moving in the direction of God from man. This was not primarily due to a wrong idea of Baptism, but to a false idea of God. Now a false idea of God leads to a false Church.

(b) The relation of faith to Baptism
The true Church is where faith exists, and this means a recognition that everything comes from God. The greatest single danger in the Church is that faith in God may be obstructed. This happens when the virtue and knowledge of Baptism have vanished. Ordinances, rites, sects, votaries, may intrude to such an extent that Christians forget they have been baptized. As Luther says: 'We ought, when baptized, to have been like little children, who are not preoccupied with any cares or any works, but entirely free, redeemed, and safe merely through the glory of their Baptism.'[33]

The blessings conferred in Baptism are not rendered ineffectual because the recipient is unconscious of them. The spiritual status which a baptized person receives is not invalidated because it is not understood by him. Moreover, it is impossible for anyone to merit in any way the blessings which are bestowed in Baptism. When a child is brought to the font, no question of merit, good works, privilege or preferment arises; there is only the helpless, waiting child about to receive the grace which a gracious God offers to it. Luther foresaw a reasonable objection to all this. He knew that it may be argued that a child is incapable of accepting baptismal faith and cannot receive the promises of God. Here again the visible presence, the prayers and faith of a believing congregation are of inestimable importance. 'On this matter I agree with everyone in saying that infants are helped by vicarious faith: the faith of those who present them for Baptism. The word of God, whenever uttered, is powerful enough to change

[32] Ibid.   [33] Ibid. p. 271.

the hearts even of the ungodly, and these are not less unresponsive and incapable than any infant. Further, all things are possible in response to the prayers of a believing Church when it presents the infant, and this is changed, cleansed, and renewed, by their infused faith. . . . What cannot the faith of the Church and the prayer of believers remove, seeing it is believed that Stephen converted the Apostle Paul by this power?'[34]

(c) Priests by Baptism

What does this mean save that believers are priests *from* Baptism and *for* Baptism; from Baptism in that they become priests by their own Baptism, and for Baptism in that the believing Church exercises faith on behalf of all who come. Luther states this in unmistakable terms: 'The fact is that our baptism consecrates us all without exception, and makes us all priests.'[35] And again: 'Everyone who has been baptized may claim that he has already been consecrated priest, bishop, or pope, even though it is not seemly for any particular person arbitrarily to exercise the office.'[36] Luther was not alone or original in this teaching as we see from the following passage: 'From that day and that hour in which thou camest out of the font thou art become to thyself a continual fountain, a daily remission. Thou hast no need of a doctor or of a priest's right hand. As soon as thou descendedst from the sacred font thou wast clothed in a white robe and anointed with the mystic ointment; the invocation was made over thee, and the threefold name came upon thee, which fills the new vessel (that thou wert) with this new doctrine'[37] (St Laurentii).

Baptism signifies death and resurrection; it is the anointing of every priest in the general service of the Church. The priesthood of all believers, according to Luther, begins at the font. Although it begins there, it is the symbol of the whole life of the Christian. 'All our experience of life should be baptismal in character, viz., the fulfilment of the sign or sacrament of Baptism. We have been freed from all else that we might devote ourselves to Baptism alone, that is to say, death and resurrection.'[38] In an impressive passage Luther elucidates this, pointing out that it is the fulfilling and completion of justification: 'For, when the minister submerges

---

[34] *Reformation Writings*, I.271.   [35] Ibid. p. 113.   [36] Ibid. p. 114.
[37] C. Gore, *The Church and the Ministry*, p. 91; quoted from *Dictionary of Christian Biography*, S. V. Laurentius.
[38] *Reformation Writings*, I.267.

the child in the water, that signifies death; but when he again lifts it out, that signifies life. That is how Paul explains it in Romans 6: "We were buried therefore with Him through Baptism into death; that, as Christ was raised from the dead through the glory of the Father, so we also might walk in newness of life." We call this death and resurrection a new creation, a regeneration, a spiritual birth; and it ought not to be understood allegorically of the death of sin and the life of grace, as is the custom of many, but of a real death and a real resurrection. . . . When we begin to have faith, at the same time we begin to die to this world and to live to God in the future life. Thus, faith is verily both death and resurrection; and this is that spiritual baptism into which we are submerged and from which we rise.'[39]

This is the new dispensation. Through Baptism and faith comes the new birth which consecrates each individual as priest of Christ, that is, as one who partakes in the redeeming grace of Christ, and is set in God's kingdom. Christians are born through baptism into communion with the death and resurrection of Christ. And so Luther attacks the Roman Priesthood, which, in place of faith as the anointing of the Spirit, sets an episcopal anointing as constituting priesthood in the New Testament sense, and so displaces this from the personal level to which it belongs, to the level of an office. It is in this sense that we regard all Christians as being baptized into the Royal Priesthood, and whatever doctrinal development may follow from this it is at least certain that they must *follow* from it, since everything begins with Baptism. The antithesis which is sometimes drawn between faith and Baptism is merely a supposition and has no foundation in facts, as Denny put it: 'Baptism and faith are but the outside and inside of the same thing.' Baptism itself is the proclamation of the Gospel, since it must result in justification of which Baptism is the visible sign. All the same, the sacramental life of all believers reaches its earthly consummation in the Sacrament of the Lord's Supper, and to a consideration of this third 'mark' of the Church we must now turn.

III. THE SACRAMENT OF THE LORD'S SUPPER

One of the significant truths which has emerged during the history of the Church is that the means of revelation easily diverts

[39] *Reformation Writings*, I.265.

attention from that which is revealed. For instance, the temptation to Israel was to make the people, through whom the revelation was mediated, the end of revelation. Eventually Israel lost the distinction between the grace of God and the means of His grace so that her people became less concerned about the Holy One than the holy things associated with His appearance. At various times in history this error has recurred. Professor Bergendoff claims that it happened during the Middle Ages: 'Claiming Jesus Christ as its foundation and boasting of an apostolic succession which comprehended its bishops in the one Catholic faith, the medieval hierarchy had reared a temple for Western Christendom. To this shrine it held the keys, and on its altar a sacrifice was offered which made the priesthood the channel of the grace of God. Again the attention had shifted from the immediacy of the relationship of the individual with his God to the *means* which somehow were to guarantee the fruits of the revelation. A structure had been carefully built of which the ordained household should confidently affirm: "The Lord dwells here." Again men believed they had found the way to command and control the spiritual power of the world.'[40]

'Few errors so excited the opposition of Luther as this implied doctrine that the Church had achieved power over God.'

Whether the Reformers were right in drawing such conclusions from the religious situation of their day may be a debatable point, but there is no doubt whatever that they genuinely believed that the religion of the Middle Ages was an attempt to 'command and control the spiritual power of the world'. The Appendix to the third Article of the Confession of Augsburg states the problem as the Reformers understood it: 'There was added an opinion which increased private masses infinitely, that Christ by His passion satisfied for original sin, and appointed the Mass in which an offering should be made for daily sin both mortal and venial. From this came a common opinion that the Mass is a work blotting out the sins of the living and the dead by the fact of its being offered (*ex opere operato*).'[41] It is sometimes pointed out that this was the *common* and not the *official* teaching of the Church of Rome, but this seems to be a quibble about terms because this was, after all, the teaching which had percolated to the ordinary

---

[40] *World Lutheranism of Today*, p. 21.
[41] H. E. Symonds, *The Council of Trent and Anglican Formularies*, p. 126.

Christian and it could only have become common by the fact that it had been proclaimed with official approval.

The Sacrifice of the Mass

Three features characterized the Roman conception of the Mass, and, in order to avoid any suspicion of prejudice, we shall state these in the modified form in which we find them in the English Writers of the sixteenth century.

(1) *The Eucharistic rite is a Sacrifice*

One of the Caroline divines, Bishop Jeremy Taylor, says:
'This also His (Christ's) ministers do on earth; they offer up the same sacrifice to God, the sacrifice of the cross, by prayers and a commemorating rite and representment. . . . Our very holding up the Son of God and representing Him to His Father is the doing an act of mediation and advantage to ourselves, in the virtue and efficacy of the Mediator.'[42]

Some of this language may sound strange in the ears of many modern Protestants, and some may even be repelled by it, but it should be remembered that for thousands of Christians the fact that this sacrifice is offered is the glory as well as the hope of their religion. All the same, it is phrases like 'Our very holding up of the Son of God', with their attendant anthropocentric implications, which we must remember when we come to Luther's trenchant reply.

It should be added that the prevalent notion was that the Eucharist was a representation before God (and not one made to the worshippers). In this sense it was the antithesis of the Lutheran view which thought of the Eucharist as a proclamation to the worshippers.

(2) *The Eucharistic rite is a* propiatory *Sacrifice*

'If we compare the Eucharist with Christ's sacrifice made once on the cross, as concerning the effect of it, we say that that was a sufficient sacrifice . . . and both of them propitiatory for the sins of the whole world . . . the force and virtue of that sacrifice could not be profitable unto us, unless it were applied and brought into effect by the eucharistical sacrifice.'[43]

[42] H. E. Symonds, *The Council of Trent and Anglican Formularies*, p. 114.
[43] Ibid. p. 124.

Even Ridley asks: 'Now when we come unto the Lord's board, what do we come for? to sacrifice Christ again, and to crucify Him again, or to feed upon Him that was once only crucified and offered up for us?' And in answer to Pie's question about the unbloody sacrifice, Ridley answered: 'It is called unbloody, and is offered after a certain manner and in a mystery, and as a representation of that bloody sacrifice: *and he doth not lie, who saith Christ to be offered.*' We cannot avoid the conclusion that the sacrifice of the Cross and the sacrifice of the Mass are regarded as possessing equivalent powers and that the first is only efficacious in the light of the second.

(3) *The worthiness of the Communicant*

Symonds states that some Anglicans consider the sacrifice to consist in the symbolical actions dealing with the bread and wine. 'But', he continues, 'even they would deny that the Eucharist was a "nude commemoration", for they would insist on the Real Presence of Christ as given to the *worthy* communicant. It must be added that few Anglicans of the present day who accept the doctrine of the Eucharistic Sacrifice would deny the doctrine of the Real and Objective Presence of Christ on the Altar.'[44]

It must be stated at once that not one of these viewpoints is acceptable to Luther. Man is not in a position to offer sacrifice to God, he is only in a position to receive from God. There is no propitiatory power whatever in the Eucharist, and only the once-for-all Atonement of Christ is effective for the remission of sins. The question of worthiness should not arise, for the believer does not approach Christ on the basis of his own worthiness but through faith alone. Both self-effacement and triumphant faith are combined in the line:

'Thy presence makes the Feast.'

The Mass: A Promise or a Sacrifice?

Did Luther reject the idea of sacrifice? In the sense in which sacrifice is understood in the above paragraphs, Luther most decidedly rejected it. Dr Rattenbury's statement that 'Anything in the nature of sacrifice was repulsive to Luther'[45] is misleading, because Luther retained the sacrificial idea but separated it entirely from the mass. Why did he do this? Because he came to

---

[44] *The Council of Trent and Anglican Formularies*, p. 124.
[45] *The Eucharistic Hymns of John and Charles Wesley*, p. 157.

the conclusion that the Eucharist was the testament of God to man and not the sacrifice offered by man to God.

(a) Christ's Testament

'The first point stands infallibly fast. The mass or sacrament is Christ's testament which He bequeathed to be distributed after His death, among those who believed on Him. For His words run, "This cup is the new testament in my blood".'[46] Let us inquire, therefore, what a testament is, and, at the same time, it will also become clear to us what is the mass, what its use, its fruit, and its abuse.

Without question, a testament is a promise made by a man in view of his death. In it, he bequeaths his heritage, and appoints heirs. A testament, therefore, (i) anticipates the death of the testator; (ii) embodies the promise of the heritage; and (iii) appoints the heirs. That is how St Paul discusses a testament in Romans 4, Galatians 3 and 4, and Hebrews 9. The words of Christ show the same quite plainly. Christ testifies His own death when he says: 'This is my body which is given. This is my blood which is shed.' He names and designates the bequest when He says: 'In remission of sins.' Similarly He appoints the heirs when He says, 'For you and for many', i.e. those who accept and believe in the promise of the testator. Faith here makes men heirs, as we shall see. So Luther holds that the mass is God's promise of testament made for the remission of sins; it is confirmed by the death of Christ, and it is available for all who will accept and believe. 'The mass is, as I have said, the gift of the promise, offered to all men by the hand of the priest.'[47]

(b) Christ's Example

To those who maintain that the mass represents a good work or a sacrifice, Luther answers: 'Christ's example is on our side. At the Last Supper when Christ initiated this sacrament, and instituted this testament, He did not offer Himself to God, or perform any "good work" for others. He took His seat at the table, He offered the same testament to each, one by one, and gave the same sign.'[48] This was offering a promise to each individual and the question of offering a sacrifice, at that stage, did not arise. The words and example of Christ are sufficient for Luther.

[46] *Reformation Writings*, I.233.   [47] *Reformation Writings*, I.248.   [48] Ibid. p. 247.

(c) The Sacrifice of Thanksgiving

As has been said earlier the Reformers did not completely erase the words 'priest' and 'sacrifice' from their vocabulary. The Lutheran Confessions deal at some length with the idea of sacrifice, but in them it is mainly a sacrifice of thanksgiving. The truth is that we cannot receive anything without offering our sacrifice of thanksgiving and surrender. Luther would have endorsed Charles Wesley's verse:

> *Thy bright example I pursue,*
> *To Thee in all things rise;*
> *And all I think or speak or do,*
> *Is one great sacrifice.*

Lutheran theologians today are striving against the misrepresentation and devaluation of the priesthood of all believers, which does not mean, 'We do not need a priest and we do not want a priest', for it possesses a much more positive content when it is interpreted in the light of biblical teaching. A German theologian expresses it as follows: 'The profession of a Christian in the world must thus be understood and fulfilled as a priestly office. The priesthood of believers must witness to the priestly office of Jesus Christ through word and deed. There is no passive attitude toward Christ's sacrifice (i.e. enjoying the fruits of His sacrifice) without simultaneous participation on our part in the action of His sacrifice. If we understand it in this way, the priesthood of all believers is vastly different from any quietism which has frequently been described as the specific danger of the Lutheran Church. At the same time this priesthood is a strong link between faith and charity, faith in Christ and service to the world. Such knowledge based upon the Bible is of great importance for the understanding and ordering of Christian worship.'[49]

There is nothing in this passage to suggest that sacrifice intrinsically belongs to an office, nor is there any reference to it as a 'good work', and this is because participation in Christ's sacrifice is possible in one way only—by faith. Luther always pursues the theology of 'faith' with a remorseless consistency. Faith gives meaning to the mass and it has no meaning apart from faith. 'Prayer is something quite different from the mass. Prayer can be extended to comprehend as many people as I choose; the mass

---

[49] Wilhelm Stählin, *Ways of Worship*, pp. 212ff.

covers none other than him who exercises his own faith, and then only in so far as he exercises it. Neither can the mass be given to God or to other men; rather God bestows on men through the agency of the priest; and men receive it through faith alone, apart from all works or merits.'[50] The greatest single danger of the sacrifice of the mass was that it tended to become a purely legal and official transaction and this was a denial of personal relationship. By whom is faith offered and exercised? The following answer is given in Vatja's impressive work: 'Luther only placed the idea of sacrifice in a different position from Roman theology. He fought the concept of sacrifice in the Roman mass because it was conceived as independent of personal relationship: one could perform the sacrifice merely by carrying out the ritual of the mass (*ex opere operato*). But, for Luther, the priest who, as ecclesiastical holder of office, conducts divine worship (proclaims the Word and dispenses the sacrament), does not perform the sacrifice at all, for the sacrifice belongs not to the person as official, but to the person as Christian, that is, to the congregation, who—listening to the Word and communicating in the sacrament—receive the gift of God in faith.'[51] Then Vatja goes to the heart of the matter and states in two simple sentences what is the vital contrast between Roman and Lutheran theology: 'This faith in the gift of God is the priestly office of the congregation at worship. Faith is what constitutes Christian priesthood.'

If we affirm that no sacrifice is offered in the mass, what then is the function of the officiating priest? In order to answer this question we must recall that Luther regards the mass as the testament or promise of Christ in respect of remission of sins. It follows that the priest proclaims the promise by giving the bread and the wine. Christ is present and gives what He has to the believer and receiver. All that Christ has won is given to us—forgiveness, life, and eternity. The priest proclaims in word and in deed that the sacrifice of Christ still avails for us all. The promise remains and has never been broken. This duty does not demand any magical powers, since the priest only announces: 'The body of our Lord Jesus Christ which was given for you.' This is a pronouncement of the promise and it is nothing more. Faith in this promise establishes a real contact between believers and their living Lord. The Roman says: 'If there is no priest,

[50] Vilmos Vatja, *The Theology of Divine Service in Luther*, pp. 269ff.   [51] Ibid.

there is no salvation'; the Lutheran says: 'If you accept the promise of Christ, that is enough.'

Now a promise must be believed and accepted. It does not lose its virtues even if it is not believed and accepted, but only when it is appropriated in this way does it reach its true fulfilment in the life of the believer. He who receives the bread and wine shows forth to all that he believes and accepts the testament or promise of Christ. He must eat and he must drink. He thereby accepts the promise of Christ in its fullness, for he cannot accept it partially nor can it be accepted on his behalf. Christ offers all; the Christian receives all—and the reverse can never be true.

Yet according to the Roman system the priesthood existed principally to offer up a sacrifice. This meant that two vital truths were undermined: first, the fact that God is the central figure in the mass as in all things; secondly, the believing congregation were robbed of their highest privilege—the sacrifice of faith. Philip S. Watson has shown how Luther was concerned to assert the former of these in his teaching in general and not least in his teaching on the mass: 'For men to offer sacrifices in the hope of placating and propitiating God, is in Luther's eye a mark of false religion and idolatry; and he therefore sets the sacrifice of Christ in absolute opposition to all sacrifices offered by men. He opposes it most sharply of all to the sacrifice of the mass, which cannot but seem doubly blasphemous to him, inasmuch as it is offered by men in order to obtain favour from the God who has shown Himself freely and eternally favourable in Christ. In the mass, Luther ceaselessly insists, we do not offer a sacrifice to God, but we receive gifts from Him; we do not repeat Christ's sacrifice, but we remember it and share its benefits, for it is eternally sufficient and complete. Christ's sacrifice, moreover, like His satisfaction, is entirely a divine work; it is God's sacrifice to Himself, to which He was moved by nothing else but His inestimable love for men. When Luther speaks of Christ's work in sacrificial terms, therefore, it is clear that he does so in order to assert yet again his theocentric point of view. Christ's sacrifice, like His merit, means *sola gratia*.'[52]

The Recipients of the Promise

Who are the recipients of the promise? There is not the least

[52] *Let God be God*, p. 121.

doubt in Luther's mind about the answer to this question. 'The gift of the divine promise is offered to *all* men.' And again: 'You will easily understand this as the plainest truth, if you hold it firmly that the mass is a divine promise, which can benefit no one, be applied to no one, intercede for no one, be communicated to no one, except only to the believer himself by the sole virtue of his own faith. Who can accept, on another's behalf, the promises of God, which require faith from each one individually?'[53]

The very means whereby believers were to receive the promise, that is faith, had been almost eradicated, and the believing congregation which ought to have possessed high privileges, sat in silent, passive, and often ignorant participation. They were permitted to watch the drama instead of being part of it.

Why was the Cup denied to the laity? In this most holy Sacrament, which was the seal of divine promise to the believing congregation, a wedge was driven between clergy and laity. Hence the sacrament which was instituted to bring all believers into faith-union with their living Lord became the most blatant and shameful example of disunity. Luther is bewildered by this dividing of believers into different categories: 'In the matter of the mass and the sacraments, we are all equals, whether priests or laity.'[54] The vital question is: Is the sacrament for some or for all? Luther proves from two sayings of Jesus that it is indisputably for all.

(*a*) Each Evangelist attaches the mark of universality to the Cup, but not to the Bread. Jesus said: 'All ye drink of it', and this was not giving permission but issuing a command.

This denial of the Cup to the laity means that they are denied of something which Christ instituted.

(*b*) This is supported by another saying of Jesus: 'This is my blood, shed for you and for many for the remission of sins.' 'Here', says Luther, 'you may see very plainly that the blood was given to all, and that it was shed for the sins of all. No one will dare to say that it was not shed for the laity, for it is clear who was addressed. Did He not address all? He used the words, "For you". It follows that the distinction between priest and layman is false, for when Christians come to the service of Holy Communion they are there in their priestly dignity and the officiating

[53] *Reformation Writings*, I.244.
[54] Ibid. p. 251.

priest acts on behalf of all.'[55] At the Eucharist 'our priest or minister stands before the altar, having been publicly called to his priestly function; he repeats publicly and distinctly Christ's words of institution; he takes the Bread and the Wine, and distributes it according to Christ's words; and we all kneel beside him and around him, men and women, young and old, master and servant, mistress and maid, all holy priests together, sanctified by the blood of Christ. We are there in our priestly dignity. . . . We do not let the priest proclaim for himself the ordinance of Christ; but he is the mouthpiece of us all, and we all say it with him in our hearts with true faith in the Lamb of God Who feeds us with His Body and Blood.'[56]

(c) Our worthiness is no criterion. It is a mistake to suppose that the efficacy of the Sacrament is dependent upon worthiness. It is dependent upon two factors: God's promise to us, and our faith in the promise. Indeed, it is the frenzied attempts to make ourselves worthy that have taken the true meaning out of the sacrament. Our vain attempts at self-justification only show how we have misunderstood the all-important truth that God alone justifies. If someone sets our own worthlessness against the magnitude of the bequest, what shall we answer? Luther says: 'I am receiving what I receive, not as my deserts, nor on account of any special claim on my part. I know I do not deserve it and that I am getting more than I have earned; in fact, I have earned the opposite. But by the generosity of my benefactor, I am making a perfectly valid claim.'[57] Once again the sovereignty of pure faith is asserted and this is a sufficient preparation.

Luther returns in another passage to the character of the benefactor. We do not and cannot know Him apart from faith. The Holy Spirit awakens faith within us, but it is faith not in the elements, or in the priest, or in our own merits and self-righteousness, but in the disinterested love of our Benefactor. 'Thus the believer draws near to Christ, that loving and bounteous testator, and becomes a new and different man through and through. . . . How could he help loving so great a Benefactor, who offered, promised, and presented to him, in his unworthiness and while deserving something quite different, this great wealth and also

---

[55] *Reformation Writings*, I.219.
[56] Lindsay, *History of the Reformation*, I.444.
[57] *Reformation Writings*, I.236.

an eternal inheritance?'[58] These blessings are not for those who are worthy; they are for those who believe.

Professor Skydsgaard sums up the Lutheran position in the following words:

(*a*) 'Holy Communion is first and foremost *communion with Christ*. Here the Christian enters into direct communion with his living Lord.'

(*b*) 'The Communion is a fellowship between the members of Christ's Body. It is a social-fellowship meal, where Christ binds men together in love, mutual help, and responsibility, both bodily and spiritual. And it is a meal through which the body of Christ is built up all down the ages.'

(*c*) 'The Communion is the eschatological Feast of Joy, where the Church looks forward to the Great Messianic Feast beyond the grave. The Holy Communion, as the Church's sacrifice of praise and thanksgiving, forms the culminating point in our worship.'

Our study has shown that these three factors are always present in the Lutheran conception of Holy Communion; all believers enter into direct communion with their Lord; all believers share in the sacrifice of praise and thanksgiving, which is the sacrifice of the whole Church. We contend that these three factors embody and amplify the doctrine of the priesthood of all believers, and it is impossible to understand or interpret Lutheran theology apart from this basic truth.

> *Feast after feast thus comes and passes by,*
>   *Yet, passing, points to the glad feast above;*
> *Giving sweet foretaste of the festal joy,*
>   *The Lamb's great bridal feast of bliss and love.*

This, surely, is the great divine Event to which all believers move in sure hope and confident faith.

IV. THE KEYS OF CHRISTIAN DISCIPLINE AND FORGIVENESS

(1) *Roman Interpretation*

In order to understand Luther's doctrine of the Keys, we shall state plainly the doctrine promulgated by the Roman Catholic Church. This is stated by O. R. Vassal-Phillips who is commenting on *On the Unity of the Catholic Church*, by St Cyprian.

[58] *The Nature of the Church*, ed. R. Newton Flew, p. 80.

(a) There is one Cathedra or Chair. Cyprian says: 'There is one God and one Christ, and there is one Church and one *Chair*, founded by the voice of the Lord upon Peter.'[59]

(b) The Church was built on Peter. Father Chapman writes: 'We find St Cyprian almost each time he mentions St Peter calling him "Peter upon whom the Church is built".' St Jerome, writing to the Pope of the time says: 'I am in communion with your Blessedness, that is, with the Chair of Peter. On that Rock I know that the Church was built.'

(c) The Primacy was given to Peter. If the Church was built upon St Peter—a truth which, as we have just seen, St Cyprian was never tired of urging—then it would seem to be an obvious deduction from this fact alone that upon Peter was *thereby* bestowed the Primacy. As a building depends upon that upon which it is built, so those who are built upon another depend upon him upon whom they are built. Moreover St Cyprian does not fail to remind his readers that St Peter received the Keys. He terms them 'The Keys of the Church'. He writes: 'The Church is one and was founded upon one, who also received the Keys of it, by the Voice of the Lord.' Now it will not be disputed that one upon whom not only the Church was founded, but who also received the Church's Keys, was thereby given the Primacy in that Church.

(d) A man who deserts the Chair of Peter can hardly trust that he is in the Church of Christ. St Cyprian writes: 'The whole number of Catholic Bishops throughout the world agree in recognizing Cornelius as Bishop of Rome.'

A definite stiffening in the idea of the primacy of Rome undoubtedly took place in the second and third centuries. How much of this was due to the teachings of Montanism it is difficult to say. One of the ironies of Church history is that a movement which set out to remove tendencies toward a rigid ecclesiastical development, ended in strengthening and confirming those things which it sought to remove. Montanism drew attention to three important truths, namely, that it is possible for the Holy Spirit to manifest Himself by other than sacerdotal means; that the laity (including women) are priests unto God and possess the privilege of leading in worship and prophesying;

---

[59] '*On the Unity of the Catholic Church*' *by St Cyprian*, trans. by O. R. Vassal-Phillip, pp. 72ff.

that there is a succession of the Word which is more important than the apostolic succession. Tertullian, who became one of the leaders of the Montanists, is voicing their views when he says: 'All advancement to better things must be by that Vicar of the Lord, the Holy Ghost.' 'The power of binding and loosing belongs not to the bishop but to the prophet, who, as the organ of the Spirit, determines whether the repenting offender is forgiven of God.' The importance of these two statements should not be overlooked. The first moves the emphasis from the institution to the Holy Spirit, and the second assumes that the Keys were not given only to the special priesthood but to the spiritual priesthood of all believers who also were organs of the Spirit. Montanism failed, however, and its failure led to a tightening up of the whole ecclesiastical system. As a result, the canon became the complete oracles of God, and the Spirit's special gifts were limited to the twelve apostles. To the Twelve belonged all authority, and the channel of communication became solely the apostolic office. It is true to say that from the grave misunderstanding which arose then, the Church has never recovered. Tertullian defined the position of his adversaries by saying that 'the Church is now the whole number of bishops'. To this episcopate it was given to preserve the unity and holiness of the Church by the use of the keys. So it happened that the failure of Montanism underlined and strengthened that very traditionalism and authority against which it had been a protest. The important point for our study, however, is not that Montanism failed, but that such a protest should be made as soon as the Cyprianic tendencies in the doctrine of the Church and Ministry became evident.

Were the Keys committed to Peter only or to the whole Church?
The Roman view is that the former is the case. The Rhemish New Testament contains the following note on Matthew 16[19]: 'To loose is as the cause and the offender's case requireth; to loose them of any of the former bands, and to restore them to the Church's sacraments and communion of the Faithful, and execution of their function; to pardon also, either all or part of the penance enjoined, or what debts soever a man oweth to God or the Church, for the satisfaction of his sins forgiven. Which kind of releasing or loosing is called "indulgence". Finally, this

"whatsoever" excepteth nothing that is punishable or pardonable by Christ on earth; for He has committed His power to Peter. And so the validity of Peter's sentence, in binding or loosing whatsoever, shall, by Christ's promise, be ratified.'[60] The same thing is stated succinctly by the Lower House of Convocation in England in 1559: 'We affirm: 1. That, to the Apostle Peter, and to his lawful successors in the apostolic see, there has been given as the vicars of Christ, the supreme power of pasturing the Church militant of Christ, and of strengthening their brethren. 2. That the authority to treat of or to define whatever belongs to the faith, the sacraments or ecclesiastical discipline has hitherto belonged, and ought to belong, to the pastors of the Church alone, whom the Holy Ghost has placed in the Church of God for this purpose, *and not to laymen*.'[61]

Luther shows that Christ did not give His keys to Peter and his successors personally, but to the whole Church and congregation. 'Christ gave it "the keys" and said, in Matthew 18: "What you bind on earth shall be bound in heaven." Similarly, he said to the one individual, Peter, *in the room of and standing for the one and only church* (Matt 16): "Whatsoever thou shalt loose...", etc.'[62] Moreover, the words of Jesus refer to a promise of forgiveness rather than a conferring of power: 'In the place where it says, "Whatsoever thou shalt bind", Christ is calling out the faith of the penitent, by giving a certitude based on the words of the promise, that, if he be forgiven as a believer here below, his forgiveness holds good in heaven. This passage makes no mention at all of conferring power, but only deals with the service performed by the administrator promising the words of forgiveness.'[63]

(*a*) The power of the keys is given in answer to Peter's confession of faith. The question is: 'Who possesses this faith, who *does* believe?' And the answer is: 'All believers.' The keys are not entrusted to any individual but to the Church and congregation. Peter receives the keys on behalf of the whole Church. In order that faith may always be exercised, the keys are given through Peter to all. If some fail, others will be there to believe.

(*b*) Yet sometimes Luther gives the impression that Christ never yielded the power of the keys at all. By conformity to

---

[60] C. Eliot, *Delineation of Roman Catholicism*, p. 195.
[61] P. Hughes, *The Reformation in England*, III.22.
[62] *Reformation Writings*, I.88.   [63] Ibid. p. 281.

Christ, Christians participate in the power of the keys. The latter remains Christ's, however, and is shared by believers. This conformity takes place mainly through Holy Communion: 'The eating calls forth the faith of the partakers, so that, when their conscience has been confirmed by faith in these words, they may have the certitude, as they eat, that their sins are forgiven. Nor is there anything said here about power, the administration being alone mentioned.[64]

(c) Luther has yet another interpretation. The power of the keys is given away, not to an individual even as a representative, but to the Church with the ministry of preaching, and the Church here means the believing people who are living members of Christ's body. 'And if they claim that St Peter received authority when he was given the keys—well, it is plain enough that the keys were not given to St Peter only, but to the whole Christian community. Moreover, the keys have no reference to doctrine or policy, but only to refusing or being willing to forgive sin.'[65]

We should not overlook the fact that when Jesus refers to the keys He uses the plural form: 'Whatsoever, *ye* shall bind on earth' (Matt 18^{18}). Also in John 20^{22}: 'Receive *ye* the Holy Ghost.'

The second reference reminds us, as Dr Flew has pointed out, that the gift of the Holy Spirit was for all, and not simply for the Eleven. 'All are called to bear witness' (Lk 24^{28}).[66] So in the Johannine narrative there is no evidence whatever that the Eleven are separated from the other disciples present. All receive the Holy Spirit (20^{21}) as the promise of the Spirit is given to all in Luke 24^{49}. Again, according to the Lucan tradition Jesus sends out the Seventy as well as the Twelve.'

Now if the words 'Receive ye the Holy Ghost' refer to all, we cannot accept the view that the rest of the verse refers only to the Eleven disciples. So, if the keys do not belong solely to Peter, neither do they belong only to the Eleven. This means that they are not given to the episcopate. If the keys were not given to the whole Church, we cannot understand Matthew 18^{17}: 'But if he [thy brother] will not hear thee, then take with thee one or two more, that in the mouth of two or three witnesses every word may be established. And if he shall neglect to hear them,

---

[64] *Reformation Writings*, I.281. [65] Ibid. p. 120.
[66] *Jesus and His Church*, p. 243.

tell it to the Church.' All who belong to the Church by faith and baptism are included here.

It will be seen, therefore, that the power of the keys is not to be regarded as legislative power, which always offers forgiveness as a reward for good works; nor must we think of this power as the possession of supreme knowledge, for it is just this error which has attributed to the Pope secular and external powers which have been regarded as the inevitable accompaniment of his spiritual authority. The power of the keys is the power to offer and proclaim to all men those blessings of the Gospel which Jesus has won for all by His death and Resurrection. To the Church is given the inestimable privilege of declaring to men the terms of divine pardon, as well as the power of delineating the conditions under which that offer of pardon may be accepted. The power to loose is the continued proclamation of the Gospel of forgiveness, the word of Him 'who hath loved us and loosed us from our sins'; the power to bind is the power to ensure those proper conditions in the Church so that judgement as well as mercy may be unceasingly proclaimed in it. The first is referred to by Peter himself when he says that God 'made choice among us that the Gentiles by my mouth should hear the word of the Gospel' (Acts 15^7); in this sense and in this alone was Peter given a special commission. The second is referred to in Acts 15^{23}ff when the Church in the exercise of its disciplinary powers laid down certain specific conditions under which the Gentiles might be admitted into the Christian Church. The reference which pervades all this is that the Gospel is the Word of mercy and judgement, and that the task of setting this forth is the task of the whole Church; by fulfilling this ministry the priesthood of all believers is exercised. Nowhere is this thought more explicit than in the words of R. H. Strachan: 'The retaining of sins means that the Church is empowered to pass the judgement which Jesus could pass. To those earliest disciples, as representatives of the Ecclesia, is given "the last and final word on the sins of frail humanity: the last and decisive word in removing the wrongs of our tangled world; the last and decisive power of judgement on the distinction between right and wrong. It is a dangerous gift, fraught with grave responsibility *and only to be exercised by the Spirit of Christ working in and through His People.*'[67]

[67] *The Fourth Evangelist*, p. 319. (Quoted in *Jesus and His Church*, p. 245.)

In the discussion of the fourth 'mark' of the Church we have noticed that the cogency of the argument rests squarely on the inescapable fact that the power of the keys is committed to all believers, in the exercise of whose priesthood lies their most urgent and primary task.

V. A CALLED AND CONSECRATED CHRISTIAN MINISTRY

(a) *The doctrine of the Two Realms*

It is Karl Barth's considered opinion that Luther destroyed Protestantism by his doctrine of the Two Realms.[68] We can best understand Luther's doctrine of the Ministry if we begin with his teaching about the two realms. He begins with the irrefutable fact that God is governing the world. He does not imagine that anyone will question this truth. But it immediately raises another question which seems equally important: How is God governing the world? To the question, 'Where is the Church?' —the answer is: 'It is where God is governing the world through the Word and the Sacraments.' By governing the world through the Word and the Sacraments, the Church becomes a reality. It is just this fact of God's governing through the Ministry of the Church which creates the Church. The Church is being created all the time by the preaching of the Gospel, which is nothing less than the proclamation of God's government of the world. The world is God's kingdom—the sphere, that is, where God rules.

God must find a means whereby He may govern the world. It cannot be imagined that God exercises His rule in one sphere only. It is God's prerogative to rule always and everywhere. He may rule through the medium of the Church; He may also rule through the medium of the State. There is a principle here which is too often overlooked. God appears to acknowledge and bless many features of the pattern of the Church which are not acknowledged by the whole Church. The majesty and scope of the divine purpose may not always fit into the narrow limits of an institution even if that institution is chosen of God. There are wider realms in which He may govern. The history of the Church bears witness that God chooses from time to time to supersede His own appointed institutions if those institutions fail

---

[68] See *The Germans and Ourselves* (Barth), and *Church Dogmatics*, Ch. 8, 'God's Commandment'.

to continue to be the instruments of His will. This failure arises again and again from human rebellion in many forms. The divine government does not cease when one sphere of activity is closed. It must be reasserted that God is governing the world; He *must* rule. If He may not rule through His own appointed institutions, through the Word and the Sacraments, He will find other means whereby to exercise His rule. The State as well as the Church is the servant of God, so the State comes within the orbit of the divine activity and is one of the realms in which He rules. If there are occasions in history when the Church has failed to obtain reform from the spiritual authorities, then God fulfils His purpose through the existing temporal powers. It is altogether too glib to suggest that Luther was acting on grounds of political expediency when he called in the help of the Princes in the affair of the Peasants' Revolt. 'He had previously denounced the princes as scoundrels; now they are ministers of God and martyrs if they are slain by the rebels.'[69] Luther's actions were generally based on his theology, and political expediency is the last accusation which should be made against him. Let us examine the facts. Luther appealed to the religious authorities to help and protect the peasants and to bring about the necessary reforms. If these reforms had been forthcoming, the matter would have ended there. If the religious authorities had heeded Luther's appeal, the revolt might well have been averted. The Church took no action and the peasants rebelled. Since the Church took no action, Luther called for the help of the temporal authorities to restore order. What are the theological grounds for Luther's course of action in this affair? 'Those who exercise secular authority have been baptized like the rest of us, and have the same faith and the same Gospel; therefore we must admit that they are priests and bishops. They discharge their office as an office of the Christian community, and for the benefit of that community. Everyone who has been baptized may claim that he has already been consecrated priest, bishop, or pope, even though it is not seemly for any particular person arbitrarily to exercise the office.'[70] The religious authorities and the temporal authorities share the same status, it is only in function that they differ. 'There is no real difference between laymen, priests, princes,

---

[69] Townsend, *Claims of the Free Church*, p. 263.
[70] *Reformation Writings*, I.114.

bishops, or, in Romanist terminology, between religious and secular, than that of office or occupation, and not that of Christian status.'[71] And again: 'Those now called "the religious", i.e. priests, bishops, and popes, possess no further or greater dignity than other Christians, except that their duty is to expound the word of God and administer the sacraments—that being their office. In the same way, the secular authorities "hold the sword and the rod", their function being to punish evil-doers and protect the law-abiding.' If this is true, 'Secular authorities should exercise their office freely and unhindered and without fear, whether it be pope, bishop, or priests with whom they are dealing; if a man is guilty, let him pay the penalty.'

After pointing out that Luther had no naïve or exaggerated opinion about the rulers of Germany, Rupp sums up the matter as follows: 'Luther regarded the abuse of spiritual power as far more deadly than that of temporal power. He is writing, moreover, in an emergency situation, in which the Church has failed to obtain reform from the spiritual authorities who have become themselves an obstacle to amendment. In this case, reform becomes the common concern of the whole Christian estate. In this emergency, the persons most fit to intervene on behalf of all are the secular authorities, since it is their God-entrusted office (*amt.*) to wield the sword of government and administration, and to protect the whole community. Therefore, when necessity demands, the first man who is able, should as a faithful member of the whole body, do what he can to bring about a truly free council. No one can do this as well as the temporal authorities, especially since they are also fellow Christians, fellow priests.'[72]

The fact that the State is regarded as the servant of God does not mean that it is never a disobedient servant. Sometimes a false government arises and then God governs in spite of it and not with its co-operation. But it is not the state only that is guilty of this. Sometimes a false Church arises also. While it is true that the Church is the means which God uses, it may also become the means which the devil uses. Man may attempt to destroy God's government; he may in various ways seek to destroy the spiritual and civil government of God. When this happens, the devil governs. This is why Luther thought the Roman Church

---

[71] Ibid. pp. 115-16.
[72] G. Rupp, *Luther's Progress to the Diet of Worms*, pp. 83-4.

as anti-Christ. Yet Luther did not hold that the true Church ceased to exist at Rome, he knew that the Word of God was proclaimed there, and where the Word of God is proclaimed God governs through it. All the same, it is possible for man to destroy the only means which God may use. If the Church abuses the Sacraments, it is an abusing Church, and becomes the Church of the Devil. If the Word of God is used as an instrument of human power, it means that the Church is being ruled by the devil and not by God. Luther genuinely felt that by using the Word of God as the Pope used it, Rome had become the Church of the devil. Any person, or system, or ceremony, which does not allow God to rule is damaging and not helping the Church. Of course, the Church may become false, and it becomes false when its conception of the Ministry is wrongly understood. Is the Ministry a divine institution and the gift of God to the Church, or is it a special Order possessing supernatural powers through whom alone God may do His work?

(b) *The Ministry as a divine Institution*

According to Luther the Ministry is the gift of God to the Church, which is quite in line with Luther's conception of grace. 'As long as grace is mainly thought of as an "infused transforming power", it is quite natural that it should be mediated by the sacraments, among which the Eucharist is foremost, but in Luther it is understood as *favor dei*, the favour of God, so it is just as natural that it confronts man through God's Word or Gospel.'[73]

This idea of grace lies behind Luther's conception of ordination which is very different from that of Rome. The fundamental significance of ordination for Roman Catholicism is that the priest receives power to consecrate and offer sacrifice. Luther's view is that the Word is not received through ordination but through a call to service (*ministerium*), and if ordination does take place, it is not integral to the ministry. Anyone who has received true calling holds the ministry independently of ordination. It follows that ordination is only a public confirmation of calling, and what is received in calling is not some special gift of grace or power but a commission.

'Within the aforesaid *congregatio sanctorum* there is a special

---

[73] Dr Gosta Hök, 'Luther's Doctrine of the Ministry', *Scottish Journal of Theology*, VII.1.16.

priesthood, instituted by God Himself, as a ministry whereby God's work of salvation may be carried on, through the preaching the Word and the administration of the Sacraments.'[74] But this is 'not in the sense that these things are dependent for their validity upon a special status conferred by a special ordination; they have their validity solely in the virtue of Christ's word and institution. The words of the Confession state clearly that the "special priesthood" is of God's ordering, and does not merely exist—as it says, "for the sake of order". Rather it is given to the Church by Christ as a gift (Eph 4^{11}ff); as a ministry in the Church and for the Church, in order that God's Word may always be preached and the holy Sacraments administered, and the Lordship of Christ be thereby set forth.'

Ministers are called to serve not to rule, and it is their duty to serve in such a way that eventually God may rule in all the world. All Christians, ministers and laity, stand together as servants of God's purpose. Christ imparted no special power to any select company of His followers. As Luther says: 'For Christ established in His Church neither emperors, nor potentates, nor despots, but *ministers*—as we learn when the apostle says: "Let a man account of us as ministers of Christ and dispensers of God's mysteries." When Christ says, "Whosoever believes and is baptized, shall be saved", this is to evoke the faith of those about to be baptized, so that they might have the assurance, based on this promise, that if they were baptized as believers, they would receive salvation. And, in founding this ceremony, He imparted no power whatever.'[75]

(c) Confirmation of Calling by the Congregation

The call to preach is the call of God. No one is allowed to preach without being legally called. It is a divine call because God is the Person who calls. The preacher stands in his vocation called and sent by God. All the same, Luther is careful to emphasize (*i*) that all Christians, being priests, possess equal authority, (*ii*) that no one may exercise it without the confirmation of the Congregation of the Faithful, and (*iii*) that in exceptional cases a Christian may be called to exercise that authority by administering the sacrament in the interests of the sacrament itself. Luther deals with these three points in detail:

---

[74] R. Newton Flew, *The Nature of the Church*, p. 83.
[75] *Reformation Writings*, I.280.

(i) 'When a bishop consecrates, he simply acts on behalf of the entire congregation, all of whom have the same authority. They may select one of their number and command him to exercise this authority on behalf of the others. It would be similar if ten brothers, kings' sons and equal heirs, were to choose one of themselves to rule the kingdom for them. All would be kings and of equal authority, although one was appointed to rule.'[76] Of course, the one who has been chosen will then be recognized by the others as the one who has been called to exercise authority. It is the same in the Church. Ordination means that the minister is recognized by the whole Church as one who has been called to serve it in particular ways. The commission comes from God, but the confirmation of the divine call generally comes through the congregation. Ordination is no more and no less than the public recognition and proclamation of the fact of the divine commissioning through the call of the congregation. A man may be appointed to this ministry only by a congregation where the ministry of preaching is shared by all who have a common priesthood stemming from a common baptism and faith. This is a conception which Luther never abandoned.

This view has sometimes been considered an over-simplification of ordination. But what exactly does a man receive at ordination? Does he receive '*character indelibilis*', or an undefined magical power, or 'special' grace? Luther rejects all such notions. In any case, we cannot understand ultimately the quality of God's grace, and we are on very uncertain and speculative ground when we attempt to distinguish the nature of grace given on one occasion from that given on another. Believers come under *favor Dei*, the favour of God, which does not and cannot change; it is the functions for which it is bestowed which are different. It is wrong to suppose that something is bestowed in ordination which is denied to all other Christians. 'The power of the congregation to call rests on the fact that all Christians possess the rightful and true ministry of preaching, besides the functions included over and above—baptism, administration of communion, hearing of confession, and so on. Luther refers here to 2 Corinthians 3^6. That we were made ministers of a new covenant, not of the letter, but of the Spirit, is a word addressed to all Christians. But a minister of the Spirit preaches grace and forgiveness of sins. All

---

[76] *Reformation Writings*, I.114.

Christians, therefore, have been entrusted with the Word. Luther refers also to 1 Peter 2⁹. All Christians have God's Word and are under obligation to see to its propagation.'[77]

(ii) Although all possess this power and authority, they will not always put them into practice. There may be occasions, however, when in the interests of the sacrament itself, they will be called upon to exercise these powers even though they are not ordained. 'To put it more plainly, suppose a small group of earnest Christian laymen were taken prisoner and settled in the middle of a desert without any episcopally ordained priest among them; and they then agreed to choose one of themselves, whether married or not, and endow him with the office of baptizing, administering the sacrament, pronouncing absolution and preaching; that man would be as truly a priest as if he had been ordained by all the bishops and the popes. It follows that, if need be, anyone may baptize or pronounce absolution, an impossible situation if we were not all priests.'[78] In such cases it is especially important to notice that this course is adopted *in the interests of the sacrament itself*, since it is better that the sacrament should be administered by one who is not ordained than that fellow Christians should be deprived of the privilege altogether. It is also important to notice that even in such cases one is chosen by the congregation, for a company of believing people are no less a congregation of the Faithful whatever their circumstances may be and wherever they may gather for worship.

(iii) A common misunderstanding may arise from the foregoing and it is important to clarify the situation at once. Luther holds that the power to ordain those who are set aside for the work of the ministry is within the province of the whole Church, but this does not mean that the holder of office at any given time is 'made' a minister *merely* by an act of orderly vocation from the congregation. Office is not created by the exercise of it. Similarly, a layman is not 'made' a priest by the occasional exercise of his privilege as a member of the Royal Priesthood. Priesthood is not created by the priestly act; on the contrary, it is his membership of the Royal Priesthood which enables him to exercise the priestly function. This principle is generally accepted in the Lutheran Church as Heinrich Hermelink makes clear in the following

---

[77] Dr Gosta Hök, *Scottish Journal of Theology* (March 1954), p. 19.
[78] *Reformation Writings*, I.114.

words: 'The holiness of the sacraments is not the result of an act of sanctification performed by a priest ordained and sanctified to that end, but of the Divine Grace of the Word, which is to be preached and made clear by the symbol. In principle, therefore, all believers of our Church may administer the sacraments as "priests". It is their bounden duty to give Baptism if the life of a child be in danger, should there be no minister at hand. But it is also possible for unordained believing members to give Communion in the Lutheran Church so long as the order prescribed by the Church is observed and the minister's permission is granted.'[79]

No one may exercise the functions of the Ministry without the confirmation of the Congregation. In the Early Church even the deacons were not called by the apostles until the whole congregation had assembled and taken its part in their appointment. That God calls through men consequently means for Luther that he calls through the congregation.

'Just because we are all priests of equal standing, no one must push himself forward and, without the consent and choice of the rest, presume to do that for which we all have equal authority. Only by the consent and command of the community should any individual person claim for himself what belongs equally to all.'[80]

Two qualifications are therefore demanded for the ministry: the minister must be—(1) anointed and born to be Christ's priest, and (2) rightly, properly, and publicly called. 'For, praise God, we can present to the Christian a proper Christian Mass, as ordained and instituted by Christ and in accordance with Christ's and the Church's intention. At the altar stands our vicar, bishop, and curate, rightly, properly, and publicly called, previously consecrated by baptism, anointed and born to be Christ's priest.'[81] The Christian is a member of the universal priesthood by baptism, but he is given a special task within that priesthood by the call of God which is confirmed by the congregation. This is what Luther means when he says: 'It is true we are all priests, but we are not all vicars.' The minister's call is mediated through the congregation. Prince, councillor or bishop may represent the congregation. The Lutheran stands alongside the Anglican in that God calls through the congregation. The ministry, therefore,

---

[79] *The Ministry and the Sacraments*, ed. Dunkerley, p. 154.
[80] *Reformation Writings*, I.115.
[81] Quoted by H. H. Kramm, *Theology of Martin Luther*, pp. 77ff.

is a divine institution. He stands alongside the Congregationalist and against the Anglican in that the divinely instituted ministry is not placed above the congregation, but in it, in the fellowship of all believers, proclaiming the Gospel which is the right of every believer. Here we have the road which leads to a proper understanding of the priesthood of believers. Believers are not only priests in vocation, they have also a right to preach. Not all exercise this right, though all may. It is in this way that believers exercise their priestly function by confirming the call and appointing those who shall exercise it. In principle it is true that everyone may preach the Gospel. If the essence of the ministry is the proclamation of the Gospel, everyone who has been baptized may proclaim it. But if everyone preached without authorization from anyone, they would not be preaching the Gospel. This is because the Gospel is a word from God, and it is necessary that the ministry should be appointed by God and recognized by all.

That which qualifies the congregation to fulfil this important task is the fact that each member is called of God to a ministry of the Spirit. Luther refers to 2 Corinthians 3^6, which states that 'we were made ministers of a new covenant, not of the letter, but of the Spirit', and he points out that this is a word addressed to all Christians. All Christians have been entrusted with the Word. Since all Christians possess God's word, they are all under an obligation to see to its propagation. John 1^{16} banishes any notion of special conditions or the bestowal of 'special' grace: 'For of His fulness we have *all* received, and grace following upon grace.'

The position may be summarized as follows: Because Christians share in Christ's High Priestly Ministry, they are all priests—yet they are not so for their own sake, but for others. Every Christian may offer the sacrifice of himself, may pray and preach, may take upon himself the responsibilities which belong to him as a member of the congregation. All this he may do because none of these things belongs to the ministry (i.e. in its restricted sense) as a right. Priesthood belongs to Christ, and Christians possess it by their baptism and their faith, i.e. by sharing in what belongs to Christ. This priesthood is inward and spiritual and there is no other priesthood in the New Testament. The ordained priesthood is a necessity and is God's gift to the Church through the Church. The minister is first and foremost a member of the universal priesthood; his calling is confirmed by the congregation and charged with special duties. At his ordination he is publicly recognized, proclaimed and commissioned by the whole Church, and in this way he becomes in St Paul's phrase 'servant of all' (1 Cor 9^{19}).

VI. PUBLIC WORSHIP, WITH PRAYER, PRAISE, AND THANKSGIVING

(a) *The Sacrifice of Prayer*

It is just because prayer, praise and thanksgiving are often thought of as something which man *offers* to God that Luther deals with this question with great caution. His strict, thoroughgoing theocentric emphasis is revealed in almost everything he writes. He dislikes the suggestion that he must be placed in a position where he must offer anything to God. He is afraid, and rightly so, that whatever he gives may be deemed inadequate. He does not wish to have anything whatever to do with the salvation of his own soul, for he prefers to leave all that with God. It is fair to say that he only found peace when he was able to do this.

'I want to make my confession in all seriousness that, even if it were possible for a free will to be given to me and I were also presented with an instrument with which I could achieve salvation, I should not like to accept the offer. In the midst of so many difficulties and dangers, and in the contest with many devils round about us, I should be in no condition to keep my feet and withstand attack. A single devil is more than all men can tame.... Even in regard to the best that I can do, the doubt would remain whether it was satisfactory to God, or whether he did not require more of me. This is the experience of all who have sought salvation by works, and accords with what I myself discovered after years of pain and toil and effort. But God has taken the care of my salvation out of my hands, and taken it wholly on Himself. He has promised to save me, not according to my conduct or my works, but by his own mercy: and I am now happy and at peace.'[82]

Therefore, the first thing to be asserted is that our offering of prayer, praise and thanksgiving, must not be regarded as an attempt to take care of our own salvation.

Again, in 'A short and good exposition of the Lord's Prayer

[82] W. J. Kooiman, *By Faith Alone*, p. 152.

forwards and backwards', Luther points out that the beginning and the end of the Lord's Prayer are centred in the glory of God. All our prayers should be summed up in the words, 'Thine is the kingdom, the power and the glory', and in so far as we forget or fail to say this we are seeking our own glory. Indeed all our praying should be primarily for His sake and not our own. 'In order that we should not desire the kingdom of God for our own sake, the hallowing of the divine name is put in the first place; so that we should pray in this sense to be blessed and for the coming of God's kingdom, not in order that it may go well with us, but that the name and honour and glory of God the Lord may be praised and magnified.'[83] This point is further emphasized in Luther's comment on the meaning of the first petition in 'The Lord's Prayer': 'Grant that in all we have, or say, or do, we may praise and honour Thee alone, and not endeavour to promote our own repute or seek our own fame: but only Thine, to whom all things belong. Keep us from the shameful wrong of ingratitude.... Prevent us from desiring anything whether in time or eternity, which is not to Thy honour and glory.'[84]

Why does Luther stress this truth? Because unless we fully realize that to God belong all power and glory there is no point in our praying at all. Prayer, after all, means receiving God's gift and not the fulfilment of man's desire. Again comes the thought that we must leave God to do the work since we cannot do it ourselves. Now prayer needs the aid of faith, and if this is present, nothing else is necessary. Luther felt that the element of faith had been overlooked and that the efficacy which belongs to prayer alone had been given to the mass. 'They trust in the efficacy of the mass, and they do not ascribe its efficacy to prayer. The error has gradually increased in this way until they ascribe to the sacrament what belongs to the prayer, and they bring to God what they ought to receive from Him as a gift.'[85] Prayer is the voice of faith and that is why it is welcomed in the sight of God. 'We ought also to bear in mind that the prayers are of no avail either for him who offers them, or for those on whose behalf they are offered, unless the testament be first received in faith. It is faith which prays, and its voice alone which is heard.'[86] The prayer of faith banishes all self-assertion, and trusts, not in the prayer that is offered, or

---

[83] Philip S. Watson, *Let God be God*, p. 40.   [84] *Reformation Writings*, I.91.
[85] Ibid. p. 247.   [86] Ibid.

the one who offers it, but in God. It will be obvious that this privilege of prayer is not confined to any particular section of the Christian community but to all. Dr Vatja goes so far as to say that it is the 'sacrament of the faithful': 'Prayer is the priestly sacrament of the faithful, through being priest-with-Christ. For all prayers, including those offered during mass, are directed to God through our mediator Christ. The prayer to God is God's way to man, is Christ become man, and in whom man meets God, and without whose mediation, he cannot approach God. . . . Christ is his intercessor to the Father. And so every prayer is a plea in which, as Luther says, One who is great in the sight of God is called upon, and for whose sake God is willing to forgive sins and to grant what one asks. Christ is the altar on which the praying person is sacrificed and through whom prayer reaches God. In this sense, prayer and the sacrifice of prayer fuse into a unity.'[87]

This wider priesthood is open to the Christian in intercessory prayer. Such service is not the privilege of a few specially consecrated people, it is the corporate activity of the whole Church. Rupp sets it in its true perspective: 'Faith, then, is no mystic abandonment, but the appropriation of this "mighty duel" in which Jesus Christ has conquered sin, death, and the devil. Luther goes straight from this thought to that of the priesthood of all believers, and it is plain that the heart of the matter for him, lies in no individualist conception of private judgement, or the denial of priesthood altogether, but rather that solidarity of Christian communion expressed in the ministry of intercession: "As priests we are worthy to appear before God to pray for others".'[88]

We may say, then, that Luther understands by 'spiritual sacrifices' not ritual actions but the living service which the Church is to offer to God. Two kinds of priesthood stand out in his theology. First, there is the Priesthood of Jesus Christ, which means that He is eternally active in His self-giving to the world, which is the expression of divine love. In addition to the priestly work of Christ, however, and as an outcome of it, there is a priestly service which the Church of Christ is expected to render as the manifestation of her union with her Lord. This is the Church's expression of her love and duty toward her Master, and

---

[87] V. Vatja, *The Theology of Divine Service in Luther*, pp. 269ff.
[88] *Luther's Progress to the Diet of Worms*, p. 88.

in this consists her Royal Priesthood which is the equivalent of the priesthood of all believers.

Many Protestants find it hard to accept the priestly function of the Church, yet the fact remains that Christians are priests, not as independent individuals but in so far as they are loyal fellow-members in the Church which is the Body of Christ, and as they share in that sacrificial activity which is common to all, and is inspired by the indwelling presence of the Holy Spirit. Dr Vatja, who has examined this aspect of Luther's teaching with great care, has pointed out that it must be viewed from two angles. First, we must view it as something which God has done *for* man; and secondly, as something which God is doing *through* man.

(1) 'Prayer as sacrifice means, on the one hand, the crucifixion of the "old man", but also, by its expression in the congregation of the Church, it demonstrates that Christ is priest on behalf of His people. When the "old man" is crucified through being priest with Christ, new life streams in, which expresses itself in conformity with the sacrifice of Christ and in the dedication of oneself for the sake of the "others". So intercession becomes priestly devotion to one's fellow men in the sacrifice of prayer before God.'[89]

(2) This means that there is imparted to the Christian a unique sense of mission, for he realizes that nothing happens to him in the spiritual realm for his own sake alone but for the sake of all. This means that there is a missionary obligation placed upon him and that he can no longer isolate himself from the sins and woes and cares of the wider world in which he is set. 'In the Church, the communion sanctorum, the whole world is opened to the Christian, and he is sent forth into it by God Himself in the priestly service of intercession. In the intercession of faith, the "new man" stands before the face of God, not to gain something for himself, but, as a successor to Christ, to give himself up for his fellow men and call down God's blessing upon them. . . . Just as the Father gives His gifts to friends and foes, so too the priestly intercession of the Christian goes out over a related circle of believers in order to reach the lost and godless.'[90] It is possible for the Christian to receive everything from God, and still to be the means of stemming the divine activity in the world. Selfishness in respect of the free blessings of Christ must be regarded as a grave offence. So a

[89] V. Vatja, *The Theology of Divine Service in Luther*, pp. 300ff.   [90] Ibid.

warning is added, and this warning touches the doctrine of the Christian's priesthood at its most solemn point because it is at the point of its deepest responsibility. As he is sent forth into the world in priestly intercession, 'he confesses that his justification is presented to, and received by him, that it is of grace, and he therefore gives his justification to others. For in the moment in which he might wish to keep it for himself, it would cease to be God's justification and become his own justification, which would be condemned to death without hope of resurrection.'[91] These may appear to be hard words, but it is a hard task to which the Christian is committed. In short, being priest with Christ means no less than being priest for others, and it is in this unconditioned sacrifice of dedication and intercession that the Christian is truly united with the sacrifice of Christ.

(b) *The Sacrifice of Praise and Thanksgiving*

The preaching of the Word may easily become objective, that is, the exercise of a function without any relation to the world in which we live. In this sense, the preaching of the Gospel may become an end in itself. This is not Luther's idea. If the Gospel is preached, there must be a response from a believing and confessing congregation. A praising congregation is part of the proper proclamation of the Gospel. Praising God in response to the preaching of the Word may, and sometimes does, lead to a tension and even an enmity between the Church and the World. This tension, however, is as desirable as it is inevitable. Indeed, persecution is sometimes a sign that the Church is fulfilling her purpose in the world. It will be remembered that the early Christians suffered and died not because they talked about Christ but because they worshipped Him. Their biggest crime against the State was their refusal to worship anyone except Christ. They were forbidden to sing, 'We praise Thee, O God, we acknowledge Thee to be the Lord', because these words involved a conflict of loyalties. All the same, no imperial order could silence their song. Only death could stop them, and that is why so many of them suffered martyrdom. Their worship cost them their life, but they knew what worship meant.

Luther did not regard worship as a soporific; on the contrary, it was a mighty activity of the spirit which made heavy demands

---

[91] V. Vatja, *The Theology of Divine Service in Luther*, pp. 300ff.

upon those who were partakers in it. Luther does not hesitate to say that the praising congregation which responds to the Word proclaimed actually *creates* the Church. There is no Church apart from the power of the Gospel; no Church apart from the giving of the Word on the one hand, and the receiving of the Word by the congregation on the other. The Holy Communion is the culminating point of Lutheran worship just because it is the Church's 'sacrifice of praise and thanksgiving'.[92] In his 'Short Exposition of the Decalogue' Luther says: 'Praise, glorify, bless, and call upon God's name; count your own name and glory as nothing at all if only God be praised; for He alone comprises all things, and brings all things to pass. Everything taught in Scripture about praising God, glorifying Him and giving Him thanks: and about His name and the joy He gives, applies to keeping this commandment' (the Second).[93]

(1) To praise God is to acknowledge that God is the Giver of all things. 'Our will, when compared with Thine, is never good, but always evil. But Thy will is always entirely good; it is to be loved and sought in the highest degree, and beyond all else.'[94] God is the Giver of all that is good, and we are asked only to receive it. Our receiving it is an act of acknowledgement and a thanksgiving. We are not the creators of goodness, for this is the divine prerogative. We are not in a position to give anything except sacrificial praise, but, to give this is our bounden duty. God's act of grace is primary; our thanksgiving is secondary, and the one is the result of the other. In other words, grace prompts our response. Luther regards the leper who turned back to thank Jesus as one who was 'bearing back home to God the grace and goodness received'. Then he comments: 'Oh, how few there are who return thus, scarce one in ten.' The Psalmist refers to the same theme: 'If I were hungry, I would not tell thee; for the world is mine' (Ps 50^{12}). This, surely, is decisive: God needs nothing but gives everything.

> *Before Thy ever-blazing throne,*
> *We ask no lustre of our own.*

(2) To praise God is to renounce self-praise.
To cause anyone to neglect God's praise is a grievous sin.

---

[92] See *The Nature of the Church*, ed. R. Newton Flew, p. 80.
[93] *Reformation Writings*, p. 80.   [94] Ibid. p. 93.

'Grant that our evil deeds and infirmities may provoke no one to dishonour Thy name, or to neglect Thy praise. Prevent us from desiring anything, whether in time or eternity, which is not to Thy honour and glory.'[95] Yet not to give God praise is to dishonour Him, for all praise belongs to Him. The whole point is that we cannot give honour to God without in some way sacrificing ourselves. An act of praise to God is therefore an act of self-sacrifice. If we expect any reward for this praise we are placing it in the category of good works and this inevitably leads to self-praise. We cannot praise God without denying ourselves.

(3) To praise God is to confess our sins.

'There is joy in the presence of the angels over one sinner that repenteth.' Repentance brings joy to God. It follows that the man who confesses his sins praises God. One of the things which troubled Luther was that confession, which should be made to God, had become a means of oppression and extortion. Faith in things other than God had become the custom, and the result was idolatry. 'One might specify such things as running about on pilgrimages, the perverse worship of saints, . . . various beliefs in works and in the practice of ceremonies; by all of which faith in God is lessened, while idolatry is fostered, as is the case nowadays.'[96] All these methods of penance had replaced the true confession of sins before God. Yet God delights in confession; confession praises God.

(4) The Sacrifice of Praise.

This is the kind of sacrifice which Luther did accept, and Vatja sees this also as an expression of the Christian's priesthood: 'The priestly sacrifice of praise as expressed in confession of sin, and the song of praise must always be considered in Luther together with God's work itself, for God acts through Law and Gospel, wrath and love: priesthood is being priest with Christ. So Luther held that the confessing of sin and the proclamation of the forgiveness of it is a sacrifice of praise. The Christian community is seen thereby as the home of this sacrifice. . . . While the Church receives this work of God, and in preaching and the sacraments, stands out before the world, she confesses before the world that God is acting in and through her. From this point of view, the priestly sacrifice is an expression of priesthood on behalf of one's

---

[95] 'The Lord's Prayer', *Reformation Writings*, I.91.
[96] 'Penance', ibid. p. 285.

fellow men. The believers become instruments through which the Holy Spirit works, and our fellow man is drawn into the faith.'[97]

It is clear, then, that in Luther's teaching, the sacrifice of praise and thanksgiving is an expression of the priesthood of all believers, and as was the case in our consideration of the other 'marks' of the Church, we find here also that this basic doctrine is prominent.

VII. THE HOLY CROSS: i.e. suffering in many forms through which the Church must inevitably pass.

The German Church has known what it has meant to exist not only under the Word but also under the Cross. In some respects every age is an age of persecution. Those who are followers of the 'Man of Sorrows' cannot hope to avoid sorrow and suffering. If they seek to avoid these things, they are not following. The way of Christ was the way of rejection, and since the servant is not greater than his Lord, he must be content to live under the Cross. Although all this is true of the Church as a whole, it is not without significance that Luther as a representative of the German Church regarded the possession of the Holy Cross as one of the marks of the Church.

It is undoubtedly true that the Church becomes much more clearly definable in time of conflict than at any other time. These tensions are sometimes within the Church and are doctrinal; and sometimes they exist between the Church and the State. When National Socialism fell upon Germany in 1933 and the State began to use the Church as an instrument of State propaganda, the Lutheran, Reformed and United Churches met at the first Confessing Synod at Barmen to protest. They declared: 'The witness of Holy Scripture for us is to Jesus Christ as the one Word of God, whom we must hear, and in life and death must trust and obey. We reject the false doctrine that the Church can or must as the source of its message recognize besides and beyond this one Word of God any other events or powers, forms or truths, as revelation of God.'[98] Although this attitude of the State toward the Church was to be feared, there is no doubt that its results were quite surprising. A visible unity emerged between the

---
[97] *The Theology of Divine Service in Luther*, pp. 300ff.
[98] R. Newton Flew, *The Nature of the Church*, p. 54.

three Churches which had not been known before. In fact, the Church under the Cross became the Church united under the Cross. 'In describing the nature of this common act of confessing which the Church struggle evoked, various cardinal points have to be noticed. In the act of confessing there occurred an act of common and public witness to Jesus Christ, Crucified and Risen, as Lord of Lords. In it the Church specifically separated itself off from the sovereign claim of the totalitarian political power, and attacked its ideology and its self-made gods. The act of confessing was at the same time a witness to a divine judgement, executed in political persecution upon the evangelical Churches in Germany and their history, and also a general confession of sin.'[99] These three factors which emerged under the struggle are of the utmost importance. The Church bore witness to the sufferings and victory of Christ; engaged openly those hostile forces which would have robbed God of the honour that was His; and acknowledged that judgement is a divine action, which, whenever it is made manifest, should result in a confession of sin. At all times of stress two truths emerge in a clearer light and receive fresh emphasis; they are the solidarity of the People of God, and the Doctrine of the Neighbour.

(a) *The Solidarity of the People of God*

Two statements by Luther will assist us to understand what this solidarity means: 'I believe that He bore His sufferings and endured the cross for my sake and that of all believers; and, in so doing, blessed all suffering and every cross.'[100] In the other passage Luther shows how the prayers and service of the entire fellowship strengthen each member of it. 'I believe that in this universal fellowship of Christendom, all things are in common, and the property of any belongs to all, and no one has anything of his own. Therefore all the prayers and good works of the entire fellowship must be of benefit to me and every believer, and must assist and strengthen us, and this at all times in life or death. Thus all bear one another's burdens, as St Paul says.'[101] The first quotation tells us that all suffering is bound up mystically but unmistakably with the sufferings of Christ. The second tells us that the entire fellowship exists for the benefit and strengthening and building up of each believer.

[99] *The Nature of the Church*, p. 55.   [100] *Reformation Writings*, I.86.   [101] Ibid. p. 88.

Luther well knew that formal religion was not enough. All the external paraphernalia of religion was meaningless until and unless it was seen in the context of suffering. Church attendance, Christian service, and obedience to rules did not signify the Church under the Cross, and may even signify a Church without a Cross. The Church must always be ready for the 'mighty duel', prepared for the struggle against all that is evil, and at no time must she shrink from defending herself in crisis even though her message may appear to be a '*scandalon*' in the eyes of the world. The Church does not exist for self-edification, self-satisfaction, self-glorification, but in order to obey the command of Him who said: 'Go ye into all the world', even though it is a world in which there is much tribulation. The command to advance in the name of Christ and in spite of every hindrance is unmistakable. There is no advance in the kingdom of Christ without struggle, and so the Church is always the Church under the Cross. Luther holds that we become most conscious of our oneness with Christ and with all Christians when we partake of Holy Communion. 'All the spiritual possessions of Christ and the saints are communicated to him who receives this sacrament: again, all his sins and sufferings are communicated to them and love engenders love and unites all.'[102] Also the knowledge that the Christian is surrounded by all those spiritual powers which are the inheritance of the universal Church is surely an enriching thought. Indeed, it means that the Christian knows no fear: 'For Christ has so cared for us that we do not need to tread the way of death alone, but walk with the attendance of the whole Church . . . and the Church bears it more strongly than we ourselves, so that we know that the word of Elisha applies to us, which he said to the timid young man . . . "Lord, open the eyes of the young man that he may see." So it happens with us too, that we ask that our eyes may be opened and we should see, with the eyes of faith I mean, that there is nothing to fear, for "as the mountains are about Jerusalem so the Lord is round about his people now and for ever".'[103]

Now if it is true that we are bound to one another because we are bound to Christ in faith, and that there is an ultimate Christian estate (Stand) in which all believers are counted priests and kings,

---

[102] Quoted from G. Rupp, *The Righteousness of God*, p. 314.
[103] Ibid. p. 315.

we may be sure that this holds important consequences for our understanding of guilt, penitence, and service.

We may best understand the meaning of the solidarity of guilt by referring to some striking words of John Donne: 'No man is an Iland, intire of it selfe; every man is a peece of the Continent, a part of the maine: if a clod be washed away by the Sea, Europe is the lesse, as well as if a Promontorie were, as well as if a Mannor of thy friends or of *thine owne* were; and man's death diminshes me, because I am involved in Mankinde; and therefore never send to know for whom the bell tolls; It tolls for thee.'[104]

Now the Church in any country is a part of the Christian continent; from the Christian standpoint there is no such thing as an isolated, self-existent community. The universal Church is one, and therefore the guilt of any part of it is the guilt of the whole. This inescapable sense of guilt as well as a profound sense of solidarity have characterized the attitude of Luther's successors in modern Germany. It was the cry which rose from the ashes of Berlin as the leaders of the Church realized their crushing burden of responsibility: 'Today we confess that long before He spoke in His anger God besought us in love, but we refused to listen. Long before our Churches collapsed in rubble, our pulpits were desecrated and our prayers had grown dumb. . . . Long before the sham of law and order broke down, justice had been counterfeited. Long before human beings were murdered, they had been reduced to non-entities.'[105] Yet none of us who claims Jesus as Lord can expect to be exonerated from a responsibility of this kind. Paradoxically enough the Christian's individual relatedness to God is the very reason for the solidarity of the universal Church. This thought is aptly expressed by Dr J. A. T. Robinson: 'A man is *a* man because God calls everyone by His own name to a wholly unrepeatable relatedness and an indivisible responsibility to Himself, to return a unique answer to the Word of his Creator.' Herein lies the significance of man's spirit; the significance of the body lies in the fact that it is 'the symbol, not of individuality, but of solidarity. It is that which binds every individual, divinely unique as he is, in inescapable relatedness to the whole of nature and history and the totality of the cosmic order. It is the bond of continuity and unity between man and his environment, between

---

[104] Quoted in *For Whom the Bell Tolls*, Hemingway.
[105] Stewart Hermann, *The Rebirth of the German Church*, pp. 13-14.

individual and community, between generation and generation.'[106]

The basis of this solidarity is biblical: it is the outcome of the doctrines of Creation and the Holy Spirit. Since we have a common origin we have also a common life. We are literally akin. The aboriginal who cried in amazement when he saw red blood trickling from a missionary's finger, 'His blood is red', was discovering for the first time what many had known for a long time as a biological fact without realizing its theological implications. Yet this sort of solidarity which is based on the doctrine of Creation is very different from that which is connected with the doctrine of the Holy Spirit. The one is natural and inevitable as well as inescapable, but the other implies a responsibility which is *voluntarily accepted* which is a very different thing. Those in whom the Spirit dwells are thereby linked not only with God in Christ but with one another. The concept of the organic unity of believers is an inevitable consequence of belief in their individual inspiration. There is no such thing as a solitary disciple, for in accepting Christ the believer enters in a life already widely shared: he not only shares a common loyalty, but one and the same Spirit dwells in the whole society, and so he shares a common responsibility too. It is a universal fact that any deep awareness of God is accompanied by a sense of sympathy and unity with mankind. It is, however, only in the context of a personal relationship with Christ that a wide responsibility is recognized. 'Am I not', said Mackay of Uganda, 'the link between dying men and the dying Christ?'[107] Is not this a true understanding of the solidarity of the whole Church? 'To be a link between dying men and the dying Christ is the prerogative of *everyone* who accepts his place in the Christian Mission.'[108] There is no higher conception of the priesthood of all believers than that which is implied in the foregoing statement. All Christians are involved in Mission and Responsibility because each Christian is the link between dying men and the dying Christ. If Mission and Responsibility mean that we share the joys and triumphs of the Faith, they must also mean that we share its suffering and guilt. Nowhere has this been recognized more clearly than in the Stuttgart Declaration which was made on 18th and 19th October 1945. It says:

'The Council of the Protestant Church in Germany greets the

[106] *In the End—God*, pp. 86-7.
[107] Quotation from Max Warren, *The Christian Mission*, p. 66.
[108] Ibid.

representatives of the World Council of Churches. We are the more grateful for this visit as we know ourselves to be one with our people in a great company of suffering and in a great solidarity of guilt. With great pain do we say: Through us endless suffering has been brought to many peoples and countries. What we have often borne witness to in our own congregations, that we now declare in the name of the whole Church. . . . We accuse ourselves for not witnessing more courageously, for not praying more faithfully, for not believing more joyously, and for not loving more ardently.'[109] And as they resolve, under the direction of Christ who is the only Lord of the Church, to make a new beginning, they find great strength in the knowledge that they are united with the Churches in other lands: 'Our hope is in the God of grace and mercy, that he will use our Churches as His instruments and will give them authority to proclaim His Word and to make His will obeyed among ourselves and among our whole people. That in this new beginning we may be aware of our wholehearted unity with the other Churches of the ecumenical fellowship fills us with deep joy.'[110]

Universal guilt demands universal repentance, and so the following words were added: 'This is [a time] for universal repentance whereby each member of Christ's body may acknowledge his share of responsibility for his omissions and commissions.' Although in some ways, we are estranged from Christ by sin and guilt and suffering, we should be estranged for ever unless He had taken upon Himself this threefold burden of responsibility. Through the High Priesthood of Christ, sin, guilt and suffering become our point of contact and not the point of alienation. So the priesthood of all believers can no longer be regarded as a doctrine which the Church *may* believe; it is rather an experience through which the Church *must* pass. Guilt, suffering and penitence are the marks of its very existence—it is always and everywhere 'the Church under the Cross', and we assert our oneness with a universal fellowship as well as our individual need when we sing:

> *My faith would lay her hand*
> *On that meek head of Thine,*
> *While as a penitent I stand,*
> *And here confess my sin.*

[109] Hermann, *The Rebirth of the German Church*, pp. 136-7. [110] Ibid.

(b) *The doctrine of the Neighbour*

Much of what has already been said in this section concerning the Church under the Cross is no more than a modern interpretation of Luther's doctrine of the Neighbour. Firstly, we must show that Luther's teaching upon this subject is not simply an adjunct to his main doctrines but rather that it springs from the heart of his theology.

Faith receives God's gifts. Faith is a relationship not between man and man but between man and God. On the other hand, there exists a relationship between man and man and this is based on love. Love means distributing to our neighbour that which we have received from God. Man is justified by the righteousness of Christ and therefore he has no need of works. If man takes his works and offers them to God, he is committing a double offence: he is offering them to God who does not need them, and he is taking them from his neighbour where they truly belong. Since God does not require man's works, they must be offered in service to man's neighbour.

Now all this springs from the fact that the Christian shares the priesthood of Christ. This means that we are engaged in a twofold activity: we are engaged in the work of faith and hope (praying and praising) which is always directed toward God; and secondly, we are engaged in the work of love and sacrifice (offering and serving) which is always directed toward man.

This activity must not be regarded as simply a human activity. We have already observed that the Ministry is seen as God's own activity in the midst of the congregation. It is because this activity is not limited to a specifically called Ministry that it must be placed on the same level as other ministries. Yet if there is no specifically called Ministry, not only will the preaching of the Gospel be neglected, but the service of one's neighbour in the earthly vocations will be neglected too. These other vocations are also part of the service of love which is expressed in the priesthood of all believers.

Once again, this divine activity is seen to be directly connected with the preaching of the Word. Because the doctrine of justification by faith in its outworking in man's life contains both faith and love, the preaching of the Gospel leads to the establishing both of vocations which serve faith and those which serve love.

In both it is Christ who is proclaimed. Each is, in some sense, a proclamation of the Gospel. When justification by faith is proclaimed, it binds a man to God in faith and to his neighbour in love. *Therefore*, both vocations—the Ministry, and the vocations of secular life which serve love to one's neighbour, spring from the same source and arise out of the same Gospel. Since the ministries which serve faith and those which serve love take their origin in the same source, they possess the same dignity and are different aspects of the same priesthood.

To begin by an imitation of Christ, and then proceed to faith, is a common error. The right order is to start in faith and proceed to love, i.e. to that kind of service which cannot be dissociated from the Cross. The ultimate end is suffering and it cannot be otherwise. The Christian begins in faith, develops in love, and this love involves suffering, it means carrying the cross. So every aspect of Christian work, whether it be the proclamation of the Gospel or service to one's neighbour is really an expression of suffering love, and this is the mark of the Church under the Cross.

With these observations in mind we may turn to Luther's teaching upon this subject as it is found mainly in 'the Freedom of a Christian'.

(1) *Sufficiency of Faith*

Luther begins with a definition of freedom: 'A Christian is free and independent in every respect, a bondservant to none. A Christian is a dutiful servant in every respect, owing a duty to everyone.'[111] These two axioms are clearly found in 1 Corinthians 9, where St Paul says: 'Though I am free from all men, I have made myself a servant to all.' Again in Romans 13: 'Owe no man anything, except to love one another. But love owes a duty, and is a bondservant of what she loves.'

The overriding theme is that God makes everything serve the purpose of man's redemption. Nothing is permitted to hinder God's redemptive purpose in the world. In this sense, therefore, everything is at the service of the believer. In his *Short Exposition of the Creed* Luther puts it as follows: 'Since He is almighty, there is nothing I need that He cannot give me, or do for me. Since He is the creator of heaven and earth, and Lord of all, who is there that can deprive me of anything, or do me harm? Yea, there can

---

[111] *Reformation Writings*, I.357.

be no event whatsoever, but that it will all turn out to my benefit, and serve me, since He, whom everything obeys and serves, Himself seeks my good.'[112]

Since he possesses a sufficiency of faith a Christian must serve his neighbour. As in all things he is served, so in all things he, in turn, must serve. In Christian thought this is not illogical since 'the Son of Man came not to be served but to serve, and to give His life a ransom for many'. 'All that we do must be designed for the benefit of our neighbour, because each one has sufficient for himself in his faith. (The Christian) should have no other thought than of what is needful to others. That would mean living a true Christian life; and that is the way in which faith proceeds to work with joy and love.'[113] Here again, the example of Christ is brought before us as sufficient evidence: 'Have the same mind as you see in Christ who, although He was filled with divine form, and had sufficient for Himself, and His life and works and suffering were not necessary to Him in order that He might become devout and be saved, nevertheless He emptied Himself of all these things, and assumed the form of a servant. He did and suffered everything with no other object than our advantage. Thus, although He was free, for our sakes He became a servant.'[114]

Luther brings the discussion to the highest level when he says: 'To my neighbour, I will be, as a Christian, what Christ has become to me',[115] and just as Christ did not keep to Himself the riches He possessed, so neither can we. To become the instrument whereby the blessings of Christ are made available to all is to exercise our common priesthood, for 'all the good things of God should flow from one man to another, and become common to all, so that each one may be as concerned for his neighbour as for his own self'.[116] But if all things come to us by the mercy of God, it is also true that these blessings should flow back to God in service to our neighbour. 'I must offer even my faith and righteousness before God on behalf of my neighbour',[117] for it is thus that our priestly service comes full circle and fulfils its true and only purpose—it is given through Christ to us, and then offered in service for others to Him whence it came. It follows that any suggestion that the priesthood of believers detracts in any sense from the Priesthood of Christ is quite mistaken. Whale has drawn

---

[112] *Reformation Writings*, I.85.   [113] Ibid. p. 375.   [114] Ibid. p. 376.
[115] Ibid.   [116] Ibid. p. 379.   [117] Ibid.

attention to the fact that Luther's theocentric emphasis is clearly manifest in what he says on this subject: 'All is of God and all is for God, but the divine agape comes down from the eternities as a parabolic curve which returns thither by way of human priesthood; the priesthood of all believers to one another. A Christian is a channel, open upwards to heaven by faith, and outwards to the neighbour through love. All that the Christian possesses has been received from God that he may pass it on. He has nothing of his own to give; he is an instrument through which redeeming love is further mediated.'[118]

It is, according to Luther, the Christian's willingness to offer up himself in this way that he becomes a priest 'of God's own making', for his verse states it thus:

> *Thus by the power of grace they were*
> *True priests of God's own making,*
> *Who offered up themselves e'en there,*
> *Christ's holy orders taking.*

(2) *Spiritual Priesthood*

(i) Spiritual priesthood is the gift of Christ to His people.

Luther points out that the kingship and priesthood of the eldest son in the Hebrew family are really a type of the offices of Jesus Christ. 'This is a figure symbolizing Jesus Christ who is that selfsame human Son of God the Father by the Virgin Mary. He is therefore a king and a priest—but in the spiritual sense. His kingdom is not earthly, nor does it consist in earthly things, but in those of the spirit, such as truth, wisdom, peace, joy, salvation, and the like.'[119] Now it is this spiritual priesthood and this alone which Christians are called upon to share: 'Since Christ has the primogeniture with all appropriate honour and worth, He shares it with all Christians who are His, that, through faith, all may be kings and priests with Christ.'[120]

(ii) The Privilege and Responsibility of Spiritual Priesthood.

The privilege is immeasurable: 'For ours is a spiritual rulership, exercised even to the extent of repressing the body. . . .

---

[118] J. S. Whale, *The Protestant Tradition*, p. 98.
[119] *Reformation Writings*, I.365.   [120] Ibid.

This is surely a high and noble dignity, a proper and all-powerful lordship, a spiritual royalty.'[121] Christ has given us so much that to ponder it can be a frightening experience: 'Faith is received and grows when I am told why Christ came, how men can use and enjoy Him, and what He has brought and given me. This takes place whenever a proper explanation is given of that Christian freedom which we have from Him: how we are kings and priests with power over all things; and how everything we do is well-pleasing to and granted by God.' On account of the power which the Christian has received from God, his prayers prevail with God. Since the Christian can receive no greater honour than this, it behoves him to use the powers which God has bestowed upon him. 'By virtue of his kingship he exercises authority over all things, and by virtue of his priesthood he exercises power with God, for God does what he asks and desires.'[122]

Nor can this all-important task be delayed. It is possible to receive the privilege and to neglect the responsibility. All is ready now, and much harm is done to the kingdom of God by our slackness. All Christians are called upon to use the Word of God and the Grace of God while they are made available.

The Bread of Life is here for you to eat,
And here for you the Wine of Love to drink.

These heavenly gifts are given to all that they might be offered to the world in terms of love and service. But too often the chance is missed. 'Therefore embrace the opportunity while you have the chance of it. Gather the harvest while the sun shines and the weather is fine. Use the Word of God and the Grace of God while they are there. You must remember that the Word of God and the Grace of God are like a passing shower which, once gone, does not come back again. The Jews had it, but it passed over; and now it is theirs no longer. . . . You . . . must not dream that you are going to have the opportunity from now onward until the end of time; unthankfulness and contempt will not persuade it to remain with you. So be up, and lay hold, as many as can arise and hold fast.'[123]

It will be seen, then, that Luther did not argue for less priesthood, but for more. All our life-work or vocation should be the

---

[121] Ibid. p. 366.   [122] Ibid.
[123] W. J. Kooiman, *Justification by Truth*, pp. 132-3.

expression of our spiritual priesthood. Unless our priesthood is actually regarded as a vocation its significance is lost. The Christian religion must find its true expression not apart from the world, but in it. Professor D. D. Williams has declared with truth: 'Protestantism came into being through a new understanding of what it means to live as a Christian in *this* world',[124] for spiritual priesthood is the translation of the heavenly gifts and graces into the terms and conditions of our earthly life. Any superficial notion is banished when vocation is viewed in terms of the Christian's sacrifice. Dr Vatja describes Luther's doctrine of vocation in the following words: 'So it is quite natural that the concept of vocation should appear as the bearer of the Lutheran concept of sacrifice. Vocation means that the man of faith takes upon himself, and uses in faith, the various offices and positions created by God, as being offered and ordained by God. He dies as "old man" in devoting himself to his fellowmen; and just in this devotion is he united with the death of Christ and so possesses the new life which is concealed in the death of his own age and revealed in the service of his fellowmen. In the freedom of his conscience he identifies himself with the work which God is carrying out for the benefit of all men. *Amid earthly life he brings the life of Christ to mankind.* He is the channel through which God's love flows down to earth. His work takes place in faith and issues out of faith. God is honoured as Creator while man is sacrificed, and man is sacrificed in so far as the various gifts of creation which are received from the Creator are offered in the service of loving one's fellow-men. Christian work in vocation is a function of Christian priesthood; it is its physical sacrifice. The vocation is a work of faith, a divine service in the orientation of earthly things.'[125]

The possession of the Holy Cross is nothing less than the possession of the Christian priesthood. In the consciousness of his oneness with all Christians and in the strength which this sense of universal fellowship imparts, the Christian offers himself in the sacrifice of loving service to all mankind.

We conclude, therefore, that this consideration of Luther's 'marks' of the true Church, suggests that the doctrine of the priesthood of all believers underlies the whole of his teaching, and, as

---

[124] Quoted in W. Robinson, *Completing the Reformation*, p. 7.
[125] *The Theology of Divine Service in Luther*, pp. 300ff.

an appropriate summary of the foregoing pages we cannot do better than quote the words of Dr Schlink: 'Out of the spiritual experience of the Church under Word and Cross, there emerged important ecclesiastical insights. Thus gathering for divine service as the centre of the idea of the Church, the essential significance of the Communion for the edifying of the Body of Christ, the unity of the Church today with the Church of all ages in the liturgy, as well as the reality of the gifts of the Spirit as the concrete form of the general priesthood of all believers—all these were realized anew. Thus right in the middle of all these needs and tasks and gifts, the New Testament affirmation concerning the Church began to speak to us in an entirely new way and to show us our path.'[126]

---

[126] *The Nature of the Church*, ed. R. Newton Flew, p. 57.

2
John Calvin

IT IS FREQUENTLY supposed that John Calvin did not emphasize this aspect of Reformation doctrine. A careful examination of his works, however, makes it clear that if he did not use the precise phrase which Luther used, he did in fact relate the doctrine to the *triplex munus*, to the doctrine of the keys, to the Ministry, to the idea of vocation, and to the necessity of offering spiritual sacrifices.

1. THE THREEFOLD OFFICE OF CHRIST

We have already noticed that in Luther's teaching the priesthood is not transferred from priest to layman but from priest to Christ. It is upon this truth that Calvin lays great stress. It was Calvin who properly revived the *triplex munus* which speaks of Christ as Prophet, Priest, and King.

'Three things chiefly to be regarded in Christ: viz. His offices of Prophet, King, and Priest. For He was appointed both Prophet, King, and Priest; though little were gained by holding the names unaccompanied by a knowledge of the end and use. Moreover, it is to be observed that the name Christ refers to those three offices: for we know that under the Law, prophets as well as priests and kings were anointed with holy oil. Whence, also, the celebrated name Messiah was given to the promised Mediator. But although I admit that He was so called from a view to the nature of the kingly office, still the prophetical and sacerdotal unctions have their proper place, and must not be overlooked.'[1]

Calvin goes on to explain his substitutionary notion of the *triplex munus*. In doing this he is not bound by a single, clear-cut explanation. Here we notice an elasticity in Calvin's outlook which is in striking contrast to the rigidity of Luther's thinking. Calvin is a typical Western-European and his mind is not dominated by one principle. An antithesis which may not trouble Calvin at all may be unbearable and untenable to the Teutonic

---

[1] *The Institutes of the Christian Religion*, II.xv.36-7.

mind of Luther. Calvin invariably sees both sides of a problem and does not hesitate to state them. Luther states a principle and endeavours to bring everything else into line with it. As we have already noted, the single dominating principle in Luther's teaching was Justification by Faith alone and everything else had to be fashioned according to it. Calvin has two interpretations of almost everything. We notice this when we consider his teaching on the knowledge of God and his doctrine of the Church. His attitude to the priesthood of all believers is no exception to this twofold interpretation. Quite unashamedly he holds the following points of view: There is no priesthood save that of Christ who is the only High Priest. Secondly, it is the business of every Christian to offer spiritual sacrifices because he belongs to a royal priesthood.

At first sight, these two interpretations may appear to be irreconcilable. The first states that there can be no priesthood of believers; the second states unequivocally that all are priests. How are we to understand these seemingly contradictory statements? It is precisely Calvin's substitutionary notion of the *triplex munus* which throws a revealing light upon this antithesis.

The substitutionary idea is mentioned in connexion with each office, Prophet, King and Priest: Isaiah 61[1-2]. 'We see that he was anointed by the Spirit to be a herald and witness of his Father's grace, and not in the usual way; for he is distinguished from all other teachers who had a similar office. And here, again, it is to be observed, that the unction which he received, in order to perform the office of teacher, *was not for himself, but for his whole body*, that a corresponding efficacy of the Spirit might always accompany the preaching of the Gospel.'[2]

The eternal sovereignty of the King of Kings (Dan 2[37]) will be shared by those who submit to His rule.

'I come to the Kingly office, of which it were in vain to speak, without previously reminding the reader that its nature is spiritual: because it is from thence that we learn its efficacy, the benefits it confers, its whole power and eternity. Eternity, moreover, which in Daniel an angel attributes to the office of Christ (2[44]), in Luke an angel justly applies to the salvation of his people (1[33]). But this is also twofold and must be viewed in two ways: the one pertains to the whole body of the Church, the other is proper to each member.'[3]

[2] *Institutes*, II.37-8.   [3] Ibid. p. 38.

Just as the Death of Christ is the undisputed characteristic of our Lord's Priesthood, so also identification with His Death marks the beginning of the priesthood of all believers.

'With regard to his priesthood, we must briefly hold its end and use to be, that as a Mediator, free from all taint, he may by his own holiness procure the favour of God for us. . . . Wherefore in order that Christ might fulfil this office, it behoved him to appear with a sacrifice. For even under the law of priesthood it was forbidden to enter the sanctuary without blood. . . . The sum comes to this, that the honour of priesthood was competent to none but Christ, because by the sacrifice of his death, he wiped away our guilt and made satisfaction for sin.

'. . . For, as has been said, there is no access to God for us or for our prayers until the priest, purging away our defilements, sanctify us, and obtain for us that favour of which the impurity of our lives and hearts deprives us. Thus we see, that if the benefit and efficacy of Christ's priesthood is to reach us, the commencement must be with his death.'[4]

Calvin leaves no doubt that the believers' priesthood is one of the direct benefits of Christ's death.

'. . . Christ now bears the office of priest, not only that by the eternal law of reconciliation he may render the Father favourable and propitious to us, but also *admit us into the most honourable alliance*. For we, though in ourselves polluted, *in Him being priests* (Rev. 1[6]), offer ourselves and our all to God, and freely enter the heavenly sanctuary, so that the sacrifices of prayer and praise which we present are grateful and of sweet order before Him.'[5]

It has been necessary to quote at length Calvin's own words on this matter so that we may know how firmly he held this doctrine of the sole priesthood of Christ. As far as he is concerned, Christ is the only Priest and Pontiff in the New Testament in whom are incorporated all priesthoods, and Calvin has some weighty words to say to those who are 'not content with the priesthood of Christ'.

Christ is Prophet, Priest and King, not for Himself alone, but for the Church, and so on the ground of His substitutionary priesthood the whole Church has a corporate priesthood. But the New Testament nowhere speaks of a believer as *hierus*, any more than it speaks of him as a *basileus* or a *hagios*. If these words

[4] *Institutes*, II.43.   [5] Ibid. pp. 43-4.

are used in the singular, or are to be used in the singular, they inevitably refer to Christ Himself alone. He is the one Priest, the one King, the one Holy One—but *in Him*, and in His name, we may speak as the New Testament does, of priests, saints, and a kingdom which the Church is. This means that the Church has a corporate priesthood by participating through *diakonia* in Christ's priestly ministry.

II. THE PRIESTHOOD OF CHRIST AND DEPENDENT UNIVERSAL PRIESTHOOD

Secondly, the priesthood of believers is based upon the fact that Christ is our Mediator and receives us into the fellowship of His service for mankind. In Calvin's words, Christians 'trusting to their Mediator, appear with boldness in the presence of God'. It is noticeable that Calvin speaks less about Christ the High Priest than as Priest but his favourite term in this connexion is 'Mediator'. His emphasis upon the meaning for believers of our Lord's mediatorship is unmistakable.

(1) There was no possibility of man approaching God without a Mediator. 'Had man remained free from all taint, he was of too humble a condition to penetrate to God without a Mediator.'[6]

(2) It is just because Christ understands as no other can understand the state of our alienation, that He is able perfectly to accomplish the task of mediation: 'That no one therefore, may feel perplexed where to seek the Mediator, or by what means to reach Him, the Spirit, by calling Him man, reminds us that He is near, nay contiguous to us, inasmuch as He is our flesh.' And, indeed, he intimates the same thing in another place, where he explains at greater length that He is not a high priest who 'cannot be touched with the feeling of our infirmities; but was in all points tempted like as we are, yet without sin' (Heb 4^{15}).

(3) Because Christ is Mediator He is able to transfer to us that which is His by nature so that it may become ours by grace. 'This will become still clearer if we reflect, that the work to be performed by the Mediator was of no common description: being to restore us to the divine favour, so as to make us, instead of sons of men, sons of God; instead of heirs of hell, heirs of a heavenly kingdom. Who could do this unless the Son of God should also become the Son of man, and so receive what is ours and to transfer to us what

[6] *Institutes*, II.II.2.

is His, making that which is His by nature to become ours by grace?' Nowhere is Calvin more explicit than in the following passage: 'For we, though in ourselves being polluted, *in Him being priests*, offer ourselves and our all to God, and freely enter the heavenly sanctuary.'

(4) The Cross is the indisputable sign of our Lord's Mediatorship: 'Since from the earliest age ... there was never any promise of a Mediator without blood, we justly infer that He was destined in the eternal counsel of God to purge the pollution of man, the shedding of blood being the symbol of expiation. Thus, too, the prophets, in discoursing of Him, foretold that He would be the Mediator between God and man. It is sufficient to refer to that very remarkable prophecy of Isaiah (53^{10}) in which he foretells ... that as a priest "he was made an offering for sin".'

(5) Christ is the *Eternal* Mediator, otherwise we should be perpetually shut off from God. Dr Denny is right when he says that Christianity cannot be recognized or guaranteed in anyone save Christ. 'He is the Mediator of it, to whom it owes its character. To introduce into it, no matter how we define their relation to Him, official *mediators*, is to relapse from the Melchizedek priesthood to the Aaronic; it is in principle to apostatize from Christianity. . . . There is not, as in the nature of the case there could not be, any trace in the New Testament of a Christian priest making sacrifice for sin, and mediating again (in the Aaronic, official, mortal, never perfect and never to be perfected fashion) between God and man.'[7]

Calvin makes it clear that Christ is our Eternal Mediator on account of His work as our High Priest. It is inevitable that minds as dynamic and penetrating as those of Luther and Calvin should disagree violently on some points. Calvin was never happy about Luther's teaching on the ubiquity of Christ's body. The contention that God is 'unrestingly active in all His creatures' did not at all appeal to Calvin. If he could not accept Zwingli's view that since Christ was risen and glorified, His presence must be localized in heaven, he was equally dissatisfied with Luther's notion that Christ could not be localized anywhere and that His body was therefore ubiquitous. Calvin desired to fasten attention upon the one Mediator. He would have supported the view that God is only 'unrestingly active' in One—His Son. Any other view would

[7] Hastings, *Dictionary of the Bible*, IV.100

have seemed to Calvin to detract from the supreme glory of the sole Mediator. The office of the Lord as Mediator was indispensable and indisputable. Calvin could not brook the slightest reference to other mediators. God was uniquely manifested in Christ. Christ is the way and the sole way whereby man may approach God. God offers His grace through the Mediator and man receives God's grace through the Mediator. The crucial question for Calvin is: 'What shall man do when he realizes that God has provided such a Mediator?' His uncompromising statements on the sovereignty of God would be alarming and even intolerable if he did not state with equal candour and clarity the fact that God in His mercy has provided a Mediator. The position of the Reformers is stated clearly by Professor Warfield: 'Calvinism asks with Lutheranism, indeed, that most pointed of all questions, What shall I do to be saved? and answers it as Lutheranism answers it. But the great question which presses upon it is, How shall God be glorified?'[8] It follows that the end of human existence as, indeed, of all other existences, is the glory of God. Again, we are in a dilemma—we can neither behold God's glory nor glorify God apart from Christ. It will not be difficult to understand that the New Testament doctrine of the priesthood of believers is firmly based upon the Mediatorial office of Christ.

III. PRIESTHOOD AND VOCATION

Apart from Calvin's teaching on the *triplex munus* and the sole Mediatorship of Christ, in what sense does he believe that believers are priests unto God? Firstly, he emphasizes the *calling* of the Christian. John M. Barkley in *Presbyterianism* considers that Luther's failure to relate this doctrine to other tenets of the Faith has led to confusion: 'Calvin accepts the priesthood of believers (*Inst.* II.7.1; II.15.6; IV.14.9) but without falling into the error of Lutheranism, which was the failure to relate this doctrine to the other tenets of the faith, and led, as it needs must, to disorder and abuses.' On the other hand, Professor T. M. Lindsay is of the opinion that the peculiar merit of Luther's interpretation is that he succeeded in relating this doctrine to the faith as a whole. After explaining that by formal principle Dr Dorner means the principle of the Word of God, and by material principle the doctrine of Justification by Faith, Professor Lindsay goes on to

---
[8] *Calvin and Calvinism*, p. 358.

say: 'What have been called the formal and material principles of the Reformation are united in and spring out of this simpler but deeper impulse. The right of entrance into God's very presence, the Reformers believed, had been conferred by Him on all His people; but the right of entrance into God's presence is what is meant by priesthood, and the one principle of the Reformation is the priesthood of all believers—the right of every believing man and woman whether lay or cleric, to go to God directly with confession seeking pardon, with ignorance seeking enlightenment, with solitary loneliness seeking fellowship, with frailty and weakness seeking strength for daily holy living.'[9] It is clear from Professor Lindsay's exposition that he firmly believes that this doctrine is the basic principle of the Reformation and that it explains Luther's doctrine of God, Justification, Pardon, Scripture, and Sin. The conclusion to be drawn from our study of Luther was that the logical corollary of the doctrine of Justification by Faith was the priesthood of believers, but this contention does not at all affect the observation of Professor Lindsay that the Lutheran doctrine of the priesthood of all believers is seen in relation to, and not in isolation from, other tenets of the Faith.

Just as Calvin placed emphasis on 'Calling' or 'Vocation', and so related this truth to all others, so Luther emphasizes Justification and relates this to other tenets of the Faith. For Calvin, a man is a priest because he finds his 'calling' in God. Dr Dakin sums up the teaching of Calvinism as follows: 'Life is regulated by one's calling. God has assigned distinct duties to each and none may presume to overstep his proper limits. Every man's mode of life is a sort of station assigned to him by the Lord that he may not always be driven about at random, . . . And everyone, from magistrate to the father of a family, will bear the inconvenience of his calling, its cares, uneasiness, and anxiety, persuaded that God and no other has laid the burden on him.'[10] All this is the logical development of Calvin's dominating thought—namely, that all things must ultimately be brought into line with the calling of God, with the divine choice. He insists that 'the divine will is the perpetual rule to which true religion is to be conformed'. Our calling as Christians is in the divine Will. So, in fact, it is impossible to understand Calvin's doctrine of the priesthood of believers apart from his teaching on election. This point

[9] *History of the Reformation*, p. 185.   [10] *Calvinism*, pp. 221-2.

JOHN CALVIN   73

is emphasized by Barkley: 'All men are priests in their daily vocation. All are priests though their duties vary according to their calling. The only real farmer is a Christian farmer; the only real doctor is a Christian doctor; the only real mother is a Christian mother; the only real man is a Christian man; the only real woman is a Christian woman; and so on covering every detail and aspect and station in life. Apart from Christ we are not what we ought to be.'[11] Only 'in Christ' have we real worth. Man is the 'servant' of God.

It is because Calvin believes that all are priests in the sense already mentioned that he deplores the use of the term 'clerk' to describe the ministerial office: 'All who receive this training (for the ministerial office) were designated by the general name of *clerks*. I could wish that some more appropriate name had been given them, for this appellation had its origin in error, or at least, improper feeling, since the whole Church is by Peter denominated *clerum*, that is, the inheritance of the Lord (1 Pet 2^9).'[12]

In speaking of this inheritance Calvin cannot forget that Israel was called to a 'Kingdom of priests', and the inheritance has a deeper meaning and a richer content when it is offered in Christ. On this point Calvin states: 'Moses declared the end of the adoption of the Israelites to be, that they should be "a Kingdom of priests and an holy nation" (Ex 19^6) . . . wherefore, Peter elegantly transposes the words of Moses, teaching that the fullness of grace, of which the Jews had a foretaste under the Law, is exhibited in Christ, "Ye are a chosen generation, a royal priesthood" (1 Pet 2^9). The transposition of the words intimates that those to whom Christ has appeared in the Gospel, have obtained more than their fathers, inasmuch as they are all endued with priestly and royal honour, and can, therefore, trusting their Mediator, appear with boldness in the presence of God.'[13]

We must not overlook the vital significance of the beginning of this passage, for it is important for our understanding of Calvin's teaching of the Christian vocation. 'Moses declared the end of the *adoption* of the Israelites to be, that they should be a kingdom of priests.' The believer is adopted by God into a believing community. This gives added meaning to the phrase 'priesthood

[11] *Presbyterianism*, p. 18.
[12] Quoted in Ainslie, *The Doctrines of Ministerial Order in the Reformed Churches of the Sixteenth and Seventeenth Centuries*, p. 6.
[13] Ibid.

of believers' since there is no such thing in Calvinism as a detached individual. As Barkley puts it in a reference to the definition of 'Adoption' in the Shorter Catechism. 'Adoption is an act of God's free grace, whereby we are received into the number—and have a right to all the privileges—of the sons of God.' What do the words 'received into the number of the sons of God' signify? Undoubtedly, they express the social aspect of conversion, just as justification expresses the personal aspect. The two are complementary. Man stands before God as an individual, and discovers that there is no such thing as a 'detached' individual, he is a member of the community. A Christian is related to, and is responsible to, the 'family' into which he is adopted. He is responsible for the family's good name and welfare in the world. He has a duty to the brotherhood and to the world. It is here that we begin to understand why the Pauline teaching on 'Adoption' has frequently been connected with the privilege of the believer as a member of the royal priesthood. As a son he becomes aware of his status before God, as a priest he understands his duty toward man. Dr Denny clarifies this idea in the following words: 'Sonship and priesthood are two figures under which we can represent the characteristic relation of man to God, his characteristic standing toward God, in the new relation instituted by Christ. Formally distinguishable, they are really experimentally the same. Christ Himself was perfect priest only because He was the true Son of God; His priesthood, though it was His vocation, was grounded in His nature: it had nothing official in it, but was throughout personal and real. So it is with the priesthood of believers: it also is involved in sonship, is one element or function of sonship, and only as such has it any meaning.'[14]

IV. THE POWER OF THE KEYS

We have already noticed that the basis of Calvin's interpretation of the doctrine of the priesthood of all believers is to be found in his doctrine of the *triplex munus*; that the believer's priesthood is inseparable from and dependent upon the Priesthood of Christ our sole Mediator; that the believer's 'Calling' or 'Vocation' is primarily a recognition of his sonship and the exercise of his priesthood. We shall now see how the believer's priesthood is further elucidated in Calvin's teaching on the power of the keys.

---

[14] Hastings, *Dictionary of the Bible*, IV.100.

Calvin's fundamental contention is the same as Luther's, namely, that the Roman hierarchy had taken upon itself privileges which belonged to the whole Church. He stresses the fact that 1 Peter 2⁹ refers not only to the apostles but to the whole Church: 'Let us now attend to the ceremonies which they employ. And first all whom they (Sorbonnists and Canonists) enrol among their militia they initiate into the clerical status by a common symbol. They shave them on top of the head, that the crown may denote royal honour, because clergy ought to be kings in governing themselves and others. Peter thus speaks of them: 'Ye are a chosen generation, a royal priesthood, a holy nation, a peculiar people' (1 Pet 2⁹). But it was sacrilege for them to arrogate to themselves alone what is given to the whole Church: these men wrest it to a few shaven crowns, as if it had been said to them alone, 'Be ye holy: as they alone had been purchased by the blood of Christ: as if they alone had been made by Christ kings and priests unto God.'[15] In this passage also, Calvin challenges the Roman understanding and interpretation of the phrase 'kings and priests'. The high privileges of every believer were undermined by the introduction of the shaven head as the mark of clerical status. This complete misrepresentation of scriptural truth as well as the blatant externalizing of spiritual things, fired Calvin into strong protest.

The Canonists, however, were perfectly logical in these matters because they firmly believed that the power of the keys was given to Peter only. So Calvin carefully examines this question of the keys. He reaches the same conclusion as Luther but on different grounds. Luther holds that the context of the passage indicates that Peter is the mouthpiece of the rest. All the disciples are asked who they say Christ is. They do not anwer, however, each for himself, but all at once through Peter. All in a body, therefore, they confess their faith through Peter and all in a body receive the power of the keys in answer to the confession.

As we have already noticed, Luther holds that the power of the keys goes to no specific individual but to the Church and congregation. Immediately after receiving the power, Peter failed, which proves that his faith could not be depended upon. Nor could the faith of the other disciples be depended on as later events showed. Jesus had said, 'Ye shall be scattered,' and His

[15] *Institutes*, III.505.

words were true, 'They all fled to their own homes'. Some returned to the labours of former days. Yet the faith of the Church could never disappear, for the gates of hell would not prevail against it (Mt 16^{18}). According to Luther the Church is the believing people and there will always be someone who believes when others fall into unbelief.

Calvin approaches the subject from a different angle altogether, but, as we have said, reaches the same conclusion. 'Christ (they say) constituted Peter Prince of the whole Church when He promised to give him the keys. But what He then promised to one, he elsewhere delivers, and as it were, hands over, to all the rest. If the same right, which was promised to one, is bestowed upon all, in what respect is that one superior to his colleagues? He excels, they say, in this, that he receives both in common and by himself, what is given to the others in common only. What if I should answer with Cyprian, and Augustine, that Christ did not do this to prefer one to the other, but in order to commend the unity of the Church? For Cyprian thus speaks: 'In the person of one man He gave the keys to all, that he might denote the unity of all; the rest, therefore, were the same that Peter was, being admitted to an equal participation of honour and power, but a beginning is made from unity that the Church of Christ may be shown to be one' (*De Unitate Ecclesiai*).[16] Augustine's words are: 'Had not the mystery of the Church been in Peter, our Lord would not have said to him, I will give thee the keys. For if this was said to Peter, the Church has them not; but if the Church has them, then when Peter received the keys, he represented the whole Church (*Hom. in Joannem*, 50).' Again, 'All were asked but Peter alone answers, Thou art the Christ; and it is said to him, I will give thee the keys, as if he alone had received the power of binding and loosing; whereas he both spoke for all and received in common with all, being as it were, the representative of unity. One receiving for all, because there is unity in all' (*Hom*. 124).[17]

If Calvin's contention is true, then the very foundation upon which the Roman hierarchy is built is insecure. It is clear that 'the binding and loosing power first bestowed upon St Peter is not represented in the New Testament as an exclusive privilege of the Apostles. It is the common privilege of the Christian society—even of a small branch of it—when acting in agreement (Mt 18^{19})

---

[16] *Institutes*, III.112.   [17] Ibid.

and solemnly assembled in Christ's name as its ground of union (18[20]).'[18] As to the question which was raised in the quotation from Calvin as to how an ordained priest can be regarded as superior to his colleagues, Calvin gives the answer himself: 'In communion with Christ we become *colleagues of His* priesthood.'

This point can only be properly understood in the light of the Roman view on the Ministry. This view is that a special spiritual estate (*ordo*) links the ministerial office with the sacraments by a twofold and indissoluble connexion. In the first place, the office of priesthood was instituted by Christ together with the sacrifice of the mass and for the sake of celebrating the mass. In the second place, the priesthood, as the sacerdotal order, receives a sacramental and ineffaceably qualifying consecration (*character indelebilis*) through the special sacrament of Holy Orders. The Tridentine theologians state that the power of the keys is only a secondary condition for the institution of the ministerial office.[19] Secondary it may be, but it was a Roman Catholic theologian who wrote: 'The power of the priest to administer the sacraments is a real *potestas supranaturalis*',[20] and although this is modified in the same paragraph, 'The Ministry of the priesthood in the Church is only a visible representation, an *instrumentum animatum*, of the one invisible Mediator—*Sacerdos Christus*', the fact remains that this supranatural power resides in the keys. According to this view power to consecrate is a *character indelebilis* which the priest receives when he is anointed. Power to administer the sacraments was given by Christ to Peter, by Peter to his successors, and by these, in an unbroken chain, to those who now hold the ministry. This implies a succession of Order and not of Faith and cannot be reconciled with Calvin's view that all believers become 'colleagues of His Priesthood'. Luther holds that the ministerial office as *office* (*ministerium*) is *instituted by God*. It is based upon the universal priesthood of the faithful which takes rise with baptism, and at the same time it points back to apostolic model and apostolic instruction to appoint office-bearers by orderly calling through the congregation. . . .' Calvin, on the other hand, nowhere speaks of the ministerial office as instituted *by* God but he does refer to ministers as 'ministers *of* God' (*ministri Dei*). As

---

[18] Hastings, *Dictionary of the Bible*, IV.30.
[19] See *Council of Trent*, Sess. 33.
[20] *The Ministry and the Sacraments*, ed. R. Dunkerley, p. 52.

far as Calvin is concerned the universal priesthood of the faithful takes rise not with baptism but with the consciousness of election, and the believer becomes aware of his election through the inward witness of the Holy Spirit.

In Protestant circles there is frequently much controversy as to what is actually *given* through the Sacraments and often the ultimate answer seems vague and unconvincing. Perhaps it is sometimes felt that it would be easier to understand the deep meaning of the ordination service if it were thought of as a Sacrament. We must not forget, however, that the Roman priest is ordained specifically to administer the Sacraments. To the question 'What is given in the Sacrament of Holy Orders?' the answer open to the Roman Catholic is: 'The power of the keys.' Protestants, believing that they are already 'priests unto God' believe that Ordination possesses a prophetic significance in that it imparts authority to proclaim the Word. Therefore, it is not regarded as a Sacrament but as a symbol of authorization. One of the reasons why Calvin stopped short of speaking of the Ministry as 'instituted by God' was because he felt this was perilously near the conception of ordination as a sacrament. Indeed, Calvin deals with this question in a very practical way. His examination of the external vocation of pastors includes four points: 'The candidate, the way in which he is elected, the body which possesses electoral authority, and the ceremony of initiation to his pastoral duties.'[21] Out of four points, three are concerned with the election and initiation of the pastor. This means that Calvin believes that it is in the whole Church that true succession resides. This raises the whole question of the meaning of the Ministry in Reformed theology, and this subject must now be considered in greater detail.

V. PRIESTHOOD AND MINISTRY

The first point to be emphasized is that the Ministry remains intact even after the Reformation. The Reformers' interpretation of the priesthood of all believers did not lead them to reject a ministerial order. Priesthood and Ministry are not identical terms and should not be confused. The Second Helvetic Confession does not fall into this error: 'Accordingly, there are great differences between a priesthood and a ministry. For the former is common to all Christians, as we have just now said, but

[21] *The Ministry and the Sacraments*, ed. R. Dunkerley, p. 457.

the same is not so with the latter. And we have not removed the Ministry out of the midst of the Church when we have cast the papistical priesthood out of the Church of Christ.'[22] The Reformers, of course, were aware that there were dangers in recognizing a ministerial order. They knew that there were dangers in institutionalism and in the false separation of clergy and laity and of Church and world. Yet these dangers were a continual reminder to them that the Church stands in need of continuing reformation in the light of the Word, and by the Holy Spirit, the only reforming power in the life of the Church. The reformers knew that order, and structure, and organization were necessary for the life and witness of the Church, but they also realized that no particular historical form of these was necessary for salvation. Whatever form or order is recognized, however, it is a mistake to set it over against the congregation. The Ministry has its function within the community of believers and is not above it. Writing of the Ministry, Dr A. A. van Ruler makes an important observation: 'But notice that the confrontation is not vertical but horizontal; God and man, ministry and people, are set over against each other *within* the *Ecclesia*, and in a spirit of love.'[23] Ministry, then, is within the universal priesthood; it is neither apart from it nor above it, but functions within the whole community. And this brings us to another important aspect of the Reformed doctrines of the Ministry.

It was a *reformed* Ministry.

The point is strikingly made by Zwingli: 'It is true we are all fully ordained to the priesthood . . . but we are not all apostles and bishops.'[24] While it is true that a form of Ministry is to be found after the Reformation, it must not be, according to the Reformers, after the pattern of Rome. The chief work of the Roman priesthood was the offering of a sacrifice for the living and the dead in the celebration of the mass. This meant that their priesthood was sacerdotal. It is possible, however, to renounce the sacerdotal idea and still to hold on to a view of the Ministry which places it *above* and not within the Christian community. As Pastor C. Westphal observes: 'It must be recognized, however, that the triple ministry of Calvin no longer appears to us to convey

---

[22] P. Schaff, *Creeds of the Evangelical Protestant Churches*, p. 281.
[23] *World Presbyterian Alliance Report* (August 1953), p. 3.
[24] Usteri and Vogelin, II.279.

all the requirements of the ministry of the Church as described in the Scriptures. The Reformation brought about the essential revolution in denouncing the "Judaic" character of the Roman Catholic priesthood and in bringing back to light the priesthood of all believers. The Church has only one Priest, a High Priest with "an unchangeable priesthood" (Heb 7^{24}). She is the priest of the people and she testifies the one mediation of redemption.'[25] Emphasis upon the priesthood of all believers meant that sacerdotalism was done away. In Dr Macleod's words: 'Every theory of the ministry that is in any way inconsistent with the free access of every believer to God through Christ as the one Mediator between God and man, is alien to the spirit of Christianity. No Ministry can relieve the individual soul of its responsibility or rob it of its privilege of personal and immediate approach to God. The Gospel interposes no sacrificial system or priestly caste between the Father of our spirits and His children.'[26] The common error that the phrase 'Priesthood of Believers' is synonymous with 'private judgement' is most unfortunate and is certainly a misrepresentation. If the doctrine meant no more than that, it is hardly likely to have survived the devastating conflicts of the Church during twenty centuries. Those who dismiss it as merely 'private judgement' have never troubled to examine its full meaning. Of course the Reformers emphasized 'private judgement', but it was always 'informed' judgement, and it was always controlled, checked, and corroborated by the corporate testimony of the congregation. Indeed Calvin himself fully realized that uncontrolled private judgement meant subjectivism, eccentricity, anarchy, and chaos. Such was to him the position of a 'nefarious herd' proclaiming pestilential doctrine.[27]

Rather is the priesthood of believers to be understood as a spiritual privilege, a moral obligation, and a personal vocation. The spiritual privilege is freedom of access to the presence of God; this implies a moral responsibility to the corporate fellowship of the Church through which the believer has learned of his spiritual privilege. It also carries with it the responsibility of regarding his secular vocation as the sphere in which his priesthood is exercised.

On what grounds is free access to God possible? The answer

---

[25] *World Presbyterian Alliance Report* (August 1950), p. 3.
[26] *The Church, Ministry and Sacraments*, p. 34.
[27] See Calvin's *Opera*, V.173, VII.53.

JOHN CALVIN

of the Reformers is that it is possible on the grounds of justification by faith alone. The faith which justifies is the gift of God lest anyone should think that it may be engendered in man's mind or produced by any human effort whatsoever. The way to God is opened up to us, not by a sacrificing priesthood but by

> *That only offering perfect in Thine eyes,*
> *The one true, pure, immortal sacrifice.*

Calvin's view of the transcendent majesty of God was such as to make man's approach to God a formidable experience. Indeed, it was only possible at all with the aid of the Holy Spirit. What is the relation of the Holy Spirit to the Reformed doctrine of the Ministry? 'Reformed theology protests against two extremities. One of these over-emphasizes the secret work of the Holy Spirit so far as to make even the ecclesiastical ministry itself superficial. The other considers the ministry so high that it even binds the Holy Spirit to it, attributing thus such a huge power to the ministry that it endows it with the glory of a full court of appeal in spiritual matters. The Reformed Confessions find the following way out between these extremities: they emphasize that God has the power to enlighten men directly without the external ministry of the ecclesiastical servants (2 Helv. Conf. 1), nevertheless He regularly realizes His plan through His ordained ministers.'[28] The truth is that we have no standing before God apart from the Holy Spirit. The principle that all men may be the channels of the Holy Spirit must be jealously guarded, and any attempt to regard ecclesiasticism as the exclusive channel of the Spirit must be firmly resisted. Calvin's twofold emphasis is unmistakable. All believers are conscious of the continuing intercessions of Christ, the High Priest, and of the inner action of the divine Spirit in their hearts. The case of the Reformers is that if believers possess this twofold divine assistance in their approach to God, they need no other. A popular hymn expresses the same thought:

> *Christ is our Advocate on high;*
> *Thou art our Advocate within.*

---

[28] *The Ministry and the Sacraments*, ed. R. Dunkerley, p. 198.

VI. MINISTRY AND SUCCESSION

The Reformers did not abolish 'episcopacy', they affirmed it. But it was not monarchical or diocesan episcopacy that they affirmed. They believed in presbyterian succession which left no room for superior rank and exclusive power. 'The Reformers found that in the New Testament the terms "presbyter" and "bishop" referred to the same person (Acts 20^{17-32}). This meant that every presbyter was a bishop.'[29] Presbyterianism, of course, has its own interpretation of succession, but it is a succession of Ministry and people together. 'The functions which it continues in its ministry are apostolic functions, and of this continuity a visible expression exists in the *"perpetua successio presbyterorum"*; which has been maintained in the Church from before the Reformation.'[30] There is biblical evidence for this idea of a continuity of true believers: 'The Reformers attacked the whole idea of a "lineal succession", but they never denied a succession "in Christ". All that was attacked was a particular conception of succession. They maintained that "they continued stedfastly in the apostles' doctrine and fellowship, and in breaking of bread and in prayers". The continuity of the Church and Ministry rests in the Lordship of Christ' (Mt 28^{18-20}).[31]

It will now be obvious that the office of the ministry to which the Reformed Church attaches great authority and reverence is not that of a *sacerdos*. Sacerdotium in the sense of the Royal Priesthood is common to all individual Christians; but the office of the ministry belongs only to those who have been specifically called to the service of the Church. There is no gradation of authority in the range of the servants of God. Apostles, prophets, bishops, pastors, elders, doctors, possess in equal measure the power of ministry—it is the power to serve.[32] This idea of equality of ministers is an important principle which has been preserved only in Nonconformist theology and practice. Dr Vincent Taylor declares: 'Presbyterians and Free Churchmen believe that it is a particular merit of their existing Church Order that all their ministers, including Moderators and Presidents, are of the same

---

[29] J. M. Barkley, *Presbyterianism*, pp. 26-7.
[30] *The Ministry and the Sacraments*, ed. R. Dunkerley, p. 177.
[31] *Scottish Journal of Theology* (June 1956), p. 156.
[32] See 2 Helv. Conf. 18.

status.'[33] This serves to underline Dr Barkley's words: 'Every presbyter is a bishop.' The idea which these two Nonconformist theologians are stressing is not a novel doctrine of the Ministry, it is the logical application of the Reformation principle of the priesthood of all believers. Equality and parity of status are implicit in the doctrine, and notions of gradation are not only artificial but quite foreign to the Reformed idea of Ministry. If the Reformers had failed at this point, it means that while they had succeeded in setting the Ministry *within* the universal priesthood, they would have introduced invidious distinctions within the Ministry itself. Had they done this, they would have committed the offence they so strenuously sought to avoid. Rejecting, however, on the grounds of the priesthood of all believers, the distinction between clergy and laity, by the same token they refused to recognize distinctions within the ranks of the Ministry.

VII. MINISTRY AND ORDINATION

'Every minister', as the London Assembly of 1654 states, 'hath a double relation, one to the Church Catholic indefinitely, and another to that particular congregation over which he is set.' It is for this reason that in Irish Presbyterianism two prayers are offered, one is a prayer of ordination to the Ministry of the Church Catholic, and the other a prayer of induction into a particular congregation. It is important, however, to ensure that the distinctive nature of Ordination is not lost. An induction or inauguration service in a local Church is something very different from ordination to the whole Church Catholic. It is important that such a local ceremony should not even *seem* to be an Ordination, an impression which is not always avoided. If local ceremonies derogate in any sense from the unique significance of Ordination, they are to be discouraged. The Anglican Induction Service adequately fulfils its purpose without any possibility of confusion with Ordination. In the Reformed Churches the position is not always so clearly defined. An instance of this confusion lies in the fact that an Elder is repeatedly ordained. It is true that the laying on of hands takes place only at the first ordination, but the very phrase 'first ordination' is a misnomer, for ordination is distinctive and unrepeatable. At his ordination the Minister or Elder becomes a chosen servant of the universal

---

[33] *Expository Times* (June 1951).

priesthood; this is the basic fact, and any other local ceremony is subordinate to it whatever name it bears.

The minister's ordination cannot be separated from his inward call. The external and formal ceremony is the confirmation of the minister's inner call. Calvin expounds this as follows: 'If anyone would be deemed a true minister of the Church, he must first be duly called; and, secondly, he must answer his calling. . . . But as we have already touched on the necessity of executing the office, let us now treat only of the call. The subject is comprehended under four heads, namely, who are to be appointed ministers, in what way, by whom, and with what rite or initiatory ceremony. I am speaking of the external and formal call which related to the public order of the Church, while I say nothing of that secret call of which any minister is conscious before God.'[34] The inner call of God to the Minister is always to be assumed, and the external call of the Church is the Church's seal upon what is already a fact in a man's own experience. In other words, the Call of God lies behind the individual's experience and the Church's corroboration of it. With this in mind we must turn to two important questions: Who ordains? and, Who is the inspiration of all ministry? 'The Reformed Church holds and maintains that the office and commission of the ministry are derived from the divine Head of the Church. Ordination is an act of Jesus Christ by His office-bearers, which means by prayer with the laying on of hands by His ministers lawfully associated in Presbytery. Orders, therefore, because it is Christ who ordains, are to the ministry of the Church, Catholic and Apostolic.'[35] The answer to the second question is that the Holy Spirit inspires ministries of all kinds. The ministry of the Church is indivisible. All ministries are varying expressions of the one indivisible ministry, and all form part of a common ministry or priesthood of the Church. The whole community is responsible for each of the ministries granted to it. It is certainly true, as Calvin said, that the signs of the Church are the Word and the Sacrament. But the Word is given to the Church on condition that she declares it and incarnates it in her life as a community. In so far as she succeeds in doing this, she is exercising her common priesthood.

While the members of the congregation are fulfilling their

---

[34] *Institutes*, IV.III.10-11.   [35] *Scottish Journal of Theology*, IX.II.155.

common priesthood in various spheres, it is the duty of the minister to present his people as a living spiritual sacrifice to God, for only by this means can they effectively do their work. Calvin corroborates the view of St Paul, namely that the offering of the congregation to God in this way is the priestly function of the ministry: 'Doubtless this is the priesthood of the Christian pastor, that is, to sacrifice men, as it were, to God, and not as the Papists have hitherto haughtily vaunted, by offering up Christ to reconcile men to God. He does not, however, give here the name of priests to the pastor of the Church, simply as a perpetual title but intending to command the honour and power of the ministry. Paul availed himself of the opportunity of using this metaphor. Let then the preachers of the Gospel have this end in view while discharging their office, even to offer up to God souls purified by faith.'[36]

Perhaps the relation of the Ministry to the universal priesthood is best expressed in one of John Calvin's prayers: 'Grant, Almighty God, that since Thou hast designed to take us as a priesthood to Thyself, and hast chosen us when we were not only of the lowest condition, but even profane and alien to all holiness, and hast consecrated us to Thyself by Thy Holy Spirit, that we may offer ourselves as holy victims to Thee. O grant, that we may bear in mind our office and calling, and sincerely devote ourselves to Thy service, and so present to Thee our efforts and labours, that Thy name may be truly glorified in us, and that it may appear that we have been grafted in the Body of Thy only-begotten Son; and as He is the chief and only and perpetual Priest, may we become partakers of that priesthood with which Thou hast been pleased to honour Him, so that He may take us as associates to Himself; and may thus Thy name be perpetually glorified by the whole body as well as by the Head.'

VIII. PRIESTHOOD AND SPIRITUAL SACRIFICES

(a) Spiritual Sacrifices not Expiatory

Before discussing the question of spiritual sacrifices, let us hear Calvin's words concerning those who imagine that they are able to offer expiatory sacrifices: 'All are injurious to Christ who call themselves priests in the sense of offering expiatory victims. He

[36] *Commentary on Romans*, pp. 15-16.

was constituted and consecrated Priest by the Father, with an oath, after the order of Melchizedek, without end and without successor (Ps 110[4], Heb 5[6], 7[3]). He once offered a victim of eternal expiation and reconciliation, and now also having entered the sanctuary of heaven, He intercedes for us. In Him, we are all priests, but to offer praise and thanksgiving, in fine, ourselves, and all that is ours, to God.'[37]

Clearly there are sacrifices which believers may offer to God, but even such sacrifices may be offered only *in Him*, that is, in the name and by the mercy of Christ.

(b) *Types of Spiritual Sacrifices*

Calvin states explicitly what he means by these spiritual sacrifices in the following passage: 'Under the kind of sacrifice which we have called Eucharistic, are included all the offices of charity, by which, while we embrace our brethren, we honour the Lord Himself in His members; in fine, all our prayers, praises, thanksgivings, and every act of worship which we perform to God. All these depend on the greater sacrifice with which we dedicate ourselves, soul and body, to be a holy temple to the Lord.'[38]

Although Calvin includes several activities of the Christian life under the heading of Eucharistic sacrifices—offices of charity, acts of worship, praise, thanksgiving and prayer, there is no doubt that the main emphasis is upon the sacrifice of praise: 'The prophets clearly expressed that under these carnal sacrifices there was a reality which is common to the Jewish people and the Christian Church. For this reason David prayed: "Let my prayer ascend before Thee as incense" (Ps 141[2]). And Hosea gives the name of "calves of the lips" (Hos 14[2]) to thanksgivings which David elsewhere calls "sacrifice of praise", which he explains to mean "the fruit of our lips, giving thanks to His name" (Heb 13[15]). This kind of sacrifice is indispensable in the Lord's Supper, in which, while we show forth His death, and give Him thanks, we offer nothing but the sacrifice of praise. From this office of sacrificing, all Christians are called "a royal priesthood", because by Christ we offer that sacrifice of praise of which the apostle speaks, "the fruit of our lips, giving thanks to His name" (1 Pet 2[9], Heb 13[15]).'[39] It should not be thought, however, that this idea of offering sacrifices of praise exhausts Calvin's views on

---

[37] *Institutes*, III.508. [38] Ibid. p. 473. [39] Ibid. pp. 474ff.

spiritual sacrifices. When he says, 'we offer nothing but a sacrifice of praise', he is denying the possibility of any expiatory sacrifice offered by any priesthood whatsoever.

(c) *Spiritual Sacrifices offered through the Mediator*

Our standing before God, however, is entirely dependent upon divine grace, and our sacrifice is offered through our Mediator. This implies a complete refutation of a sacrificing priesthood. The idea of man offering Christ as a sacrifice to God is unthinkable in Calvin's view. His position is clarified in the following words: 'We do not appear with our gifts in the presence of God without an intercessor, Christ is our Mediator by whose intervention we offer ourselves and our all to the Father; He is our High Priest, who, having entered into the upper sanctuary, opens up an access for us; He the altar on which we lay our gifts, that whatever we do attempt, we may attempt in Him; He it is, I say, who "hath made us kings and priests unto God His Father" (Rev 1^6).'[40]

(d) *Function of the Spiritual Priesthood*

Calvin applies to believers on account of their spiritual priesthood all the characteristics and functions of priests which he found figured and typified in the Old Testament. They are holy as chosen by God (1 Pet 1$^{2, 15}$), are sprinkled by sacrificial blood by accepting Christ's sacrifice (Heb 12^{24}), are washed with pure water in Baptism (Heb 10^{22}), are dedicated with laying on of hands (Heb 6^2), and anointed (1 Jn 2^{20}), and they are taught as they are themselves to teach (1 Jn 2^{27}). They offer sacrifices, good works, prayers and praises (Rom 12^1, Eph 5^2, Heb 4^{16}, Heb 13^{15}).

One of the staunchest followers of Calvin, Robert Leighton, follows up this exposition of the spiritual priesthood: 'The priesthood of the law represented Him as the great High Priest that offered up Himself for our sins, and that is a priesthood altogether incommunicable; neither is there any peculiar office of priesthood for offering sacrifice in the Christian Church, but His alone who is the head of it. But this dignity that is here mentioned of a spiritual priesthood, offering up spiritual sacrifices, is common to all those who are in Christ. As they are living stones built in Him

---

[40] Ibid.

with a spiritual temple, *so they are priests* of that same temple made by Him (Rev 1⁶).

'The priesthood of the law was holy, and its holiness was signified by many outward things suitable to their manner, by anointings and washings and vestments; but in this spiritual priesthood of the Gospel, holiness itself is instead of all those, as being the substance of all. The children of God are all anointed, and purified and clothed with holiness.'[41]

So the characteristic note of Reformation theology emerges once again: it is holiness of life rather than fulfilment of ceremonial that God requires. There is no doubt that the Reformation brought with it a new understanding of God's attitude to man. The medieval view that God's relationship with man was in terms of a demand or penance, or in the form of a legalistic transaction, is taken away. The explicit meaning of justification is that God had made an *offer* of *free* grace to *all* men. The Reformers knew that there were vital Christian truths at stake here, truths which the Tridentine theologians could not or would not understand. No longer was divine salvation encumbered by innumerable ecclesiastical rules, it was an offer; no longer was it conditioned by exorbitant and sometimes unpayable penances, it was free; no longer was salvation bequeathed to a chosen few who had exclusive power to dispense it to others, it was for all.

If the Reformation brought a new understanding of God's relationship with man, it also brought with it an entirely new conception of the offerings which man was able to bring to God. Leighton sums it up thus: 'As the apostle speaks (Heb 7¹²) of the High Priesthood of Christ, that the priesthood being changed, there followed of necessity a change of the law; so, in this priesthood of Christians, there is a change of the kind of sacrifice from the other. All sacrifice is not taken away, but it is changed from the offering of those things formerly in use, to spiritual sacrifices. . . . Even in the time when the other sacrifices were in request, these spiritual offerings had ever the precedence in God's account.'[42] 'A broken spirit' is a costly offering, but frequently it is the only offering that we may bring or that God will receive. The Psalmist had discovered this deep truth when he wrote: 'The sacrifices of God are a broken spirit.'

In one trenchant sentence Leighton states the reason for the

---

[41] Leighton's *Works*, Vol. III, Commentary on 1 Peter 2⁵. [42] Ibid.

failure of the Jews, which, incidentally, was the failure of the Romanists: 'This was the sin of the Jews in those times, *that they leaned the soul upon the body's service too much*, and would have done enough of that to be dispensed from this spiritual service.' He is writing in the spirit of Calvin when he declares: '1. They (the legalistic priesthood) had charge of the sanctuary, and the vessels of it, and the lights, and were to keep the lamps burning. Thus the heart of every Christian is made a temple of the Holy Ghost, and he himself, as a priest, consecrated to God . . . he is to have the light of spiritual knowledge within him, and to nourish it by drawing continually new supplies from Jesus Christ.'[43] The most interesting thing about the foregoing paragraph is that Leighton links together the priesthood of believers, the light of spiritual knowledge and the Holy Spirit. The light of spiritual knowledge is given especially to the Elect, who are consecrated to God and who are priests unto God. But the realization and confirmation of this are only possible through the inward testimony of the Holy Spirit in the believer.

2. The priests were to bless the people. And truly it is this spiritual priesthood, the Elect, that procure blessings upon the rest of the world, and particularly on the place where they live.

3. They are daily to offer the incense of prayer, and other spiritual sacrifices unto God. And as the priests offered not only for themselves, but for the people, so Christians are to extend their prayers, and to entreat the blessings of God for others, especially for the public estate of the Church. As the Lord's priests, they are to offer up their praises to God that are His due from the other creatures, which praise Him indeed yet cannot do it after the manner in which these priests do; therefore they are to offer as it were their sacrifices for them, as the priests did for the people.

4. Works of charity are spiritual sacrifices and therefore ought not to be neglected by Christian priests, that is, by any who are Christians.

Leighton's statement in which the Christian's priestly privilege and responsibility are wedded to each other clearly indicates the nature of the sacrifices which a believer may offer. As a temple of the Holy Spirit he is the custodian of all that is holy. As a member of the spiritual priesthood, 'the Elect', he is elected to a specific service. Since he is chosen not only for his own sake but for the

[43] Ibid.

sake of others, he becomes, along with the whole spiritual priesthood, God's instrument for evangelism.

Our investigations prove one thing, namely, that as far as Calvin's theology is concerned, the priesthood of all believers is not to be considered as some obscure by-path, but as a main road along which he frequently travelled. Starting with the Priesthood of Christ, he regards the universal priesthood as being dependent upon it. He then goes on to show how priesthood is the Christian's calling and vocation. This priesthood is a high calling indeed because the power of the keys is vouchsafed to the whole Christian community and not simply to official representatives. Ministers were set aside to serve the Church, not as those who are *above* the congregation, but as those who are *within* the universal priesthood. The sacrifices that are offered are spiritual and are offered by the whole Church. This means that the universal priesthood is expressed in the worship, intercessions, witness, and service of the whole community.

3
Anglicanism

ALTHOUGH the reforms envisaged in the Act of Supremacy (1536) left much to be desired, their importance must not be overlooked. This importance lay in three directions:

(1) The emphasis on the free grace of God in Justification.
(2) The omission of all mention of Transubstantiation in the account of the mass.
(3) The stipulation of three supreme doctrinal standards—the Bible, the three ecumenical Creeds, and the decisions of the first four Councils.

These factors alone do not constitute Protestantism but they contain definite Protestant tendencies. The first declares that religion is a personal relationship with God, the second diminishes the power of the official priesthood, and the third strikes at the root of Papal authority. Ultimately the conception of spiritual liberty which underlies these reforms was more significant than the political break with Rome.

Yet it is no easy task to sort out the specifically theological issues from the welter of racial, political, and social factors which were operative at that time. The vast inter-play of rival forces makes the situation difficult of analysis. Theological doctrines may easily be conditioned by current thought. 'How far was Cranmer influenced by the events of his time, by his knowledge of the apostolic, patristic or medieval Church, by Continental writers (especially those with whom he was friendly), and by his conception of the kingly office? What was the cumulative effect of all these factors upon his thinking in regard to the nature of the Church?'[1]

While allowing the force of these questions, it is also true to say that some problems are resolved only in the sphere of doctrine, and while other extraneous factors often set the problem in sharper relief, they do not in any way solve it. On the whole we may say

[1] *The Doctrine of the Church in Anglican Theology (1547-1603)*, H. F. Woodhouse (Introduction).

doctrine conditions events and is not conditioned by them. Some of those who came from the Continent saw the issues at stake more clearly, or perhaps they knew, having already had to face the issues in their own country, where to look for them. One of these visitors was Martin Bucer who came to England at the invitation of Cranmer, in April 1549, and if he did nothing else, he made it clear that external reforms would be like a house without foundation unless the doctrine of Justification by Faith was understood.

I. JUSTIFICATION BY FAITH

(a) *Rome*

If the doctrine of Justification by Faith is recognized today as the dominant problem which the Reformers had to face, it is not because it had an easy passage but because it was severely tested both by Continental and English theologians. Roman Catholic scholars also agree that this was the question at issue. Father Hughes writes: 'Once man is reconciled through the saving merits of Christ, his salvation is assured. No act of his can come between him and the eternity of heaven—save one, he must not lose faith. For, what secures to man his participation in the saving merits of Christ, what causes him *to appear before God* clad in their splendour, making him acceptable to God, just in God's sight, justified, is man's faith that he is *already* saved by the sacrifice of Christ. This faith alone is the operative element which secures to man all the rest. Such is the famous doctrine of Justification by Faith alone, the revolutionary doctrine which, in these years when Wolsey ruled England, was spreading over Europe like a prairie fire.'[2] Father Hughes repeats the error of the theologians of Trent in that he defines what he thinks the Reformers meant by Justification by Faith without any mention of the terms 'grace' and 'the Holy Spirit'. This is odd especially after three hundred years of Protestant history. Regarding the opening sentences of the above statement, it must be observed that it is not a bad thing, after all, to be sure of one's salvation, and it is a great comfort to many to realize that nothing can alter what Christ has done for the believer who exercises faith. If, on the other hand, the believer may not in any circumstances, 'appear before God', it is easy to understand

[2] P. Hughes, *The Reformation in England*, p. 121.

why the Reformers were regarded as plain heretics from the Roman viewpoint. But if the believer may not so appear, we may well ask, What is the ultimate purpose of religion, and if faith in God's justifying act is ruled out, what remains? To this extent the Roman Church failed to grasp the significance of the Reformation doctrine of the Priesthood of all Believers which means that 'faith alone is the operative element which secures to man all the rest', and if this faith is absent, all ceremonies and formalities are rendered worthless. What the Roman Church has never clearly grasped is that if the nature of faith which is implied in the Priesthood of all Believers is cast out, all other notions of Priesthood go with it. Whether ceremonial is present or absent, in the last resort, it is on the basis of faith alone that man may appear before God. If, as the Roman Church maintains, it is the privilege of the ordained Priest alone to appear before God, on what grounds does he do so apart from the 'splendour of the merits of Christ'? If the priest appears before God trusting in anything other than the saving merits of Christ, he is deceived by human arrogance and is standing on the sinking sands of self-justification. If, on the other hand, he trusts solely in the merits of Christ, do not all Christians do the same? Faith in the saving merits of Christ is not an exclusive privilege but one that is common to all believers. The Reformers could not get away from this fact and it is impossible for anyone to evade it without undermining the doctrine of Justification by Faith. Father Hughes's statement, however, creates the impression that faith is a sort of magic wand and that the Reformers thought that virtue resided in the word. On the contrary, Justification by Faith emerged as the basic doctrine of Reformation theology because the Reformers refused to accept widely accepted phrases, and gave themselves to the task of carefully examining those traditional phrases which had been handed down in the course of Church history. Some of these came under the scrutiny of Luther's penetrating mind, and they emerged representing something quite different from what had been commonly believed. Consequently, Luther not only affirmed the real meaning of Justification by Faith, but, equally important, he denied that man could be justified by anything else.

In a different situation the English Reformers also had to state not only what they meant by the doctrine of Justification by Faith, but also they had to stipulate what it involved for the life and worship of the Church. The second of these they accomplished more successfully than the Continentals, although they were greatly assisted by the German scholars who had come to reside in England.

(b) Bucer

Martin Bucer was able to view the situation impartially, and his background, education and natural talents well fitted him for the high task which confronted him. His association with Luther was a distinct advantage. 'Luther had a warm welcome in the Augustinian monastery at Heidelburg (April 1518), and he presided at a debate which was held in the lecture room. The propositions which he proposed for discussion were concerned, not so much with the question of indulgences, as with the underlying problem regarding the doctrine of justification. Among the noteworthy propositions were the following: "The works of man, no matter how specious and good they seem, are nevertheless in the last analysis, just deadly sins; whereas God's works, however puzzling or evil they may seem, are in fact eternal merits." "The law says, 'You must do all these things; yet you find it impossible'. But the Gospel says, 'Believe in Him—and lo! the whole requirement is met'." In the course of the debate Luther openly parted company with Occam's scholasticism. Instead of prejudice, he found willing ears and many whose hearts were like his own, especially among the younger monks. Here it was that he won over to the side of the Reformation several persons who were to be of great importance as the years went by, among the most earnest being John Brenz and Martin Bucer.'[3] Bucer was impressed not only with Luther's teaching but also with the vigour and direct imagery of his style. In the course of time this friendship deepened and with it Bucer's agreement with the Reformation principles was strengthened, so that when he came to England he was fully convinced of the worth as well as the truth of Luther's theological position. In addition, Bucer had played an important part in creating harmony between the German and Swiss Reformers, especially in respect of the doctrine of the Eucharist. It was largely due to his conciliatory influence that a large measure of understanding was achieved between the Lutherans and Calvinists concerning the doctrine

[3] W. J. Kooiman, *By Faith Alone*, p. 60.

of the Real Presence. With this background Bucer certainly knew at what points of doctrine theological tensions were likely to arise. Consequently, when he came to England he perceived that beneath Henry's over-elaborate theological arguments there lay two fears. First, the fear that acceptance of the doctrine of Justification by Faith would lead to secular troubles as had been the case in Germany, and secondly, the fear that if this doctrine were accepted, it would involve the surrendering of the Sacramental teaching of the Real Presence in the Catholic conception. No man was better fitted to deal with this situation than Martin Bucer, and if he was not permitted directly to dispel these fears, his influence upon Thomas Cranmer, who was instrumental in doing so, is unmistakable.

Henry, on the other hand, had learned much of his theology from one of the Catholic prelates, Bishop Stephen Gardiner, who, referring to Luther says: 'When he halted at the sacrament of the Eucharist, there rose up not a few who assailed the timidity of the man because he did not dare to follow out the full force of that proposition to the end; viz. that he utterly abolish the Eucharist also which cannot stand with that doctrine.'[4] All the same, the arguments in defence of what Gardiner called 'that foolish sophism—Justification by Faith alone' had cost Bucer a great deal, including a lifetime's exile from his native land, and he was unlikely to surrender it for the flippant reason which Gardiner put forward. It must be remembered that Charles V had hoped to pacify the Lutherans by including in the Augsburg Interim a modified form of the doctrine of Justification by Faith, and because they opposed this, Bucer and Fagius were banished from their native land. Certainly Bucer did not think he was contending for a foolish sophism, and if he did nothing else, he influenced tremendously no less a person than Archbishop Cranmer whose statement on the doctrine of Justification is pre-eminently Lutheran.

(c) Cranmer

Grace always precedes faith. It is important that this basic truth should not be forgotten. Cranmer is right in insisting that: 'Justification is not even by faith but only by grace.'[5] By this

---

[4] Constantin Hopf, *Martin Bucer and the English Reformation*, p. 177.
[5] G. W. Bromiley, *Thomas Cranmer, Theologian*, p. 29.

is meant that God always takes the initiative. The gracious work of God which is offered in Justification may only be apprehended by faith. Yet there is no contradiction in believing in 'proffered grace' and also in the truth implied in 'faith only' because it is by faith that 'we know God's mercy and grace promised by His word (and that freely for His death and passion's sake), and believe the same, and being truly penitent, we by faith receive the same'.[6]

It should not be forgotten that Cranmer was writing at a time when, according to traditional interpretation, Justification needed the support of innumerable subsidiary aids in order to do its work. Father Hughes gives a list of these aids, and laments the fact that they were no longer regarded as necessary: 'One truth alone mattered—that whoever "believed" was justified, and that by "faith" alone could man be justified. All the old notions are reinterpreted in the light of this. As to the rest, the asceticisms, the devotions, the monastic life, the processions, the pilgrimages, the statues, the relics, the sacraments, none of this was necessary.'[7] There is much truth in this statement—none of these *was necessary* to salvation, although the Reformers would not have included the sacraments in the same category as the other practices mentioned and precisely because none of the others is a sacrament. In the work of man's salvation God needs not the service of man; He requires only faith. We do not say that all the practices mentioned above are worthless, but rather that they are unnecessary, and certainly they have nothing whatever to do with Justification.

Cranmer, like Luther, was chiefly concerned to emphasize the grace and glory of God as revealed in the Person and work of Jesus. It will not do to say that Catholic orthodoxy shared this concern, for, as Professor P. S. Watson has pointed out, the principal weakness of scholasticism was that it would not 'let God be God'. Cranmer sums up the matter in these words: 'Our justification doth come freely by the mere mercy of God, and of so great and free mercy, that whereas all the world was not able *to pay any part* toward their ransom, it pleased our heavenly Father, by His infinite mercy without any of our desert or deserving, to prepare for us the most precious jewels of Christ's body and blood, whereby our ransom might be fully paid, the law

---

[6] G. W. Bromiley, *Thomas Cranmer, Theologian*, p. 29   [7] *The Reformation in England*, I.135.

fulfilled, and His justice fully satisfied. So that Christ is now the righteousness of all them that truly do believe in Him. He for them paid their ransom by His death: He for them fulfilled the law in His life: so that now *in Him, and by Him, every true Christian man may be called a fulfiller of the law*; forasmuch as that which their infirmity lacketh, Christ's justice hath supplied.'[8]

The English Reformation may be said to have begun in the mansion-house of Waltham Abbey. Here, in conversation with the Secretary of State, Gardiner, and the Lord High Almoner, Fox, Cranmer asked the crucial questions: 'Could not the question be decided without the exercise of Papal authority? Why go to Rome when there is a shorter road—that of the Scriptures? Why not ask the canonists, the divines, and the theological professors to return a scripture verdict upon the point at issue?' The question under discussion was that of the nullity of Henry's marriage with Catherine of Aragon, and Henry was only too ready to appoint Cranmer as the person most fitted to answer the questions he himself had raised. So Cranmer embarked upon a great task for a questionable reason, but the task was amply justified by its ultimate results rather than the immediate one. The importance of the resultant treatise which Cranmer presented to the King was not that it solved Henry's immediate problem, but that it laid down in England the formal principle of Protestantism—the appeal to Holy Scripture as the final authority. The result of Cranmer's work in this particular respect is writ large in the history of the Church of England.

Cranmer's achievements in the sphere of liturgical reform will be the better appreciated if we consider them against the background of the type of worship which existed in the Middle Ages.

To the common people both the ceremonial and language of medieval worship were unintelligible. They followed the ceremonial with their eyes but few of them understood what they saw. The significance of St Paul's word to the Romans had not been fully worked out: 'So belief cometh by hearing, and hearing by the word of Christ' (Rom 10[17]). True, there was drama in medieval worship, and people watched it in mute passivity as if it were only a drama. The whole emphasis was upon seeing rather than hearing, and when seeing is thus emphasized, belief takes a secondary place. The people were unable to follow the

[8] G. W. Bromiley, *Thomas Cranmer, Theologian*, p. 31.

priests' prayers because they were offered in Latin, and, more serious still, the responses were made by the clerks who assisted the priests and not by the congregation as a whole. If they could not follow the liturgy, neither could they follow the readings from the Bible, which again were in a language they could not understand. Moreover, sometimes at the mass, only the priest received the sacrament, although it was recognized that he did so on behalf of the people. Never did the people receive the Cup. All this meant that the congregation had no active share in the offering of public worship. Every circumstance we have mentioned was calculated to enhance the power of the priest and separate him from the people. Consequently, fear and superstition were rampant. It has been truly said that in the sphere of public worship the Reformation in England was a 'rediscovery of the congregation'. The introduction of the English Bible played a decisive part in this rediscovery.

II. THE ENGLISH BIBLE

In 1539 there was published a new version of the Scriptures in English. On account of its size it obtained the name of 'The Great Bible', but to the second edition there was prefaced a long and valuable prologue by Cranmer, and for this reason it has been called 'Cranmer's Bible'. The title-page of this version, said to be the work of Hans Holbein, is curious as a work of art and interesting as a page in the history of the times. About the middle of the engraving is the figure of Cranmer placing a copy of the sacred volume in the hands of one of his clergy and repeating the charge to St Peter: 'Feed the flock of God.'

No single incident in our history has done more to implement the Reformation doctrine of the Priesthood of all Believers than the introduction of the English Bible. McCrie, in *Contemporary Portraits of Reformers*, tells how it was received by the people of England: 'It was wonderful to see with what joy this Book of God was received, not only among the learned sort, and those that were noted for lovers of the Reformation, but generally all England over, among all the vulgar and common people; and with what greediness God's Word was read; and what resort to places where the reading of it was. Everybody that could bought the book, and busily read it, and got others to read it to them; and divers more elderly people learned to read on purpose. And even little

ANGLICANISM

boys flocked among the rest to hear portions of the Holy Scripture read.'[9] His words still convey the thrill of that occasion. The effect of it was even more significant, for when God is permitted to speak directly to individuals through His Word, they know that 'their redemption draweth nigh'.

III. THE BOOK OF COMMON PRAYER

The real transformation, however, in the worship of the English people took place ten years later when Cranmer issued the Book of Common Prayer. Undoubtedly this was his greatest achievement. The English Bible meant that God was able to speak to individuals through the medium of His Word; the Prayer Book meant that individuals were able to come together as a corporate body so that they were no longer passive spectators of something that they did not understand, but active participants in the general confessions and thanksgivings of the Church. The services of the Church were now within the reach of the laity, and the whole congregation was able to take part in the various acts of worship. The aim of the Reformers is expressed in the preface to the first English Litany: 'And such among the people as have books and can read may read them quietly and softly to themselves, and such as cannot read, let them quietly and attentively give audience in time of the said prayer, having their minds erect to Almighty God and devoutly praying in their hearts the same petitions which do enter in at their ears so that with one sound of the heart and with one accord God may be glorified in His Church.'

However, it was not to be expected that the first edition of the Prayer Book would satisfy everyone. Indeed, the attempt to satisfy the orthodox Catholic party as well as the Continental Reformers was a gargantuan task. Consequently, a revised edition of the Prayer Book appeared in 1552 and the hand of Bucer in this work is plainly evident. Bucer was ever anxious to include the congregation in worship, hence: 'People ought to be taught to say the responses which they do not. All ought to recite the prayer, "We do not presume", and the Thanksgiving after . . . together with the priests.'[10] Of course, it must be admitted that many of the liturgical reforms envisaged by the new Prayer Book

[9] Op. cit. p. 223.
[10] C. Hopf, *Martin Bucer and the English Reformation*, p. 65.

could not possibly be implemented at once because the whole idea of corporate worship was new. But Bucer was fighting for a vital principle: he wanted the whole congregation to be given the opportunity to exercise her corporate priesthood, but this much the Catholic Party would not allow. Bucer would not give in, and even the first rubric did not meet with his approval—'The Priest, being in the quier, shall begynne . . .'. This part was extended in the revised edition for the reasons which Bucer put forward. 'That it was an anti-Christian practice for the choir to be severed from the rest of the Church, and for the prayers there only to be said, which pertained to the people as well as to the clergy; that the separation of the choir from the body of the Church served for nothing else, but to get the clergy some respect above the laity as if they were nearer to God than laymen are: that a pernicious superstition was thereby maintained, as if priests alone were able to procure God's favour, by reading and reciting a few prayers; that in the ancient times of the Church, their temples were built in a round form, and not in a long figure as ours are; and that the place of the clergy was always in the midst of those temples; and that therefore this custom of the division of Church from chancels and of the priests saying service in them, was an insufferable abuse, to be forthwith amended, if the whole kingdom would not be guilty of treason against God.'[11] Here again, Bucer was pleading the Priesthood of all Believers, and it is to Cranmer's credit that he accepted the reasons which Bucer promulgated. This is not to say that he accepted every alteration which the revisers put forward, for he had to reassure the Catholic party as well as ameliorate the radical reformers, but it is evident that these suggestions of Bucer were in harmony with Cranmer's views on the matter. There is great force in some of these contentions of Bucer's. Ultimately the question is: Is the priest a substitute or a representative? The functions which the priest is called upon to fulfil are not carried out instead of the people but alongside them. He exercises a priesthood which they all possess, and he does this *with* them, not *for* them. Bucer's case is not a quibble; it is not simply that the exaltation of the clergy invariably involves a detraction of the laity, but rather that the congregation is deprived of the opportunity to exercise her priesthood—that is, her offering

---

[11] C. Hopf, *Martin Bucer and the English Reformation*, p. 67.

of praise, thanksgiving, prayer, and self-consecration. These noble acts of worship may not be done by proxy; they are the personal, inescapable functions of that priesthood which is common to the whole Church. To deprive Christians of this inestimable privilege is, according to Bucer, treason against God. Not all of Bucer's suggestions were implemented, but we may be grateful that the cause of Christian liberty had so fearless and forthright a champion in those days. It is important for us to remember that Cranmer supported those reforms which ultimately led to the rediscovery of the congregation, and it was this fact which had such far-reaching consequences.

IV. CRANMER'S INTERPRETATION OF THE EUCHARIST

The denial of the Cup to the laity had virtually destroyed the notion of the common priesthood, and not the least significant of Cranmer's reforms was the granting of the Cup to the laity. Again, the spiritual privileges of all Christians were recognized. No doubt Cranmer would have liked to have considered the question of the complete revision of the Communion Office so that it might more effectively reflect his changing theology, but unfortunately for us, events were fast moving to their nemesis and the time remaining to him was too short to do all he wished to do. The subject of the Eucharist was very close to Cranmer's heart, and always he regarded it as the sacrament of the People of God. He put the case for Communion in both kinds not simply to restore a lost privilege, but because he firmly believed that in the Eucharistic Service the 'whole Christ' was offered to believers. For anyone to interfere in any sense with the simple command of the Lord Jesus was blasphemy. This is why Cranmer makes the granting of the Cup one of the vital issues of the Reformation. Briefly, his teaching is as follows:

(i) *The High Priesthood of Christ*

He was always anxious to assert the sole High Priesthood of Christ. He resented any attempt made by others to enhance or embellish in any way the one sufficient Sacrifice of Christ. 'His first concern was for the glory of Jesus Christ and the fullness of His atoning work. For the uniqueness of the propitiatory sacrifice of Christ he found many passages especially in the Epistle to the Hebrews. In this priestly office "he admitteth *neither partner nor successor*. For by His own oblation He satisfieth His Father for all men's sins, and reconciles mankind unto His grace and favour".'[12] 'The result is that if there is a re-offering of Christ on the sacramental altar, an attempt is made by human priests to add in some way to the one sacrifice of Christ, or else there is a continual repetition of the "wicked act" of the "wicked Jews and Pharisees".' 'Either way injury is done to Jesus Christ Himself.' No wonder such notions alarmed Cranmer. It is true to say that in the foregoing statement the whole system of hierarchical priesthood is brought under judgement. It is presumptuous to believe that anyone may add to the glorious work of Christ. The Holy Spirit actualizes the presence of Christ and the faith of the believer realizes that presence, and this constitutes our appropriation of His Priesthood in which we all share and by which all are blessed.

(ii) *Priest and People together*

What then, is the work of the official priest? It is his great privilege to proclaim the Death of Christ, to point men and women to the Cross and bid them receive its benefits. 'The priest *should declare* the death and passion of Christ, and all the people should look upon the cross on the mount of Calvary, and see Christ there hanging, and the blood flowing out of His side into their wounds to heal all their sores; and the priest and people all together should laud and thank instantly the physician of their souls. And *this is the priest's and people's sacrifice*, not to be propitiators for sin, but (as Emissene saith) to worship continually in mystery that which was but once offered for the price of sin.'[13]

The only adequate response to such a vision of Christ is the offering of self and herein lies the most deliberate and personal expression of our priesthood. 'For if it is the office of the sacrament to bring before us the Sacrifice of Christ, its sacrificial work includes not only the application of that work, but the response of self-offering to Christ which is evoked by that sacrifice and demanded of all the recipients. In the first instance, this response is a sacrifice of "laud and praise", for it is a grateful recognition of the saving work of Christ. It is also a sacrifice of repentance and obedience. . . .'[14]

---

[12] G. W. Bromiley, *Thomas Cranmer, Theologian*, p. 85.
[13] Ibid. p. 87.   [14] Ibid.

V. THE MEDIATION OF CHRIST'S JUSTIFYING ACTIVITY

It must now be affirmed that Cranmer's emphasis upon justification by faith, his rediscovery of the congregation, and his conception of the believer's identification with the Priesthood of Christ, places all Christians under an added sense of responsibility to God. If they cannot measure their privilege, neither can they measure their responsibility. Their constant peril is lest they should accept the one and reject the other. It is important, then, to emphasize that the foregoing receives its real significance when it is studied in relation to, and not in separation from, the world in which we are called upon to witness.

Since we are justified by the merits of Christ and are identified with Him in His priestly activity, we cannot evade the questions to which F. W. Dillistone has drawn attention: 'How can we mediate His justifying activity?'[15] It is clearly the duty of all Christians to mediate the justifying activity of God, and it is in this inherent duty that the priesthood of believers is to be understood. None of the Reformers thought that the Christian could do this without the aid of the Holy Spirit, and while Cranmer sets the pace in this respect he is ably supported by several others among whom is Bilson, who writes: 'From His riches flow the fruits, blessings, and gifts of His Spirit by which the Church and every member is endowed and enriched. Thereby we are grounded in faith, moulded in hope, rooted in charity. All these come from His fullness, and in the Church Christ rules as prophet, priest and king through the Holy Spirit.'[16]

It is not only that God's justifying activity is mediated through individual Christians, but also that the Church becomes the instrument of mediation. Since the Holy Spirit actuates individual members, He also unifies them so that the whole company of believers mediates the divine justifying activity. In this way the Holy Ghost vindicates all that God has done on behalf of man.

This Justifying Activity operative by the Spirit in every Member
'The Church becomes the house and dwelling-place of the Holy Ghost, and His gifts and graces are scattered and given *unto every member of the Church*. . . . Because Christ is present by the Holy Spirit in every member of the Church all Christians are coupled

[15] *Justification by Faith*, p. 46.
[16] *The Perpetual Government of Christ's Church* (1593), p. 205.

with Christ their Head.'[17] As recipients of these inestimable privileges it is the duty of all Christians to set forth the gracious justifying activity of God. 'The reality of the Spirit's guidance, the certainty of His defence, His living and active ruling presence in the Church as representing the Risen, Ascended Lord, His ability to impart to the believer the fruits of redemption, and his power to join all believers in close fellowship, have been mentioned here, and their ideas are all developments of the great Pauline ideas contained in the words "in Christ".'[18]

Here, indeed, is the driving-force of evangelism in any age. The impact of the Church upon the world is always the impact of the divine Spirit. God is active in the life of the Church because He has chosen to be active in this particular way. But the primary impact of God's power upon the world is through the Cross, the efficacy of which is perpetuated through all believers. Therefore, there is a difference between God's justifying act (the Cross) which is unrepeatable, and His justifying activity, which is perpetuated in the life of the Church day by day. On the basis of this unrepeatable act Christians are engaged in the continuing activity. Since God has justified all in that saving act, it is the responsibility of Christians to accept all into the fellowship of the covenant thus established.

Dr Dillistone expounds justification as follows: 'The doctrine of justification by faith keeps ever before the Church's conscience the unlimited generosity of God. In what way could the Church, the individual Christian more adequately bear witness to the God whom they worship and serve than by being baptized afresh into that same Spirit of Grace and by participating in whatever measure is possible in the divine work of accepting those who by no other kind of work could ever be justified?'[19]

Cranmer and his fellow reformers have right on their side when they see a coming together of theology and ethics in the context of the doctrine of Justification by Faith, which means, according to the argument amplified above, the justifying activity of God mediated through the priesthood of all believers.

VI. CRANMER'S INTERPRETATION OF ORDINATION

The vital significance of the above considerations is in relation

---

[17] H. F. Woodhouse, *The Doctrine of the Church in Anglican Theology*, p. 33.
[18] Ibid. [19] *Justification by Faith*, pp. 48-9.

to the question of Ordination and upon this subject Cranmer's views can only be described as radical. His thoughts upon this were far ahead of his contemporaries as they are also far ahead of many of his successors in Anglicanism. His views are important because of their bearing upon the doctrine of the universal priesthood as well as for their relevance for ecumenism as it is understood today.

(1) *Ordination—a dispensable ceremony*

While this is indeed a radical view, we shall see that there is sound reasoning behind it. It will be generally agreed that grace is available both to those who are called upon to serve in secular callings as well as to those who are called to serve in the Ministry. Cranmer denies 'that there is any more promise of grace in the committing of the ecclesiastical office than in the committing of the civil office'.[20] There is here an obvious danger of Erastianism, and it is at this point that both Luther and Cranmer have been frequently misrepresented. Luther attributed ecclesiastical as well as civil authority to the Christian Princes, and to all intents and purposes Cranmer invested the same authority in the King. Further, both of them followed this course on the basis of the priesthood of all believers, Luther explicitly and Cranmer by allusion. Luther held that because the Princes were also priests unto God, they were entitled to exercise jurisdiction in spiritual as well as civil affairs. Cranmer held that commissioning to a secular office was just as important as commissioning to a sacred one, and that commissioning was not absolutely essential in either case. If it is thought that Luther and Cranmer surrendered the spiritual authority of the Church to the State, we must bear in mind the following two facts: first, that it was commonly believed that authority must be invested in someone; and secondly, that to invest spiritual and ecclesiastical authority in the State was by no means an innovation, unless we forget entirely the reign of Constantine and the teaching of St Augustine. Luther, pleading the priesthood of all believers, sincerely held that spiritual power was safer when entrusted to the German Princes than to the Roman hierarchy. He was mistaken in this assumption, but the abuse of a principle does not invalidate it. Cranmer had agreed to the transfer of spiritual authority from

---

[20] G. W. Bromiley, *Thomas Cranmer, Theologian*, p. 50.

the Pope to the Sovereign. When Queen Mary ordered him to sign the recantation, he was under an inescapable obligation to obey the person holding that spiritual authority which he had done so much to establish. He could not preach that this authority resided in the crown, and then refuse to obey. We should recognize his dilemma before condemning his weakness. But Cranmer's Erastianism is inextricably bound up with his view on the question of the Ministry. He was not prepared to believe that Prince, nobleman, or commoner were not, equally with the Priest, set aside to fulfil a divine vocation.

'The divers comely ceremonies and solemnities used in the admission of these offices are not *of necessity*, but only for a good order and seemly fashion.'[21] The conclusion is inescapable that Cranmer believed that even ordination was a dispensable or alterable ceremony. His main point appears to be that while there has to be a ministry, the mode of calling is not fixed by Scripture, but belongs to the sphere of things in which the Church can take order for itself.

(2) *The Power of the laity to make and constitute Priests*

We do not know to what extent Cranmer was familiar with Luther's writings, but if in the following passages on the Ministry, he is writing independently of Luther, we may assume that the two reformers were much closer together than is commonly thought. Cranmer's view is that the form of the Ministry is no more than a matter of organization. He even asserts that: 'At a pinch, the ceremony of consecration is unnecessary and that in special circumstances the ministry can be reconstituted, or even constituted for the first time, either by civil enactment or on the initiation of the civil power. For instance, "if it befortuned a prince Christian—learned to conquer certain dominions of infidels, having none but temporal learned men with him" it is lawful, and indeed obligatory that "he and they should preach and teach the Word of God there, and also *make and constitute priests*".'[22]

If a man is called of God, chosen by faithful Christians, presented to Christ in prayer, and equipped for service, his ministry has the divine approval and this is the important matter.

[21] G. W. Bromiley, *Thomas Cranmer, Theologian*, p. 50.
[22] Ibid. p. 51.

He is not less a priest because he is chosen by the laity. Cranmer rejects the view that divine authority is bestowed only by succession.[23] Again, the power which Luther conceded to the Christian Princes on the ground of their membership of the universal priesthood, is allowed also by Cranmer: 'If for some reason the ordinary succession of ministers failed, as happened in some of the reforming territories, Cranmer thought it both right and necessary that the Christian laity responsible for ordinary government should re-establish the ministry.'[24]

(3) The Commission and the form of commissioning

Ceremonial must always be subordinated to authentic experience. The internal calling which is the work of the Holy Spirit is the sole prerequisite of a true exercise of spiritual functions. 'For a genuine doctrine of the ministry we do not turn to the *form* of commissioning but to the Commission itself.'[25] But if, on the internal side, the calling is prompted by the Holy Spirit, on the external side, it is a matter for the whole Church. 'The underlying principle, however, is that on its external side, the appointment of ministers is not merely a question of a hierarchy but an affair of the whole Church, so that no man ought to exercise his ministry without the expressed willingness of the congregation.'[26]

First, there is the ministry which is given or committed to the Church, and secondly, there is ministry as it is exercised in various ways in the life of the Church. Since ministry is the gift of Christ to His Church and cannot be regarded as otherwise, all ministries are fulfilled in Him. If there is such a thing as an essential ministry or priesthood it must be that of Christ, and His is a priesthood which all believers share, for all are called in varying measure to fulfil the task which is committed to the whole Church. The principal error of the Middle Ages was that the ministry was regarded as possessing a single and exclusive structure which, as Cranmer observes, 'in spite of its respectable antiquity cannot claim the clear and authoritative sanction of the New Testament'.

---

[23] See above, page 43, for Luther's enunciation of the priesthood.
[24] G. W. Bromiley, *Thomas Cranmer, Theologian*, p. 52.
[25] Ibid. p. 53.
[26] Ibid. p. 54.

VII. HOOKER'S INTERPRETATION OF GOSPEL PRIESTHOOD

Even Hooker while affirming that a special power and authority is committed to the Ministry, is prepared to allow that *this authority is sometimes given immediately*, and sometimes mediately—through the Church. In this vital matter Hooker implies that the decisive factor is the Call of God: 'That God which is in no way deficient or wanting unto man in necessaries, and hath therefore given us the light of His heavenly truth . . . hath in the like abundance of His mercies ordained certain to attend upon the due executive of requisite parts and offices wherein prescribed for the good of the whole world, which men thereunto assigned do hold their office from Him, whether they be such as Himself immediately or as the Church in His name investeth, it being neither possible for all nor for every man without distinction convenient to take upon him a charge of so great importance.'[27] If this passage means anything, it means that not all need necessarily receive this authority through the Church as an institution, for 'there be such as Himself immediately investeth'. All this is consonant with Hooker's definition of the word 'Priest'.

(a) Gospel Priesthood does not imply Sacrificial Priesthood

'Seeing then that sacrifice is now no part of the Church's Ministry, how should the name of Priest thereunto be rightly applied? The Fathers of the Church of Christ with like serenity of speech call usually the ministers of the Gospel Priesthood in regard of that which the Gospel hath *proportionable* to ancient sacrifices, namely, the Communion of the blessed Body and Blood of Christ, although it have now no sacrifice. As for the people it draweth no more their minds to any cogitation of sacrifice, than the name of a senator or any alderman causeth them to think upon old age.'[28]

This opinion carries an added weight since it is drawn from one who held strong ecclesiastical views. Hooker's affirmation that sacrifice is no part of the Church's Ministry and that this truth was so widely established as to be recognized by the people as a whole is surely of the highest significance for our understanding of priesthood in the seventeenth century.

[27] P. E. More and F. L. Cross, *Anglicanism*, p. 345.
[28] Hooker, *Works*, II.179.

(b) Gospel Priesthood and the Calling of the Presbyter

On this Hooker says: 'In truth the word Presbyter doth seem more fit, and in propriety of speech more agreeable than Priest with the drift of the whole Gospel of Jesus Christ. For what are they that embrace the Gospel but sons of God? What are churches but His families? Seeing therefore we receive the adoption and state of sons by their ministry whom God hath chosen out for that purpose, seeing also that when we are sons of God, our continuance is still under their care which were our progenitors, what better title could be given them than the revered name of Presbyters or fatherly guides?'[29] It is interesting to note that Hooker not only rejects the word 'Priest' and adopts the word 'Presbyter', but that he does so on grounds of pastoral responsibility. The minister, therefore, is to be regarded not as one who offers sacrifice on behalf of others, but as one who protects and guides those who are committed to his care. In short, his chief work is that of a shepherd. It is also interesting to note that the Lutheran Churches dropped the word 'priest' and adopted the word 'Pastor'. H. H. Kramm, explaining the reason for this, says: 'The metaphor of a pastor, a shepherd, shows exactly what is meant. The shepherd is not the mediator between the sheep and the grass, the sheep have direct access to the grass. But the shepherd shows them the right way to the meadow and defends them against dangers.'[30]

Joseph Mede (1672) supports Hooker though for a different reason. 'The reason we thus speak is to avoid the name Priest which we conceive to signify *sacerdos*, that is, one that sacrificeth, such as were those in the law; but our curates in holy things in the Gospel are not to offer sacrifice, and therefore ought not to be called *sacerdos*, and consequently not Priests.'[31] So while Hooker rejects the word 'Priest' on practical grounds, those of the pastoral duties involved, Mede does so for purely etymological reasons.

(c) Gospel Priesthood is not confined to the Apostles

Hooker then ventures a definition of the word 'Presbyter' since he has also said that it is preferable. 'A Presbyter according to

[29] *Works*, II.180.
[30] *The Theology of Martin Luther*, pp. 77ff.
[31] More and Cross, *Anglicanism*, p. 320.

the proper meaning of the New Testament is he unto whom our Saviour hath communicated the power of spiritual procreation.'[32] This bears reference to a spiritual succession which is the opposite of an external hierarchy. The apostles do not claim the title for themselves alone: 'In which respect the apostles also likewise gave themselves the same title, although that name were not proper but common unto them with others.'[33]

Hooker, however, is on less certain ground in his exposition of 1 Corinthians 12[28]. He is replying to those who, upon reading this passage, have surmised 'incompatible offices where nothing is meant but sundry graces, gifts and abilities, which Christ bestowed'. 'To them of Corinth his words are these, "God placed in the Church first of all some apostles, secondly prophets, thirdly teachers, after them powers, then gifts of cures, aids, governments, kinds of languages. Are all Apostles? Are all Prophets? Are all Teachers? Is there power in all? Have all grace to cure? Do all speak with tongues? Can all interpret? But be you desirous of the better graces." They which plainly discern that some *one general* thing there is which the apostle doth here divide into all these branches, and do secondly conceive that *general* thing to be Church offices. . . .'[34]

We admit the first—one general thing was offered to all these branches; but deny the second—that the general thing was 'office'. St Paul was speaking about spiritual gifts and not about Church offices. (See 1 Cor. 12[1].) It will not do to make this passage an argument for the threefold ministry, for the apostle does not mention *only* Apostles, Prophets and Teachers, and there is certainly no marked distinction between these three and the others, for verse 27 reads: 'Now ye are the body of Christ, and severally (each in his part—*R.V.*) members thereof.'

The second passage mentioned by Hooker must be viewed in the light of modern biblical research: 'To every one of us is given grace according to the measure of the gift of Christ. He . . . gave gifts unto men. He therefore gave some to be apostles and some prophets and some evangelists and some pastors and teachers, for the gathering together of the saints, for the work of the ministry, for the edification of the body of Christ.'[35] Some New Testament scholars maintain that the comma after the word 'saints'

---

[32] More and Cross, *Anglicanism*, p. 370. [33] Ibid.
[34] *Works*, II.184-5. [35] Ibid. p. 185.

should be omitted, and on this basis J. B. Phillips translates the passage: 'His gifts were made that Christians might be properly equipped for their services, that the whole body might be built up. . . .' We may say then that these gifts were given for the equipping of the saints for the work of the ministry. We may not say that the passage implies that some were spiritually equipped in a way which was denied to others.

VIII. THE CHURCH AS A SUCCESSION OF BELIEVERS

(1) *The People of God*

Again the spiritual succession is emphasized by John Pearson (1659), who regards the Church as a succession of believers. 'And therefore to make good this explication of the Article, it will be necessary to prove that the Church, which our Saviour founded and the Apostles gathered, was to receive a constant and perpetual accession, and by a successive augmentation be uninterruptedly continued in an actual existence of believing persons and congregations in all ages unto the end of the world.'[36] Such believing persons constitute the Church, the People of God.

Now the Israelites were called to be a holy people, and those called in the New Israel are to bear the same mark. The People of God are a holy People, and if they are not holy they do not belong to God. Yet their holiness is not theirs by nature, neither is it a virtue which they may win for themselves, however hard they may strive, it is that holiness which is communicated to them by Him who is Himself holy. 'The end of constituting a Church in God was for the purchasing an holy and precious people; the great design thereof was for the begetting and increasing holiness, that as God is originally holy in Himself, *so He might communicate His sanctity to the sons of men*, . . . because without holiness no man shall ever see God.' The sole purpose of this gracious action is that 'the whole Church may be termed and believed holy'.[37]

(2) *The Holiness of the People of God*

Now if holiness is the mark of the whole Church, and if God in His mercy makes provision for communicating that holiness to believers, it follows that this offer of general grace must be evidenced in the teaching and ceremonies of the Church. And not

[36] More and Cross, *Anglicanism*, p. 30.   [37] Ibid. p. 32.

only so, it must be the Church's primary concern both to teach and to make plain God's offer of grace to man. If she fails in this one thing, she fails in all things. James I faced this question with great sincerity and came to the conclusion that the divine offer of grace was hedged around with several strictures and limitations. Apparently these insufferable conditions and innumerable media left him bewildered. He refers to them in his Confessions of Faith. One by one he delineates the barriers which have been set up between God and man, and his reason for refuting them is always the same: 'As for prayer to saints, Christ, I am sure, hath commanded us all to come to Him that are loaden with sin, and He will relieve us; and St Paul hath forbidden us to worship angels or to use any such voluntary worship. . . . But what warrant have we to have recourse to these Courtiers of God, I know not; I remit that to these philosophical Neoteric Divines. It satisfieth me to pray to God through Christ, as I am commanded.'[38]

(3) *The Priesthood of the People of God*

A Christian is first a member of the whole Christian priesthood and then a minister. It is never the other way round. Ordination does not *make* him a priest in any sense, rather it stipulates and directs in what specific ways he shall serve (minister to) the whole Church. A king is not made a king by coronation, nor a priest by ordination. In each case the symbol is but the recognition of what is already a fact, and every Christian is a member of the Royal Priesthood.

It is not easy to determine when a Christian becomes a member of the Royal Priesthood. Some Anglicans consider that it takes place at Baptism, others hold that it takes place at Confirmation. On the other hand, the rite of Unction which was frequently linked with Baptism in the Early Church would seem to indicate that sometimes the membership of the Royal Priesthood was symbolized by Baptism as well as by the anointing with oil. A. J. Mason has drawn attention to the rite of Unction: 'It would not be an emblem of the consecrating influence of the Holy Spirit in general; it would be the sign of consecration to a priesthood. . . . If the idea of the priesthood of the Christian was so prominent in the thoughts of the Apostles, there would

---

[38] James I, *Anglicanism*, p. 4.

be nothing strange in their using a ceremony which perfectly expressed it.'[39] There is, however, a more important reason for combining the two ceremonies, and that is in order that the twofold dignity of kingship and priesthood may be expressed. A deacon of the Roman Church in the sixth century wrote a letter to Senarius in which he described the baptismal ceremonies. After relating the actual baptism he shows how the newly-baptized were arrayed in white robes and then: 'His head is anointed with the unction of the sacred Chrism, in order that the baptized may understand that the kingship and the priestly mystery *have met in him*.'[40]

It is not clear, however, from Mason's subsequent argument whether he considers this combined ceremony as consecration to the common priesthood or whether this consecration takes place at Confirmation. He writes: 'Our Confirmation, too, like His, is really a consecration as well.'[41] And again: 'Confirmation consecrates the Christian to be a priest. The great division between the priestly race and the rest of mankind begins at Baptism as completed by Confirmation, and not anywhere higher up.'

From this, two important aspects of the question emerge. (*a*) Baptism and the rite of Unction would appear to be a public proclamation of the spiritual resources which are available to all Christians—the twofold blessing of kingship and priesthood, whereas (*b*) Confirmation indicates the conscious acceptance of the responsibilities and duties which are involved in the twofold blessing. They represent two sides of the same question: the first is an objective proclamation and the second a subjective experience which also embraces a definite commitment to a task.

Jeremy Taylor (1613-67) declares that 'in Confirmation we receive the unction from above, that is, that we are then most signally made kings and priests unto God to offer up spiritual sacrifices'. In a sublime passage he shows how the Anointing of the Spirit is given without measure in the New Dispensation: 'But in the Gospel the Spirit is given without measure: first poured forth upon our Head, Christ Jesus; then descending upon the beard of Aaron, the father of the Church; and thence falling upon the lowest of the people. And this is given regularly to all that ask it, to all that can receive it, and by a solemn ceremony

---

[39] *The Relation of Confirmation to Baptism*, p. 10.
[40] Ibid. p. 201.   [41] Ibid.

and conveyed by a sacrament. . . . It is the parent of boldness and fortitude to martyrs, the foundation of learning to doctors, an ocean of all things excellent to all who are within the ship and bounds of the Catholic Church: so that old men and young men, maidens and boys, the scribe and the unlearned, the judge and the advocate, the priest and the people, are full of the Spirit if they belong to God. Moses's wish is fulfilled and all the Lord's people are prophets in some sense or other.'[42]

We may say then that this is the seventeenth-century version of the Priesthood of all believers; it is an attempt to show that in Confirmation the Christian is incorporated into the Royal, Priestly and Prophetic office of Christ. The comment of a later Anglican writer may be appropriate here: 'Confirmation is an act which carries out and fulfils the intention of Baptism. . . . It is a distinct acknowledgement of the truth that there must be a conscious and voluntary recognition of our Church membership. Confirmation does not make Baptism more complete, but shows how complete it is. In Confirmation the great Father owns those whom He has regenerated, as His children, "taking them out of the hands of subordinate teachers and into His own immediate service, enduing them with the powers necessary for that service".'[43] There is no doubt that in Anglican theology there has always been a close connexion between Confirmation and the common priesthood, and in support of his interpretation Mason rebuts the theory that the common priesthood is to be interpreted in a narrow and inadequate manner. 'And thus Confirmation is, as the Fathers always taught that it was, the conferring of a real priesthood—and not a priesthood only, but a kingly and prophetic priesthood also. Such titles mean a great deal more than a right of direct access to God, or the like. They involve duties on behalf of other men. And the Holy Spirit given in Confirmation is given for a wider purpose than the enrichment and exaltation of the confirmed man himself.'[44]

IX. THE ANGLICAN EVANGELICALS

Theology

G. R. Balleine has drawn attention to three vital truths which

[42] *The Works of Jeremy Taylor*, ed. Heber.
[43] A. R. Vidler, *The Theology of F. D. Maurice*, p. 117.
[44] A. J. Mason, *The Relation of Confirmation to Baptism*, p. 461.

the Evangelicals emphasized: 'And this has led them', he says, 'to lay special stress on three important facts, which they have found specially prominent in the New Testament, facts which most of their fellow-Churchmen acknowledged to be true, but which few have emphasized as Evangelicals have done.

'(*a*) The first is that Christianity is a religion of Redemption: that the Atonement is the very foundation doctrine of the faith. "There is therefore now no condemnation to them that are in Christ Jesus"—this is the Evangel, the Good News from which they obtained their name.

'(*b*) The second point is the supremacy of the spiritual over the external, the fact that the root of personal religion lies deeper than in any sacred rites or series of moral actions; that the "abysmal depths of personality" must feel the presence of God moving upon the face of the waters; that conversion not conformity, change of heart not change of habit, is the thing to be worked for; that ritual, church-going, outward observances do not make a Christian, but the action of the Spirit of God transforming the inner life. The Evangelicals have never mistaken the machinery for the motive-power.

'(*c*) But the *chief source* of their success has lain in the third point. They have never allowed *anything*, however sacred, to come between themselves and Christ. While all Churchmen strive to teach the whole Christian faith, each party tends to emphasize some particular point. High Churchmen are apt to accent the functions of the Church and Sacraments; Broad Churchmen lay stress on the thought of the universal Fatherhood of God; but with the Evangelicals the central point has always been the Person of Christ, the glory and all-sufficiency of His work. The keynote of their message is:

> *Nothing between, Lord, nothing between;*
> *Let me Thy glory see,*
> *Draw my soul close to Thee,*
> *Then speak in love to me,*
> *Nothing between.*'[45]

The first draws attention to the self-offering of the Great High Priest; the second shows that His self-offering is all sufficient for our needs, rendering everything else unnecessary; and the third

---

[45] *A History of the Evangelical Party, in the Church of England*, pp. 206-7.

indicates that a direct and personal relationship with the all-sufficient Redeemer is the indisputable inheritance of all believers. So then, the doctrinal basis of the Evangelicals may be summed up as follows: the High Priesthood of Christ presupposes a spiritual, universal priesthood. It would be difficult to overemphasize the theological significance of the words 'nothing between'. The truth which underlies them should be viewed against the background of the Tractarian Movement, for even when the considerable contribution of that Movement to ecclesiology, theology and liturgiology is conceded, we cannot but notice and deplore the definite tendency to regard Church, Priesthood, Sacraments and Succession as indispensable intermediaries between the believer and his Redeemer. The Evangelicals, therefore, had some reason to declare that all may behold God's glory, that all may draw close to Him, and that His Word is spoken to all—nothing between. These were precious truths which the Tractarians would not own but which the Evangelicals could not surrender. These truths may be summed up in one phrase: 'Justification by Faith.'

(1) *Justification by Faith reasserted*

The reason why this doctrine was emphasized by the Evangelicals is to be found in that excellent work by Joseph and Isaac Milner (1744-97), *The History of the Church of Christ*. In those volumes Justification by Faith is made the undisputed criterion of true Christianity. Was the doctrine lost in the eighteenth century?

'That, which is most to our purpose to observe, is the awful departure, which had commonly been made, throughout Christendom, from the all-important article of Justification. While this is firmly believed and reverenced, it is impossible for men to think of commuting for their offences with heaven; and it is itself the surest defence against clerical encroachments, superstition, idolatry and hypocrisy. But the pulpits were silent on this doctrine: during the whole century false religion grew without any check or molestation; and vices, both in public and private life, increased in proportion.'[46] The thirteenth century is also castigated for a similar reason. Matthew Paris, who was not unaware of King John's crimes, was yet able to observe: 'We ought to hope and most assuredly to trust, that some good works, which he did in

[46] J. & I. Milner, *The History of the Church of Christ*, III.166.

this life, will plead for him before the tribunal of Jesus Christ. For he built one abbey, and dying bequeathed a sum of money to another.' Milner adds: 'So grossly ignorant was this ingenious and valuable historian of the all-important doctrine of Justification by the merit of Jesus Christ alone, through faith.'[47]

There is little doubt that once the sole-sufficiency of Christ is called into question, man has no option but to seek other means of soothing his conscience even though this involves deceiving his soul. In dealing with the Reformation period Isaac Milner edits and elucidates the work of his brother. He finds this a happy task, for he can expound more fully his, as well as Luther's, favourite doctrine—Justification by Faith. He discovers that there is opposition to this doctrine not only in religion but in philosophy. He finds it necessary to condemn Aristotelian philosophy for three reasons: first, because it does not recognize the sinfulness of man; secondly, because it erroneously assumes that salvation is possible by a series of external actions; and thirdly, because it knows nothing of the doctrine of grace. The Church, however, which should have been opposing such false doctrine, was indirectly supporting it.

It was this which impelled Milner to investigate the whole system. The attitude of the Church presented a serious problem. He found men in bondage to a system which, in theory, was pledged to set them free. 'Men were then bound fast in fetters of iron, their whole religion was one enormous mass of bondage. Terrors beset them on every side. . . . Persons truly serious were so clouded in their understanding by the prevailing corruption of the hierarchy, that they could find no access to God by Jesus Christ. The road of simple faith was stopped up by briars and thorns.'[48]

In order to add weight to his answer to Aristotelian teaching, Milner quotes one of Luther's letters to Spalatin: 'For men are not made truly righteous as Aristotle supposes, by performing certain actions which are externally good—for they may still be counterfeit characters—but men must have righteous principles in the first place, and then they will not fail to perform righteous actions. God first respects Abel, and then his offering.'[49]

Milner, whose gifts as a historian enabled him to trace the relation of one doctrine to another, was by the same means able to

[47] *The History of the Church of Christ*, IV.7. [48] Ibid. p. 310. [49] Ibid. p. 340.

appreciate the way in which Luther connected the doctrine of Justification by Faith with the doctrine of the priesthood of all believers. In a brief survey of this subject Milner emphasizes the unfailing logic of Luther's position. First of all he points out that not only had the clergy utterly misunderstood the doctrine of Justification but they had also played upon the fears of the people and thus forfeited the respect of the laity. In the second place, it was asserted by Milner that pardon and other spiritual blessings were not dependent upon the official priesthood since all may become partakers of the grace of Christ. In the third place, the sole condition of receiving these blessings was belief in the righteousness of Christ. All this and more Milner discovered in Luther's writings of 1518.

(*a*) 'There was no occasion to excite hatred of mankind against Priests to a greater degree. The avarice and profligacy of the clergy had, for many years past, kindled the indignation of the laity. Alas! they have not a particle of respect and honour for the priesthood, except what solely arises from fear of punishment.'[50]

(*b*) Since respect for the Priesthood had vanished, did this mean that the spiritual privileges of Christians were also banished? Again he calls Luther to witness 'that every true Christian may become partaker of the grace of Christ without pontifical indulgences'. In all this Milner was marching in step with Luther and was satisfied to accept Luther's judgement upon the matter.

(*c*) There remains one more question, namely, How does a Christian become partaker of the grace of Christ? This comes to pass, not because the Christian produces his own righteousness or merits, but because he believes in the righteousness and merits of Christ. Hence, 'A Christian may glory that he has all things, and all the righteousness and merits of Christ are his own by virtue of that spiritual union with Him, which he has by faith.'

Milner was not satisfied simply to understand Luther's interpretation of Justification; he was also anxious to discover the reasons why Rome had misunderstood it. In the reasons which he gives he shows complete agreement with Melanchthon.[51] Milner holds that Rome misunderstood the doctrine because she assumed that the Pope, cardinals, and clergy of Rome constituted the Church. He also complained that the Pope and his Bishops had exacted an unlawful obedience and that nothing short of

[50] *The History of the Church of Christ*, IV.354.   [51] Ibid. V.432.

giving up the Word of God would content them. But if they had misunderstood the nature of the Church and the Word of God, it was chiefly because they had a defective doctrine of Grace. They had obviously forgotten 'the great doctrinal point is that of faith in the merits of Christ, independent of human works, as the ground of acceptance before God'.

(2) *Reformation Doctrine not Latitudinarian*

Milner, however, has done another great service, for he has not only stated what Luther believed, but he has also shown us the doctrines which Luther opposed and his reasons for so doing. In this case he was thinking not of Rome but of those within the Protestant fold. The Lutherans in the sixteenth century and the Evangelicals in the eighteenth have sometimes been accused of encouraging baseless latitudinarian and antinomian tendencies. This is to misread history. They attacked such tendencies, and were distressed whenever they found that the doctrines they emphasized were misinterpreted and misapplied. Let it be admitted that some of the leading reformation doctrines were particularly susceptible of misunderstanding, and add to this the tendency of radical elements always to over-emphasize their case, and we shall be in a better position to understand what happened at Antwerp. Milner draws attention to the dangerous spirits there who held the following beliefs:

1. Every man had the Holy Spirit.
2. The Holy Spirit signified neither more nor less than men's reason and understanding.
3. That all men were believers.
4. That every soul would possess eternal life.
5. That he who had not the Holy Spirit was incapable of sin, because he was devoid of reason.[52]

Luther emphatically disapproved of all this and perceived that it was an attempt to give a twist to the doctrine of the priesthood of all believers and to make it something different from that interpretation which is warranted in Scripture. First, then, it must be affirmed that only those who through faith have received the Holy Spirit, possess Him. The Holy Spirit is not, and cannot be, the natural inheritance of every man. But to equate the

[52] Ibid. V.393.

Person of the Holy Spirit with human reason is as fantastic as calling darkness light. Further, all men are not believers, and any such theory is foreign to the New Testament. We may take one verse from among many to show the evidence of Scripture: 'He that believeth on the Son of God hath the witness in Himself, he that believeth not God, hath made him a liar; because he believeth not the record that God gave of His Son.' The Reformers held strong views on the calling, privileges and duties of a Christian, but they clearly recognized that while all were called to believe, all did not, in fact, believe. They would have endorsed the testimony of the visionary in Revelation, the believer is one who is washed from his sins and made to be a member of the kingdom of priests. To ascribe to everyone blessings which are clearly conditional, and to pretend that they apply to all irrespective of the response of faith, is to play havoc with Scripture and to indulge in an unwarrantable universalism. But Luther dealt effectively with all these deviations, and the important point for our purpose is that Milner is anxious to show, as indeed he does with considerable success, that Luther was no antinomian rebel but a constructive thinker whose reforms were the outcome of a dynamic theology.

(3) *Reformation Doctrine not Rationalism: Luther and Erasmus*

Milner rendered a great service to the Church in his own age by showing how Luther found the remedy for the ills which beset his generation. But others also had sought to reform the Church; Erasmus was incensed against the abuses of Rome. He often listened to their facile rationalizing: 'The Pope did not exact taxes like secular sovereigns. He gave something in return. The "something" might not admit of precise definition. But Christ had given to the Christian priesthood the power of absolution. The Pope was supreme priest, Pontifex Maximus, and possessed that power, whatever it might be, in supreme degree. What Christ could do the Pope could do; and at any rate the grant of indulgences was a time-honoured custom in the Church.'[53] Erasmus certainly attacked the system, but Luther did so at a much deeper level. It is this fact which epitomizes the difference between them. Erasmus attacked the scandalous vices of the monks; the intrigues, avarice and encroachments of the clergy;

[53] *The History of the Church of Christ*, IV, Preface, p. xi.

ANGLICANISM

and many abominable impieties and superstitions of the Romish Church. Was this enough, or was it only skimming the surface of the problem? Milner points the answer. Writing of Erasmus he says: 'Never once in his life did he look in the face what, according to Luther's judgement, was the real efficient enemy of Christ and his religion; never did he lay siege to the stronghold of self-righteousness.'[54] This then was the uniqueness of Luther's work—he saw the root of the problem, and, equally clearly, pointed to the solution. We shall always be indebted to Milner for making this plain. If Luther had stopped where Erasmus stopped, we should have had no more than a no-popery campaign, no more than another revolt of the laity against the clergy. The positive content of Luther's message should not be overlooked. He did not simply say 'the Pope is not Pontifex Maximus'; he said that all Christians, by virtue of the merits of Christ, possess a priestly privilege and dignity and service. He did not simply denounce those who prevented men from drawing near to God, he pointed to the means whereby men were accepted by God, namely, by faith. Just because Luther dealt with the problems at this deeper level—the theological level, rather than at the legal and moral level as did Erasmus, his work was more effective and permanent than that of Erasmus.

We may at least claim that Milner was confronted in the eighteenth century with the same sort of task as faced Luther in the sixteenth, namely, the preservation of Evangelical doctrine, and that he used his considerable gifts to reinterpret for his own age the truths which Luther had revived. He who studied most carefully the manner in which Cyprian and the later Fathers deviated from the biblical doctrine of the universal priesthood, was even more interested in the way in which it was reasserted in the sixteenth century. It may be hoped that sufficient has been said to show that there is no truth in the assumption that Evangelical teaching was based on a shallow theology, and that there is much truth in the assumption that if there is a definite Lutheran flavour in the theology of the later evangelicals, it is unquestionably due to the work of Milner.

X. THE ANGLICAN EVANGELICALS (ECCLESIOLOGY)

If the Evangelicals did not neglect the theological aspect of their

[54] J. G. Froude, *Life and Letters of Erasmus*, p. 210.

Movement, neither can it be said that they overlooked the ecclesiastical question. Indeed, both these aspects were far more thoroughly investigated and expounded than is commonly supposed. It is too lightly assumed that only the Tractarians showed any interest in questions of Order The man who served the Evangelicals in this respect was Charles Simeon, who takes his place alongside Milner as one of the outstanding leaders of the Movement.

(1) *Church Order and the Evangelicals*

There is no doubt that by the beginning of the eighteenth century Christians had become divided into two categories of 'evangelical' and 'formal', and this division cut right across denomination and tradition, and sometimes ignored them. Clearly it was necessary to devise a system which would comprehend both of them. The man who did most to achieve this end was Charles Simeon (1759-1836), of Holy Trinity, Cambridge. Some of the clergy, notably Wesley and Berridge, tended to regard lightly questions of Order. On the other hand, those who followed in the steps of the Caroline Divines thought that nothing else mattered.

Simeon was anxious to bring together Anglicans and un-Anglicans (we cannot say non-Anglicans because Wesley and Berridge and the rest were certainly Anglicans though not in the sense that Simeon was) by mutual recognition of one Church Order. It seemed as if Simeon was saying to the Dissenters: 'Reverence Church Order, then do what you like.' Wesley, however, held some very definite opinions about this question of Church Order as may be seen from his words to Bishop Secker of Oxford: 'I would inquire what is the end of all ecclesiastical order? Is it not to bring souls from the power of Satan to God and to build them up in fear and love? Order, then, is so far valuable as it serves these ends; and if it answers them not, it is nothing worth.'[55] It was not that Wesley had no regard for Order, but that he always considered it secondary to doctrinal questions and practical considerations. Perhaps this is why Troeltsch quite definitely regards Methodist theory and doctrine as representing the sect-type rather than the Church-type. By sect-type he meant a community of the elect, a *societas perfectorum*—and Wesley's

[55] Henry Bett, *The Spirit of Methodism*, p. 57.

description of the Church as 'the congregation of believers' lends strength to the view.

We may assume that Simeon's views on Methodism were similar to those of Troeltsch. At least, they did not differ on questions of doctrine, for 'in his celebrated interview with John Wesley at Hinxworth, Herts, on Monday, 20th December 1784, he (Charles Simeon) rejoiced to know that the differences between them were differences rather of *expression* than of opinion.'[56]

Troeltsch was emphatic in his judgement of the situation in 1911: 'The days of the pure Church-type within our present civilization are numbered, more and more the central life of the Church-type is being permeated with the vital energies of the sect and of mysticism.'[57] C. C. Richardson states the difference as follows: 'The distinction between the "sect" and "church" idea of religious community is roughly apparent in the antithesis that one is baptized as a child into a Church, while association with a sect involves voluntary, adult decision.'[58] This is but the modern interpretation of what Berridge held in the eighteenth century: 'Admission into the true Church is not by baptism but by conversion.'[59] The sect-type also presupposes that the Church is less an institution than a corporate body of believers, and controlled and guided, not by a hierarchy but by the inspiration of the Holy Spirit. This involves a principle of spiritual liberty which is not sanctioned by the Church-type. The question is: Are these tendencies present among the Anglican Evangelicals or not? There is evidence to show that the Evangelicals as represented not only by Milner and Simeon, but also by Henry Venn, James Hervey and Thomas Adams, express ideas which are consonant with the sect-type rather than with anything else. Three of their leading sentiments confirm the view put forward:

(1) They accepted wholeheartedly the theory of the Invisible Church of all true believers.

(2) They maintained that admission to the Church came not by Baptism but by conversion.

(3) While they accepted the apostolic succession of the clergy they viewed it as not much more than a historical expression of

---
[56] C. Smyth, *Charles Simeon and Church Order*, p. 185.
[57] See Troeltsch, *The Social Teaching of the Churches*, II.691-4; J. S. Whale, *The Protestant Tradition*, p. 222.
[58] C. C. Richardson, *The Church throughout the Centuries*, p. 184.
[59] *The Christian World Unmasked*, p. 457.

the pedigree and antiquity of the Church of England, although they saw no charismatic principle involved, and definitely rejected, as on their theory of the Church of the Christ they were bound to reject, *Ubi Episcopos ibi Ecclesia.*

All this may well make us wonder why they did not travel a little farther along the road and join Wesley. The answer is that they developed an emotional antipathy toward Dissent, to the congregational principle, to lay preaching and lay administration of the sacraments, which they were unable to justify theologically. They fervently disagreed with the more liberal tendencies of the Dissenters, but they could not state why. Still less were they able to put forward theological and logical arguments for their point of view. But emotional antipathy is no substitute for theological truth.

(2) *Corporate Priesthood*

(a) *Proclamation of the Word*

Standing together doctrinally, and cherishing their evangelical message, the Evangelicals soon realized that the Gospel of God was for the whole world. They rightly reasoned that if the Gospel did not involve a missionary obligation, it was not the Gospel of God. This new vision is summed up in Berridge's answer to his bishop: 'There is one canon, my lord, which saith, Go, preach the Gospel to every creature.' Also, when Rowland Hill was charged with violating Church Order, he replied, 'In preaching the Gospel in England, Scotland, Ireland and Wales, I always conceived *I stuck close to my parish*', which is reminiscent of Wesley's better-known remark: 'I look upon all the world as my parish.'

These sentiments, irregular and revolutionary as they were then regarded, have really brought us to the heart of the matter. Were the Evangelicals to obey the Dominical command or were they to obey something else? Called of God to go forth and proclaim the Evangel, were they to be restrained by questions of form, order, regulation and succession? Were they to move forward on the basis of the priesthood of all believers, or were they to delay until the official Church smiled upon their seemingly unorthodox projects and customs? Was right order or orthodoxy more important than direct obedience to the burning words of the Saviour? The Evangelicals did not see themselves as those who were at loggerheads with the Church of antiquity. They were quite sure that they were reinterpreting the message of the ancient Church in the light of their own age. Whenever this is attempted, there are some who raise the hue and cry: 'Individualism! Revolution! Heresy!' The revival of certain doctrines in order to facilitate the reorientation of the message and mission of the Church in the light of the changing centuries, has sometimes seemed heretical just because those doctrines had been too long forgotten. The new vision of the universal scope of the Gospel led to significant developments in the thinking of the Evangelicals. The Missionary obligation which was *now* deemed to be implicit in the Gospel meant, not only that they had to go beyond the parish boundary, and sometimes out-step the official sanction of the Church, but also, in the interests of their all-important task, they had to overcome the conventional distinction between clergy and laity. They quickly discovered, as Smyth observes, that 'men's fellowship in the Gospel cuts right across the barrier between Churchmen and Dissenters, and that the ministry of the Word must be impatient of conventional distinctions between clergy and laity. If the Gospel is to be preached to every creature, it may, of necessity, having regard to the conditions of the time, *be preached by any creature who has received it*, whether he be cleric or layman, or even laywoman for that matter, and whether he be within or without the Ecclesiastical Establishment.'[60] This appears to be a return to the biblical doctrine of the priesthood of all believers. The task of missionary endeavour rightly devolves upon all believers, and is to be undertaken by the Royal Priesthood which is able to draw upon the various gifts and capacities of the whole Church. Some are called to preach, others to heal, some to show mercy, others to teach, some to give, others to intercede, and in this way all the diverse spiritual and material resources of the whole Church are marshalled in the sublime task of evangelizing the world. Can anything less than this be regarded as enough? The Evangelicals saw the wide vision of the Church's task, and in seeking to realize it, they revived the doctrine which had lain dormant too long—the universal priesthood of the Church.

[60] C. Symth, *Charles Simeon and Church Order*, p. 265.

(b) Pastoral Responsibility

The Evangelicals used a term which became increasingly popular amongst them. It was the term 'Gospel-labourer'. Obviously the word is taken from the words of Jesus: 'Pray ye therefore the Lord of the harvest that he may send forth labourers into his harvest.' John Berridge wrote to Lady Huntingdon: '"But", you say, "the Lord is sending many Gospel-labourers into His Church": True; and with a view, I think, of calling his people out of it; because, when such ministers are removed by death, or transported to another vineyard, I see no fresh Gospel-labourer succeed them, which obliges the forsaken flocks to fly to a meeting. And what else can they do? If they have tasted of manna, and hunger for it, they cannot feed on heathen chaff, nor yet on legal crusts, though baked by some staunch Pharisee quite up to perfection.' It is a mistake to regard this differentiation between Gospel-labourers and the main body of clergy as mere anti-clericalism. It is, in fact, a protest against any legal interpretation of the Gospel. The real importance of the term Gospel-labourer is that it transcended the distinction between clergy and laity since it included both.

There arose among the Anglicans some religious Societies which were very similar to those founded by Wesley, and Simeon admits that he found them equally valuable for the edification of new converts. 'My judgement is that without Societies the people will never be kept together, nor will they ever feel related to their minister as children to a parent, nor will the minister himself take that lively interest in their welfare, which it is both his duty and his happiness to feel.'[61]

These Societies, however, were something more than an opportunity for spiritual fellowship; they were a training ground for the laity. They were frequently held in the homes of the members and resulted in the regular practice of Family Prayers, a custom which Simeon did much to encourage. It was his avowed wish that the laity should learn how to conduct worship in the bosom of their own families, and so there was revived the custom of regarding the father of the family as the priest in his household.

---

[61] G. R. Balleine, *A History of the Evangelical Party in the Church of England*, p. 92.

(c) Congregational Worship

This did not mean that Church worship was neglected, but even in respect of Church Worship the Evangelicals felt there was a crying need for reform. The first task was to teach the people that congregational singing was a corporate act of worship. It was the custom for the choir only to sing the metrical psalms, and therefore the congregation had no active part in the offering of praise. Indeed, it sometimes happened that during this vital part of their worship the congregation sat and rested and occasionally chatted.

Having stressed the fact that congregational singing was an expression of the congregation's corporate priesthood, the Evangelicals proceeded to teach them to stand for the singing of the hymns. This task was more difficult than might be supposed. Indeed, in many continental Churches the custom of sitting for the singing of hymns still persists. They have not supplied the answer to Romaine's question: 'When subjects go upon any joyful occasion to address their sovereign, is it the custom of any nation in the world to do it sitting?' In England, however, congregational singing during which the congregation stands, became and has remained a marked feature of an evangelical. This emphasis was yet another way in which the Evangelicals expressed the universal priesthood.

(d) Christian Service

There was another way too which must not be overlooked. Never before had the laity realized so clearly that membership of the universal priesthood involved the awakening of the social conscience, the campaigning against national evils, the Christianizing of the industrial system, and the rendering of vital Christian service in every sphere of life. What had been an idealist's dream now became a reality, and those responsible for making it a reality were laymen whose lives were fully dedicated to the cause of the kingdom of God, and who realized as their predecessors had failed to do, the duties and responsibilities of their calling. These men lived in the workaday world and learned to exercise their priesthood amid the complex conditions of a pagan environment. The priesthood of all believers had ceased to be simply an interesting aspect of Church doctrine and became a living reality in the religious life of the nation. And, as Sykes observes: 'The peculiar glory of the campaign was that it was led by Christian laymen.'[62] These laymen who together formed the Clapham Sect —Henry and Robert Thornton, William Wilberforce, Charles Grant, James Stephen and Zachary Macaulay, had come to the firm conclusion that it was not sufficient for the Christian religion to remain an unattainable idealism but that it should become a revolutionary dynamism always active in conquering evil and in transforming the conditions of the world. The whole task of the Church was set in a broader context, and with this wider vision came a deeper sense of the divine resources whereby it could be realized. In their view, if the priesthood of believers meant anything, it meant responsibility as well as privilege, the application of Christian principles as well as intercessions, and, with this in mind, they accepted their priestly responsibility and faced in the name of Christ the bastions of evil, the problems of industry, the slave-trade, illiteracy and prison reform. They carried the transforming message of the Gospel into every aspect of life, and when they were accused of being too worldly, Wilberforce answered for them all: 'My business is in the world, and I must mix in the assemblies of men, or quit the part which Providence seems to have assigned to me.'[63]

(e) The Missionary Task

Nor did the Evangelicals confine their labours to the Church in the homeland. Their sphere of service was as wide as the world, and so they founded the Church Missionary Society. Also, since they had found the inspiration of all their work in the Bible, they sent its message ringing across the world by the instrumentality of the Bible Society which they founded in 1804. These men were prodigious in their labours for the kingdom of God, and perhaps never in the long history of Christendom has the doctrine of the priesthood of all believers been more clearly grasped or more thoroughly applied than it was by them. It was they who conceived of the Church as the manifestation of divine life in the midst of society, who envisaged the Church as the dynamic society of all believers moving forward in their Lord's name to conquer all the strongholds of evil. They

---

[62] N. Sykes, *English Religious Tradition*, p. 71.
[63] G. R. Balleine, *A History of the Evangelical Party in the Church of England*, p. 99.

did not interpret the nature of the Church in terms of an exclusive or circumscribed theology, but gave to theology a richer content and a wider meaning by setting it against the practical problems of their age and by proving its adequacy for the solution of social and ethical as well as purely religious problems.

4

The Puritan Tradition

I. BEGINNINGS

THE ORIGINS of a movement are not always easy to specify, and this is particularly true of those trends in religious thought and practice which emerged in England in the sixteenth century. But in so far as every movement must have a beginning, we may safely say that Puritanism, as it is commonly understood, had its beginning between 1550 and 1580. It developed in three progressive phases which may be called the Conformist, the Non-Separatist, and the Separatist. The first group is represented by those who avoided as many objectionable ceremonies as possible by becoming lecturers or chaplains to private families. This meant that they were freed from parochial responsibility and from the necessity of reading every part of the liturgy. The second group is represented by those who, avowing their loyalty to the 'Holy Discipline', that is to the Puritan ideal, endeavoured to set it up within the established Church. The third is represented by those who, agreeing with the latter in essentials, realized that they could not consistently remain inside the Church. Bishop Hooper (1550), who is sometimes called the first Puritan, may be said to represent the first group; Thomas Cartwright (1572) represents the second group; and Robert Browne (1581) the third group. Bishop Hooper and his lineal successors, however, were largely concerned with a protest against the use of Roman vestments and had little difficulty in accepting the doctrines and discipline of the established Church. Unquestionably Thomas Cartwright may be regarded as the first of the Presbyterians, and Robert Browne as the first of the Independents. The Puritan Tradition, therefore, in its various phases and emphases, begins during those thirty years from 1550 to 1580. Puritanism may be said to embrace all the three groups already mentioned, but our main concern is with the second and third groups—the Non-Separatist and the Separatist Puritans. Two other important religious movements emerged from the Separatist-Puritans—the Baptists and the Quakers. John Smyth (1609), who had migrated to Amsterdam where he became the founder of the first (English) Baptist Church there, had originally been associated with the Separatist-Puritans at Gainsborough, and George Fox, who became the founder of the Quakers (1645), was deeply influenced by his association with the Baptist communities. The Puritan Tradition in the life of England cannot be over-stated, but before we consider in greater detail its development, we must examine the religious and political background on which it is set.

'The one definite thing that can be said about the Reformation in England is that it was an act of State.'[1] That is not to say that it was only an act of State. There was an interplay of religious, social and political forces which makes the situation in England more complex than in either Germany or Switzerland. Luther's emphasis on Justification by Faith and Calvin's emphasis on Divine Sovereignty pin-point the theological debate in those two countries. No single doctrine dominated the scene in England. However, one thing is noticeable: a sense of individual liberty and nation-consciousness seemed to emerge simultaneously. Hence the apt comment of Professor Norman Sykes: '. . . there can be no doubt at all that it was the combination of Nationalism and Protestantism which determined the peculiar character of the Reformation in England.'[2] Although it was the avowed aim of Protestantism to allow no interference from anyone between the private man and his God, the Reformation shows how easy it is to remove the priest only to install the peer. To shake off the shackles of the priest only to fall under the displeasure of the prince is a doubtful blessing. Very soon the divine right of kings was proclaimed in England with the avidity that the divine right of popes had been proclaimed in Rome. Since the Puritans had heard repeated references to the Divine Right of Popes, of Kings and Bishops, they saw nothing inconsistent in asserting the Divine Right of Believers; far from refuting the existence of powers, rights and privileges, they claimed them for all believing Christians. It was the doctrine of the Priesthood of all Believers which said all that the Puritans wanted to say, and

[1] F. M. Powicke, *The Reformation in England*, p. 1.
[2] N. Sykes, *English Religious Tradition*, p. 9.

although Cartwright borrowed many of his ideas on this matter from Wyclif, there can be no doubt that he had more success than Wyclif in applying them.

II. THOMAS CARTWRIGHT

There is no doubt that, for a time at any rate, the Lollards were effectively suppressed, yet the smouldering ashes of their cause were fanned into a flame in the late sixteenth and early seventeenth centuries. Many historians, repelled by the bigotry of Thomas Cartwright, the leader of the Presbyterians, are blind to his wide learning and considerable influence upon the life of his times. He is entitled to a unique place in the religious life of the nation at the dawn of the seventeenth century for two important reasons: First, he sought to reform the established Church from within it and by constitutional means—he insisted on 'reformation by tarrying for the magistrate'. Second, he was the only man intellectually equipped to give a considered theological reply to the Rhemists' Translation of the Bible of 1582. Some of Cartwright's great contemporaries were, perhaps, less bigoted in their beliefs but more radical in their ecclesiastical actions, and Robert Browne, John Smyth and Thomas Helwys were bent on 'Reformation without tarrying for anie'. Our present concern is with the second reason for Cartwright's important position, namely, his *Confutation of the Rhemists' Translation of the Bible*, which was published in 1618. His exposition of the Priesthood of all Believers may be summed up under six headings:

(1) Spiritual Priesthood.
(2) Spiritual Priesthood based on the Priesthood of Christ.
(3) The meaning of Sacerdotes.
(4) Priesthood and election.
(5) Priesthood and the marks of the true Church.
(6) Universal Priesthood as the basis of Cartwright's Propositions for reform.

(1) *Spiritual Priesthood*

Commenting on 1 Peter 2[9], Cartwright says: 'It is very true that all Christians are priests to offer up spiritual sacrifices; so are they all kings to maister and overrule their evil concupiscences, which make rebellion against the good notions of God's spirit in men.' Here then is the plain statement that all Christians are priests and that the function of their priesthood is to offer up spiritual sacrifices. Cartwright was sufficiently clear-sighted to know the dangers which might attend his own words and the qualification which follows in the same passage is of immense importance. He realized that the concept of universal priesthood was only safe when it was anchored to the Priesthood of Christ. He also knew that to speak of Christians being 'kings and priests' might well lead to spiritual pride on the one hand, and to antinomian tendencies on the other. Neibuhr has reminded modern Protestants of the same danger: 'The fact is that the Protestant doctrine of the Priesthood of all Believers may result in an individual self-deification against which Catholic doctrine has more adequate checks. The modern revival of Reformation theology may be right in regarding the simple moralism of Christian liberalism as just another form of pharisaism. . . . There is no final guarantee against the spiritual pride of man.'[3] The dangers of self-deification and spiritual pride can be averted only if the doctrine of the priesthood of believers is viewed in its true theological setting. When it is divorced, as has too often been the case, from those New Testament doctrines from which it springs, all kinds of dangers emerge. Just as in Luther's teaching this doctrine was anchored to Justification by Faith, so also in Cartwright's teaching, it was inseparable from the Priesthood and Sacrifice of our Lord.

There are sacrifices which all Christians may offer. In exercising their priesthood Christians should offer a twofold sacrifice: first upward toward God, and then outward toward men. In answer to the Rhemists' view that Hebrews 13^{15} specifically refers to the Eucharist, Cartwright says: 'Let it be observed therefore first, that the whole Church being exhorted to offer this sacrifice of praise, if the sacrifice of the Masse should here be meant, then every one in the Church must be a Masse Priest. The writer of the Hebrews having moved all the Church in the former verses, by the example of Christ to be content to bear reproach for His sake . . . and therefore in the next verse going into this holy service of thanksgiving to the Lord, the charitable assistance that is given to the brethren, he saith, that God is well pleased with such sacrifice: ranging this thanksgiving unto God mentioned in

[3] *The Nature and Destiny of Man*, I.215.

this verse, to one and the same kind of sacrifice with the relief that is given to the needy members of Christ.' Members of the spiritual priesthood offer spiritual sacrifices: the sacrifice of praise, thanksgiving, and service for others, but such sacrifices are possible only because *the* Sacrifice has already been made. Spiritual Priesthood is dependent upon the High Priesthood of Christ.

(2) *Spiritual Priesthood based on the Priesthood of Christ*
Cartwright continues: 'And therefore under the Gospell there is properly but one true King, Christ and Saviour, which giveth laws unto His subjects; so properly there is but one true Priest that, once offering Himselfe, made a full satisfaction for the sinnes of the world, and now liveth to make intercession for all those that come to God by Him.'[4] It has sometimes been supposed that this emphasis upon the Priesthood of Christ is contrary to the doctrine of the Priesthood of all Believers. Such a view is mistaken; it is not only mistaken, it is definitely harmful. The Priesthood of Believers rests firmly and only upon the Priesthood of Christ. If the Priesthood of Christ is not paramount in our thinking, the believers' privileges are lost. Now the conception of the Priesthood of Christ involves His redeeming work on our behalf. Professor Lindsay couples the doctrine of Justification by Faith with the work of Christ and holds that together they explain the priesthood of all believers: 'The doctrine of Justification by Faith in its simplest form means that God Himself speaks the pardon, pardons for what Christ has done and can bestow on the sinner; and that man can hear this pardon spoken only if he has faith to trust the mercy, the salvation, and the promise of God.'[5]

Cartwright drew an interesting conclusion from his theory of the Headship of Christ and one which had not previously been emphasized. Equality was a term which was very much in vogue in those days, and it generally implied an elevation of the ordinary man, an honour and dignity which were supposed to be his right and privilege. Cartwright's view of equality, however, was along different lines. It involved a levelling rather than an elevating process. Before God all men were equal in sin, equally deserving of damnation. The task of the Church was to render men

---

[4] *A Confutation of the Rhemist's Translation of the Bible*, Comment on 1 Peter 2⁹.
[5] *The Reformation* (1882), p. 187.

obedient to God. This interpretation shed a new light on the prevalent doctrine of equality, but it was the natural corollary of Cartwright's ideas on the Headship of Christ.

Whether he realized it or not Cartwright was playing a vital part in the keen struggle which was engaging the greatest minds of seventeenth-century England. Two great movements were in full swing: the first was Puritanism, the second was Science. Both were individualistic in their emphasis; the first was the individualism of a spiritual fellowship and the second the individualism of an atomic system. The second of these which thrived under the leadership of Thomas Hobbes, ultimately resulted in a conception of society composed of identical units which produced the abstract equalitarianism of philosophic Radicalism. The *first* ultimately resulted in the principle of spiritual equality implied in the doctrine of the priesthood of all believers. It is fallacious to state that all men are equal and therefore equally good at all jobs. Professor A. D. Lindsay has given the lie to this erroneous view: 'Many democrats think that jobs of which they themselves know nothing should on democratic principles be done by just anyone. It is not hard to see the entire falseness of this doctrine; what is puzzling is, why anyone should ever have believed it. But if human equality does not mean that all men are equal in all capacities, what does it mean? . . . This is the Christian answer: they are all children of one Father: the poorest of them have been described as "the least of these my brethren". They have all, as it is sometimes put, got souls to be saved, or they are all those for whom Christ died.' We notice then that Cartwright's basic assumption, namely, that all men are equal in sin and therefore are in need of redemption, is reasserted in our own day. The universal fact of man's sinful state is too easily forgotten. If this fact was more often recognized, man would prate less about equality and weep more for his sin. All the same, the matter cannot be left there. Man was not left there by a merciful God. 'If that spiritual priesthood be taken as seriously as it was by the seventeenth-century Puritans, more follows. There follows the belief that God will reveal His purposes to the individual; there follows the right of the private conscience and of the inner light. This is not the same as to say that one man's opinion is as good as another. The Puritans knew well that a man might easily mistake his own foolish imaginings for the voice of God, that spiritual priesthood meant responsibilities as well as privileges, that the gift of discerning spirits was not one easy to exercise.'[6] There can be little doubt that Cartwright was the initiator of this interpretation of spiritual priesthood.

(3) *The Meaning of Sacerdos*

The Rhemists had denied the doctrine of the priesthood of believers and had quoted St Augustine in support of their case. But St Augustine was so prolific in his writings and so comprehensive in the range of his themes that he might be quoted for the Catholic or Protestant side of almost any theological problem. However, commenting on Revelation 20[6], the Rhemists say: 'Which words be notable for their learning that thinke there be no properly called priests now in the New Testament, no otherwise than all Christian men and women, and a confusion to them that therefore have turned the name Priests into Ministers.' The reply is given in the following words: 'Because the common people in St Augustine's time, did commonly and specially call them in Latine Sacerdotes, which were Bishops and Elders, so the Scripture nameth them: he giveth warning that the word Sacerdotes in this place, doth not signifie those special officers of the Church, but *all true Christians*, which are all Sacerdotes, that is, Sacrificers, because they are members of the one high Sacrificer, Christ. But you thinke his words notable, because hee saith, that Bishop and Elders are now properly called Sacerdotes, where he meaneth not, that this term is properly appertaining to them, but that they were now, that is in his time, so called peculiarly, whereas the name is general to all Christians: For he meaneth not that Bishops and Elders be called Sacerdotes, Sacrificers properly and all other Christians unproperly: but the adverbe properly is opposite to general, and signifieth no more than specially or peculiarly. Therefore this place is rather a reproving than allowing of them that call the Ministers of the Church properly or peculiarly by the name of Sacerdotes, which is common to all Christians, men and women.'

(4) *Priesthood and Election*

Cartwright is at great pains to show that the word 'priests' is

[6] A. D. Lindsay, *The Church and Democracy*, p. 14.

not to be applied only to Bishops and Elders but to Christians generally. But he makes it crystal clear that in the midst of this general priesthood some are especially called. Indeed, rarely has the relation between the Ministry and the general priesthood been stated with greater clarity. Yet we may well ask wherein lies the difference between the two? In Puritan theology this conception of the general priesthood arises out of two conceptions which had found little emphasis in the established Church, and to these we must now turn:

(a) *The Covenant.*
(b) *Election.*

(a) The Puritan pastor devoted himself to the task of maintaining the solidarity of his little group and of retaining their loyalty. In order to accomplish these aims the leaders made the Covenant the basis of Church life. The Covenant was a solemn pledge entered into by the members, a contract with one another and with God, to adhere to the congregation and never to depart. This became the normal feature of all the separatist groups. The Covenant bound every believer first to God and then to the community of all believers.

(b) This situation demanded a definition of the phrase 'Community of all believers', and it was in seeking such a definition that the Puritans found themselves preoccupied with the doctrine of election. Having refused to identify the true Church with the nation or with society, the Puritans had no alternative but to offer an alternative doctrine. At length the statement came and it lacked nothing in impressiveness and clarity. The Church is 'an exclusive congregation of saints, unanimous in belief and uniform in practice, admitting to its communion only those who could give satisfactory proof of their divine election'.[7] So the Puritan movement out of which the Presbyterian, Congregationalist and Baptist Churches eventually emerged, were Calvinist in doctrine. Even though they did not interpret the doctrine of election as rigidly as the Calvinists on the Continent, they certainly believed that there was a firm biblical basis for it. 'But ye are an *elect* race, a royal priesthood, a holy nation, a people for God's own possession, that ye may show forth the excellencies of Him who called you out of darkness into His marvellous light'

[7] W. Haller, *The Rise of Puritanism*, p. 176.

(1 Pet 2⁹). This doctrine of election was emphasized for three reasons:

(a) It asserted a divine supremacy.
(b) It banished all thought of human merit.
(c) It banished the quite baseless assumption that the difference between the believer and unbeliever is altogether negligible. This was done by emphasizing the priesthood of all believers.

(a) The Puritans appeared on the scene when everybody's supremacy was asserted except God's. They had heard enough of Papal Supremacy, Royal Supremacy, and Episcopal Supremacy, and so they began to speak about the Supremacy of God. All around them they saw a grasping for power and authority, so they attributed all authority to God. In an age which was guilty of the sin of depriving God of His glory and giving all glory and power into the hands of a human hierarchy, the Puritans were not wrong in ascribing everything to God. This emphasis was certainly a reaction and not every reaction is noble, but this one was both theologically right and historically timely. The implications of the doctrine of election are clear: the sovereign will of God is final. Since God is supreme He is free to choose whom He will, when He will. The cause of election is solely in God. If it is asked why God should call and elect some and not others the answer is that the will of God is the highest rule of justice. What He wills must be considered *just* because He wills it. Questioned upon this theory of God's choice, the Puritans were always driven back to an assertion of God's Supremacy. Some of the questions they asked baffled their adversaries: What does God owe to man and why should God not judge man? The Puritan answer was, 'He is God', and that was a sufficient answer for them. They had the support of St Paul: 'O man, who art thou that repliest against God? Shall the thing formed say unto Him that formed it, why hast thou made me thus?' (Rom 9²⁰).

(b) This election was founded on God's gratuitous mercy, totally irrespective of human merit. The believer is chosen in Christ from the foundation of the world—this precludes any consideration of merit in him. He is adopted in Christ to a heavenly inheritance because in himself he is incapable of such high dignity. Those who are chosen are distinguished not by their virtues but by receiving the divine mercy. People do not enter into God's blessing till they are called. By connecting calling and election (2 Pet 1^{10}), Scripture evidently suggests that nothing is requisite to it but the free mercy of God. Scripture also maintains that God is no respecter of persons (Acts 10^{34}), and this means that in the election of God no regard is had to merit. God does not favour a man because that man is good. He derives the motive o favour man from His own goodness. We see then that the Puritans were Calvinists, but moderate Calvinists and for good reasons. 'We shall fail to understand Puritanism if we conceive English Calvinism in too narrow or rigid a sense. The dynamic Pauline doctrine of faith, with its insistence on the over-ruling power of God, on the equality of men before God, and on the immanence of God in the individual soul, had long appealed to the English mind, and the struggle of the English people to secure their independence from foreign power as symbolized to them by the papacy had confirmed that appeal. What Calvinism did was to supply a current formulation of historic doctrine in lucid, trenchant terms, strikingly supported by the success of the state which Calvin's genius had called into being at Geneva.'[8]

(c) If Cartwright and the Puritans in general warmly embraced a modified form of the doctrine of election, they did not accept a rigid predestination. If it is maintained that *all* men are elected to eternal life through Christ, the difference between believer and unbeliever becomes negligible. But the difference is vital. It is possible to open the gate so wide that no one is left out. The Puritans had no room for such a confusing and misleading conception of the Church. The comprehensive, all-embracing view of the Church which lightly spanned the whole of society in a country mainly pagan did not at all coincide with the Puritan conception of the Church. The Church was the Priesthood of all Believers, not a vague, indiscriminate assembly of priests and pagans, believers and unbelievers, sinners and saints. Unlike many of his contemporaries Cartwright made a distinction between election and predestination. The members of the Royal Priesthood were the *elect* of God, but it was a priesthood of those who had sealed their divine election by entering into the divine Covenant and in this way Cartwright rejected the arbitrary implications of predestination. He could not agree with the undue

---

W. Haller, *The Rise of Puritanism*, p. 8.

emphasis on predestination by some of his contemporaries, and he held that it weakened the Puritan cause. Haller is right when he says: 'If Cartwright could have had his way in 1569 all the centrifugal tendencies in Puritanism would never have been allowed to develop.' We may say, then, that believers are an elect race, chosen of God, but they are God's not because they must be (which is predestination), but because they may be.

(5) *The Marks of the True Church*

Cartwright knew that the main problems which faced the Church centred on the interpretation of the Word, order, and discipline. He knew that it was perilously easy for privilege to turn into licence. So in 1572 in his *Admonition to Parliament* he stipulates what he considers to be the marks of the true Church very much as Luther did in 1539. Luther mentioned seven marks of the Church, and, significantly enough the three which Cartwright stresses are included in Luther's seven. 'May it therefore please your wysdoms to understand we in England are so fare of, from having a Church rightly reformed accordying to the prescripte of God's Words, that as yet we are not come to the outward face of the same. . . . The outward markes whereby a true Christian church is knowne, are preaching of the word purely, ministering of the sacraments sincerely, and ecclesiastical discipline which consisteth in admonition and correction of faults severelie.'

These three marks of the true Church were designed to offset free interpretation of Scripture by unauthorized persons; a falsely-appointed, lax and ill-equipped ministry, and an undisciplined laity. Such dangers could only by averted if they were seen clearly and dealt with effectively by the whole fellowship of the Church. The Puritan earnestly believed that for discovering the truth as revealed in Scripture, the divinely appointed instrument was the minister or ministers whose gift of interpretation was sealed by the acknowledgement of the people. Although they were prevented by the Royal policy from receiving official recognition for the adoption of this policy, they certainly acted upon it, and the people chose those by whom they were to be taught and served. 'That we should judge our ideas by the principle of their conformity, not to our desires or imaginings, but to the will of God, is the duty of each man's individual conscience. But where that duty is not properly fulfilled, as so often from human weakness it is not, there is a second test implied in the phrase "all believers". The Scriptures are not of private interpretation. The revelation of God to the individual must commend itself to the fellowship.' The Puritans discovered that this was a hard lesson to learn, but Cartwright's attempt to link the fellowship of believers to the Headship of Christ was not only a practical solution but a true interpretation of the spiritual priesthood.

(6) *Universal Priesthood as the basis of Cartwright's propositions for reform*

The three great principles which characterize the Puritan movement have their origin in the doctrine of the Priesthood of all Believers. These principles are:

- (*a*) That God's free grace, mediated by the soul's faith in Christ, is the essential root of human salvation.
- (*b*) That God's will, revealed in His written Word and interpreted by His living Spirit, is the supreme law for human conduct both in the sphere of the Church and the world.
- (*c*) That the conscience must be free from merely human dictation and above all, from the enslaving rule of the priest.

Out of these three main principles Cartwright's three propositions arise. They relate to the following:

- (*a*) The appointment of ministers.
- (*b*) The parity of ministers.
- (*c*) The functions of ministers.

According to these propositions the Church is the totality of her members and the function of the members is to join in the exercise of a judgement whether a given person is called of God to be a minister, and to decide whether he shall exercise his office over them, as their spiritual guide. This is part of the Church's corporate priesthood, and, as a recent Report has it: 'All human ministry and priesthood is a continuing participation in the ministry of Christ.'[9] It follows that all Puritan principles safeguard, without unduly exalting, the place of the laity in the

[9] Report on 'Conversations', *Scottish Journal of Theology*, IX.II.172.

life and witness of the Church. The parity of ministers and their functions are not to be regarded merely as convenient arrangements but as firm expressions of biblical theology.

There is a close relationship between the Presbyterian form of government and the reformed system of doctrine. It combines authority with freedom, corporate tradition with individual experience. Officials in the Church hold offices which are divinely ordained, and yet the persons who hold these offices are elected by popular vote. The parity of the ministry is 'presbyterian' as is the governing principle of the priesthood of all believers. Presbyterianism is not Congregationalism—the pure rule of the people; nor is it Episcopalianism—the rule of divinely ordained bishops. The sovereignty of the Word of God is the ultimate authority which must govern ruling or teaching elders and people. It was the rule of the Word of God through the People of God. This sums up all Cartwright's work.

Yet, on any showing, his work was an anti-sacerdotal movement. The bitterness of the controversy was due to the existence of two irreconcilable ideals—Hierarchy and Presbytery. Hierarchy, however, had three advantages—it was 'commanded by authority, established by law, and confirmed by general practice'. There is no doubt that the attempt to graft Presbyterianism upon a system that was in essence sacerdotal was a hopeless task. The future of the anti-sacerdotal movement lay with the Separatist Puritans rather than with the Presbyterians. All the same, Browne, Barrowe, and Owen owed not a little to the pioneer work of Cartwright.

III. ROBERT BROWNE

One of Cartwright's contemporaries at Cambridge was Robert Browne (1550-1633), who is unquestionably the prophetic leader of the Nonconformist movement. It simply will not do to dismiss him as 'a radical and a crank who ended by quarrelling with his wife and going insane'.[10] Browne served sentences in thirty-two prisons, and if he was prepared to suffer in this way for what he believed, we may well inquire what was the impetus behind his faith and courage. It was he who laid down the principles of Independency.

The instrument of Reformation, Browne maintained, was the

---

[10] C. Burrage, *The true story of Robert Browne, Father of Congregationalism*, p. 30.

Church and not the magistrates. He had no hesitation in saying that the latter should be under the spiritual oversight of the Church. 'They say the time has not yet come to build the Lorde's house; they must tarrie for the magistrates and for Parliament to do it.'[11] 'Can the Lorde's spiritual government', he cries, 'be in no way executed but by the civil sword?' The magistrates have 'no ecclesiastical authority at all, but only as any other Christians'.

Having stated that the instrument of reform is the Church, Browne goes on to define what he means by the Church. 'The Church planted or gathered is a company or number of Christians or believers, which by willing covenant made with their God, are under the government of God and Christ, and keep his laws and are in one holy communion, because Christ both redeemed them unto holiness and happiness for ever, from which they were fallen by the sin of Adam.' He scorned the idea that the Church contained good and evil alike, and he had no use for a nominal membership. In this doctrine of Church membership he deviated from Luther and Calvin who never rejected the idea that the Church was composed of unregenerate as well as regenerate. The Church was ruled not by a clerical hierarchy but by the people of God.

'The Church governement is the Lordship of Christ in the communion of His offices: whereby His people obey His will, and have mutual use of their grace and callings, to further their godliness and welfare.'[12] Here again is expressed the priesthood of all believers since the believers and not the hierarchy rule the Church under Christ. Browne further elucidates this doctrine when he writes: 'The Kingdom of all Christians is their office of guiding and ruling with Christ, to subdue the wicked and make one another obedient to Christ. Their priesthood is their office of cleansing and redressing wickedness, whereby sin and uncleanness is taken away from amongst them. . . . Their prophecy is their office of judging all things by the Word of God, whereby they increase in knowledge and wisdom among themselves.'[13] This view of the Church meant that the appointment of the minister by the officials of State could no longer be

---

[11] *A Treatise of Reformation Without Tarrying for Anie*, p. 18.
[12] *A Book Which Showeth the Life and Manners of All True Christians*, p. 35.
[13] Ibid. p. 35.

tolerated. The office of judging all things by the Word was itself the gift of God but always it must be confirmed by the Church: 'The dispensation to preach is committed unto me, and this dispensation did not the magistrates give me, but God, by consent and ratifying of the Church.'[14]

Later Congregationalists have made great use of the term 'a democracy of members', but this term was not used by Browne nor yet the idea implicit in it. If democracy, as the British Commission's Report (on Congregationalism) uses it, means that the local congregation acts through plebiscite and not through representative Church government, then it is foreign to the ecclesiology of Congregationalism. Again, if it means that all members have identical duties, offices and spiritual competence, and that any group of Christians may separate themselves from the rest without any appointed minister, or any rules of Church government or without any eldership, then Congregationalism knows nothing of it. As Dr Micklem states it: 'When it is suggested that the "deacons" are simply the executive committee of the Church Meeting, and that the Church is under no obligation to listen to its minister, who is its servant, longer than it likes his message, or that a group of Christians banding themselves together without minister or sacraments or elders may call themselves a Church and claim that none may interfere with their unqualified sovereignty over all Church affairs, we are offered a very sorry parody of Congregationalism.'[15]

We may therefore sum up Robert Browne's doctrine of the Church as follows:

(1) The Church is a body of Christian believers organized according to a polity derived from the New Testament.

(2) Under his theory of Church government the priesthood of all believers becomes not only a spiritual fact but a principle of ecclesiastical polity.

(3) It is the inalienable responsibility of the whole communicant membership of the local Church to appoint its officers, and in this manner the universal priesthood is expressed.

(4) It is the duty as well as the privilege of the laity to exercise their spiritual gifts in a ministry which may be pastoral, didactic or administrative. Some of the other nonconformist bodies would

---

[14] *A Treatise of Reformation* . . ., p. 22.
[15] *Congregationalism Today*, p. 13.

also add 'prophetic'. So the members of the Royal Priesthood are equal in honour but diverse in function.

(5) In all this the key word is obedience: 'It is the duty of the whole commonalty to appoint their Church officers in the Lord, and, having appointed them, to obey them in the Lord.'[16] These words of Browne and those which follow are as applicable now as when they were first written: 'Let the Church rule in spiritual wise and not in worldlie manner; by a lively law preached and not by a civill law written; by holiness in inwarde and outwarde obedience, and not in straightness of the outwarde onlie.'[17] When modern followers of Browne speak of 'a democracy of members' they should remember that he had in mind no such thing. They are most true to New Testament polity who are most true to the theology of Browne. 'It is of the utmost importance to recognize that Christocracy, not democracy, was Browne's chief concern. He had no intention of establishing a Church order where *vox populi* should count as *vox dei*; where Churchmen could believe what they chose to, or act as they wished. He based the powers and responsibilities of the Christian commonalty upon their union with Christ, whose regal, priestly and prophetic offices they share.'[18]

IV JOHN OWEN

John Owen (1620-83) became the undisputed theologian and vigorous defender of Independency. His position is competently set forth in an impressive work entitled *The True Nature of a Gospel Church and its Government*, and an examination of portions of this document will account for its continuing influence in Nonconformist circles.

(1) *The Ministry in relation to the whole Church*

Doubtless Owen's conception of the Ministry was revolutionary when considered in the light of his own generation, but it is never destructive. He views the Ministry as God's gift to the Church, and he sees it as a special instrument which God uses in the service of the whole Church. 'All those by whom the ordinary rule of the Church is to be exercised unto its edification are; as unto their

---
[16] *A Treatise of Reformation* . . ., p. 29.
[17] Horton M. Davies, *The English Free Churches*, p. 52.
[18] Ibid.

office and power, *given into the Church*, set or placed in it, not as "lords of their faith" but as helpers of their joy.'[19] This is seventeenth-century religion at its best, for the joyous note had been pushed into the background for several centuries. The 'lords of their faith' had become instigators of fear, and this phrase, 'helpers of their joy', was as refreshing as it was beautiful. Owen used this phrase of St Paul's (2 Cor 1^{24}) with great effect. This reaffirms Luther's position that the ministry is set within the Church and not above it.

All the same, there is a certain authority which is given to the Ministry and Owen next explains its source and the manner in which it is received. 'But as the whole Church-power is committed unto the whole Church by Christ, so all that are called unto the peculiar exercise of any part of it, by virtue of office-authority, do receive that authority from Him by the only way of the communication of it—namely, by His Word and Spirit, through the ministry of the Church.'[20] This embodies the Puritan idea of succession.

(2) *The Individual member in relation to the whole Church*

Generally speaking Owen is on safe ground when he is speaking of the Church as a unit but frequently falls into serious error when considering the individual as a unit. 'Every individual person hath the liberty of his own judgement as unto his own consent or dissent in what he is himself concerned.' This is not Church order, it is anarchy, and it was the unthinking application of such theories that led to the innumerable Puritan sects which arose during the period under discussion. Such statements are fraught with danger when they are made without any reference to the Word of God, the fellowship of the Church, and the prophetic calls. Moreover, there were many who were ready to isolate such declarations from their proper context but this was partly due to the strife, tensions, and uncertainty of the times. At any rate, the ill-considered statement mentioned above was corrected by Owen when he had grasped the full significance of the priesthood of believers. He then understood that there were privileges and duties which belonged to the body of believers collectively which could not possibly be applied individually. 'That this power under the name of the "keys of the kingdom of heaven", was originally

[19] *The True Nature of a Gospel Church*, XVI.15.   [20] Ibid. p. 36.

granted to the whole professing Church of believers, and that it is utterly impossible it reside in any other, who is subject unto death, or if so, be renewed upon any occasional intermission, is fully proved by all Protestant writers.'[21] The fact that this power is given to the whole professing body of believers does not in any sense alter the fact that some, and not all, are called, chosen and ordained to use it. Although Owen maintains that the authority of Christ is invested in the whole Church, he is in full agreement with Luther regarding the necessity of the Pastoral office. On this point he writes in clear and trenchant terms: 'There is an accountable trust committed unto those who undertake this (pastoral) office. The whole flock, the ministry itself, the truths of the Gospel, as to the preservation of these, are all committed to them. Colossians 4^{17}, 1 Peter 5^{1-4}, Hebrews 13^{17}. They must give an account. Nothing can be more wicked or foolish than for a man to intrude himself into a trust which is not committed unto him.' Let no one think that Owen held a light conception of the pastoral office; there is a Lutheran ring about his emphatic words: 'Whoever therefore, takes upon him the pastoral office, without a lawfull outward call, *doth take unto himself power and authority* without any divine warranty, which is a foundation of all disorder and confusion; interests himself in an accountable trust no way committed unto him; hath no promise of assistance in or reward for his work, but engageth in that which is destructive of all Church order, and consequently of the very being of the Church itself.' 'Yet there are three things', he writes, 'which are to be annexed to this assertion by way of limitation, as:

'(a) Many things performed by virtue of *office*, in a way of authority, may be performed by others, not called to office, in a way of *charity*. Such as the moral duties of exhorting, admonishing, comforting, instructing, and praying with and for one another.

'(b) Spiritual gifts may be exercised unto the edification of others without office-power, where order and opportunity do require it. The constant exercise of spiritual gifts in preaching, with a refusal of undertaking a ministerial office, or without design so to do upon a lawful call, cannot be approved.

'(c) The rules proposed concern only ordinary cases . . . extraordinary cases are accompanied with a warranty in themselves for extraordinary actings and duties.'

[21] Ibid. p. 52.

Here again Owen is enunciating the priesthood of all believers. In (a) he states that all may do in charity what some are commissioned to do in a way of authority, and lest anyone should misunderstand his statement he lists some of the functions of the general priesthood—exhorting, admonishing, comforting, instructing, and praying with and for one another. These he regards as the moral duties of every believer. Since these duties cannot adequately be performed apart from the power of the Spirit, Owen turns his attention to spiritual gifts. The first sentence in (b), mentioned above, is self-explanatory, but the second shows a limitation of insight which has been corrected by the development of the doctrine of the priesthood of believers. Nowadays the prophetic office is regarded as the privilege of the laity as well as the ministry, and a layman may exercise spiritual gifts in preaching without ever accepting ministerial office.

The importance of the priesthood of believers is emphasized in Owen's third limitation—(c), mentioned above. Some Churches within Protestantism have long since recognized that 'extraordinary cases are accompanied with a warranty in themselves for extraordinary actings and duties'. Such cases frequently arise on the Mission Field where laymen who have responded to a call to preach and have exercised responsible pastoral duties over a long period, have been granted permission to administer sacraments on the grounds that it is a greater evil to deprive God's people of the blessings of Holy Communion than to permit a devoted layman to administer it. This course may not and perhaps should not become a regular practice in the Protestant Churches, but that it is permissible few would deny. So we find in some parts of the Mission Field the *occasional* application of a *permanent* privilege, but the fact that such a privilege exists demands emphatic assertion.

(3) *The Duties of Believers*

The duties of believers are divided into two distinct classes: there are duties that are universal, and duties 'that are peculiar to some'.

(a) *Duties that are universal*

These are described in Romans 12^{1-2}. 'These belong absolutely to all and every one that appertains unto the Church.'[22] All believers, therefore, are called out from the world, and consecrated to the service of God. Called out from the world, it is their duty to offer the priestly sacrifice of their lives upon the altar of God. Because they are an elect race separated from the world, and an holy priesthood on account of the living sacrifice which they offer, the holy will of God will be revealed to them.

Included in this sacrifice is intercession for others. Owen expresses this in a beautiful passage: 'All of them continually offered unto God by the same High Priest, who adds unto it the incense of His own intercession, and by whom they have all an access unto the same throne of grace—they have all a blessed communion herein continually. And this communion is the more express in that the prayers of all are for all, so as there is no particular Church of Christ in the world—not any one member of any of them, but that they have all the prayers of all the Churches in the world, and of all the members of them every day. ... This prayer, proceeding from and wrought by the same Spirit in them all, equally bestowed on them all by the promise of Christ, having the same object, even God as a Father, and offered unto Him by the same High Priest, together with His own intercession, gives unto all Churches a communion far more glorious than what consists in some outward rites and orders of men's devising.'[23]

If the universal priesthood may be exercised in the sacrifice of self and in the offering of prayers for others, it may also be exercised in the service which is rendered under the authority of Christ and in His name. 'It is a certain rule, that, in the performance of all duties which the Lord Christ requires, either of the whole Church, or of any in the Church, they are the first subject of the power needful unto such duties who are immediately called unto them. Hereby all things come to be done in the name and authority of Christ; for the power of the Church is nothing but a right to perform Church duties in obedience unto the commands of Christ and according to His mind.' The spiritual resources needed in order to fulfil the mission of the Church will be supplied. In this way, everything will be done according to the mind of Christ. Sometimes, as Owen states, it is a task which can only be accomplished by the whole Church.

[22] *The True Nature of a Gospel Church*, XVI.124. [23] Ibid. p. 192.

(b) Duties that are peculiar to some
It is clear that Owen here refers to those who are called to some special office in the Church. He relates three ways in which men were called to office in the Old Testament.

(i) They were so extraordinarily and immediately by the nomination and designation of God Himself: so Aaron was called to the priesthood. And afterward Samuel to be prophet.

(ii) By a law of carnal generation: so all the priests of the posterity of Aaron succeeded unto the office of the priesthood without any other call.

(iii) By the *choice of the people*, which was the call of all the ordinary elders and rulers of the Church (Deut 1^{13}): 'Give to yourselves.'

Commenting on these three ways, Owen continues: 'The first of these was repeated in the foundation of the evangelical Church. Christ Himself was called unto His office by the Father, through the unction of the Spirit (Isa 41^{1-3}, Heb 5^3), and He Himself called the apostles and evangelists, in whom that call ceased. The secondary, ordinary way, by the privilege of natural generation of the stock of the priests, was utterly abolished. The third way only remained for the ordinary continuation of the Church— namely, by the choice and election of the Church itself, with solemn separation and dedication by officers extraordinary and ordinary.'[24] Not all Nonconformists would agree about these three separate categories. It is possible, for instance, that the truth lies somewhere in a combination of the first and third, that is, the call of the Church in confirmation of the man God has chosen. But Owen's main contention is not affected by this observation. His main contention is that the only way in which a priest may be chosen is out of the universal priesthood and by means of it.

V. PURITAN PRINCIPLES

We may now briefly summarize the Puritan principles which became the basis of Nonconformist belief and practice.

(1) *Christ is the Head of the Church*

The Puritans regarded themselves as a company of which Christ

[24] *The True Nature of a Gospel Church*, XVI.55.

was the Head. John Smyth, the Baptist pioneer, adds his testimony to that of Wyclif, Cartwright, Browne, Barrowe, and Owen: 'Christ onlie is the King.' Again: 'Christ is the only true King, Priest, and Prophet of the Church.'[25] All authority in the Church belongs to Christ, derives from Him and is bestowed by Him. But if all authority ultimately belongs to God alone, it means that all life and service is owed directly to God. The early Nonconformists resisted any attempt to substitute the authority of the Church for the authority of Christ. Writing of the seventeenth-century Puritan, Sir Ernest Barker says: 'He might serve the chosen people, and through the chosen people he might serve the nation; but the service of which he always thought was the ultimate and lonely service which he owed directly to God.'[26]

This direct relationship with God was characteristically Lutheran. As Tawney states: 'God speaks to the soul, not through the mediation of the priesthood or of social institutions built up by man, but *solus cum solo*, as a voice in the heart and in the heart alone. Thus the bridge between the world of spirit and the world of sense is broken and the soul is isolated from the society of men that it may enter into communion with its Maker. The grace that is freely bestowed on it may overflow in its social relations, but these relations can supply no particle of spiritual nourishment to make easier the reception of grace.'[27]

Yet this freedom to approach God did not bring peace of heart to the Puritan. Alone he faced God. All alone he faced hell. He suffered the terrors of the medieval Christian without the comforts. He had not the massive power of the Roman Church behind him, and in the last analysis he was free only to go on struggling. The Puritan did not possess the quiet contentment of the true Calvinist. He had to prove to himself hour-by-hour by diligence, discipline, and defiance of circumstances that he was predestined for salvation. The true Calvinist had no such misgivings; he *believed* that he was predestined to be saved and that was sufficient. But if the Puritan had not the contentment of the Calvinist, neither had he the assurance of the Lutheran. Faith alone was never quite sufficient for him and it had to be buttressed by the operations of the human will and persistent human effort.

---

[25] H. Wheeler Robinson, *The Life and Faith of the Baptists*, p. 124.
[26] *Oliver Cromwell*, p. 85.
[27] Cited in J. Marlowe, *The Puritan Tradition*, p. 43.

To the Puritan, Faith was a goal to be reached; to the Lutheran, Faith was the only means of reaching the goal. The Puritan never fully appreciated the place of Faith in justification. That he accomplished so much in spite of these serious limitations is in itself remarkable.

(2) *The Principle of Religious Liberty*

The Puritan struck a blow for religious liberty that is without parallel in the history of our land. For if men owe service directly to God they must be free to offer it. This, then, is the second important Puritan principle—freedom of conscience and freedom of worship. Dr Northcott sums up succinctly the meaning of religious freedom: 'Freedom in religion is, therefore, twofold. First, the right of the individual's direct approach to God, his freedom of conscience and free choice of a community where he shall find religious fellowship. Second, the right of a religious community freely to order its own way of life and to witness to its beliefs.[28] One of the most daring and revolutionary works on this subject came from the pen of one of the earliest Baptist laymen, Thomas Helwys, who established the first Baptist Church on English soil in 1612, and during the same year issued *The Mistery of Iniquity*, which he had written during his eight years' exile in Amsterdam. This tempestuous little volume is significant for two reasons: first, because it marks the time when the English Reformation passed from the professional to the layman, and secondly, because it was the first time that a voice had been raised in England in defence of universal religious liberty. Helwys writes: 'Our Lord the King is but an earthly King, and he hath no authority as a King, but in earthly causes, and if the King's people be obedient and true subjects, obeying all humane laws made by the King, our Lord the King can require no more: for men's religion to God is betwixt God and themselves: the King shall not answer for it, neither may the King be judge between God and Man. Let them be heretikes, Turcks, or whatsoever, it appertaynes not to the earthly power to punish them in the least measure.'[29]

(3) *The Priesthood of all Believers*

The third important principle which was emphasized by the

[28] C. Northcott, *Religious Liberty*, p. 116. [29] *The Mistery of Iniquity*, p. 69.

Puritans was the priesthood of all believers. In this connexion we must notice the place which they afforded to faith, to the congregation, and to the conception of ministry.

(*a*) The Puritans were a company of people gathered out of the world because they had responded to the divine offer of salvation. They were in reality a company of *believers*. The Church was regarded by them as a divine society on earth who believe in Christ and confess Him as Lord. In Edwyn Bevan's words: 'Perhaps the greatest contribution made by the Dissenters was the continuous testimony they bore, by their very existence, to the character of Christianity as a society to which men adhere by individual conversion and choice, not by birth.'[30] All the leaders which we have considered agree that the Church is not to be identified with the State, or the Monarchy, or the Hierarchy, but rather as an independent spiritual fellowship which is founded on faith in Christ, and continues to exist by that same faith.

(*b*) When believers come together in the name of Christ they are conscious of possessing certain unique privileges, as well as realizing that certain duties and responsibilities have to be discharged. In so far as they fulfil those corporate functions which form part of their spiritual inheritance they become a 'priesthood'. Dr Townsend combines the privilege and the responsibility in the following passage: 'Wherever and whenever believers gather together in the name of Christ there is Christ Himself; and where Christ is there the Church is: such a Church is a priesthood of believers, competent after humbly seeking the mind of Christ according to the Scriptures, and praying for the guidance of the Holy Spirit, to receive believers into fellowship, to order its own forms of worship, to choose its own ministers and to discipline its own members.[31] Horton Davies rightly says that the outstanding Puritan contribution to English life was the affording of these high spiritual privileges to all members of the Christian community: 'Perhaps the most distinctive contribution of Puritanism to English life is found in the literal application of the doctrine of the priesthood of all believers. This was first enunciated by Luther, but both Lutherans and Calvinists, not to mention Anglicans, had given the State and the magistrate powers over the Church. It was the glory of the Independent

---

[30] *Christianity*, p. 197.
[31] *The Claims of the Free Churches*, p. 66.

Churches to give to all their members, regardless of personal rank or sex, equal rights in the government of their congregations.'[32]

(c) But if, as believers, the Puritans were invested with special privileges in regard to Church government, they were also personally and vitally concerned in the wider mission of the Church. Dr Townsend is right when he says: 'The ministry is the functioning of the whole membership of the Church; it is a divine vocation.'[33] This means that the members' duties are not confined to juridical functions within the congregation, but also extend to questions of pastoral responsibility and evangelism. This development had far-reaching consequences not only upon the religious life of England but in the sphere of social and political matters too. 'The English Free Churches witness to the priesthood of all believers, and the apostolate of the laity. By this principle they declare positively that each member is to be a missionary, and negatively they dissent from the double standard of Christian life (ascetic and non-ascetic) and sacerdotalism. Theirs is the true *via media* between an ultra-montanism which claims too much power for the Church, and an Erastianism which claims too much power for the State. Their assertion of the priesthood of all believers is the secret of their own contribution to democracy, by transference from the spiritual to the political sphere, and of their success in evangelism by the utilization of lay-preachers.'[34] It must be admitted, however, that it is not always clear whether the doctrine of the priesthood of believers was the *cause* of social and political movements, or whether it was an *afterthought*. There are times when it would appear to be the belated rationalizing of revolutionary strivings. One thing is certain: the idea was powerfully operative in the seventeenth century. But if a measure of doubt remains concerning the precise connexion of the doctrine with social and political events, there is no doubt, as has been shown, about its significance in the religious sphere. We must now show the prominent place which has been given to this principle in the development of doctrine in the Baptist and Congregational Churches and in the Society of Friends.

---

[32] *The English Free Churches*, p. 89.
[33] *The Claims of the Free Churches*, p. 66.
[34] Horton Davies, *The English Free Churches*, p. 199.

VI. DEVELOPMENTS IN THE BAPTIST CHURCH

Baptists remain faithful to those principles of order and worship which were laid down by John Smyth, who, during his exile in Holland, became the founder of the first English Baptist Church (1609). These principles are:

(1) 'That Christ is become the Mediator of the New Testament (to wit) the Kinge, Priest, and Prophet of the Church, and that the faithful *through Him*, are thus made spiritual kings, priests and prophets' (see Apoc 1^6 and 1 John 2^{20}). The latter passage refers to the ceremony of anointing which was common to priest and king.[35] 'And ye have an anointing from the Holy One.'

(2) The saynts as Priests offer up spirituall sacrifices acceptable to God by Jesus Christ. These sacrifices are called spirituall in opposition to the carnal or literal sacrifices performed by the sacrificing priests of the Old Testament.

(3) The actions of the Priesthood of the saynts are actions of concord or union and spiritual worship. (Deut 33^{10} and Heb 13^{10}.)[36]

(4) The brethren joyntly have all powre both of the kingdom and priesthood immediately from Christ (1 Pet 2^5, Matt 18^{20}), and that by virtue of the covenant God maketh with them (Gen 17^7, Acts 2^{39}).

(5) Therefore when the Church wanteth [this clearly means lacks] an Eldership, it hath nevertheless powre to Preach, Pray, Sing Psalmes, and so by consequent to administer the seales of the covenant (i.e. Holy Communion): also to admonish, convince, excommunicate, absolve, and all other action eyther of the kingdom or of the priesthood.[37] Believers' Baptism apart, here are the main tenets of the Baptist position. All believers being priests through Christ, offer up spiritual sacrifices, and because they function as a whole priesthood, their actions are united. Further, the authority which they possess is derived directly from Christ, confirmed by the covenant He has made with them, and by it they are enabled to minister in any sphere of service in the Church.

The Significance of the Covenant

'The New Israel . . . is the heir of the Old Israel, yet it is marked

[35] *The Works of John Smyth,* II.737. [36] Ibid. I.275. [37] Ibid. p. 315.

by vital and significant differences. It is based upon the *New Covenant*; membership is not constituted by racial origins but by a personal allegiance; the ritual of the temple and synagogue has given place to the ordinances of the Gospel and the national consciousness has widened to world horizons.'[38] This conception of the Church as a covenanted people is a characteristic of Baptist theology. The Covenant is both individual and corporate.

(*a*) The Baptists affirm that there must be a time when the believer consciously places himself under the Covenant of God. He does this by making a commitment to God, the outward sign of which is Believers' Baptism. Evelyn Underhill considers this fact the distinctive contribution of Baptist theology: 'No other Church has insisted, as the Baptists have done on the centrality of the New Testament connexion between baptism and personal faith, the importance of the great symbolic act of surrender to God; and on a realistic conversion of the whole life, inward and outward, as the condition of entrance into the Divine Society. Within that Society all are equal, and all are called to the worshipping life; the "priesthood of every believer" and the impossibility of substituting any liturgical act for personal communion with God and self-offering to God, are cardinal points of Baptist belief.'[39]

Yet one thing must be clear: it is not the rite which is significant but the personal crisis which precedes the rite. The basis of membership is not Baptism but conversion, although Baptism is the external sign of it. As a Declaration of Baptist Belief puts it: 'The basis of our membership in the Church is a conscious and deliberate acceptance of Christ as Saviour and Lord by each individual. There is, we hold, a personal crisis in the soul's life when a man stands alone in God's presence, responds to God's gracious activity, accepts his forgiveness, and commits himself to the Christian way of life.'[40] 'We value the symbolism of immersion following the Pauline teaching of the believer's participation in the death, burial and resurrection of our Lord (Rom 6^3).'[41] Baptism, therefore, indicates the believer's participation in the Priesthood of Christ.

(*b*) There is, however, a corporate aspect to all this, for, as all pass through the waters of Baptism, so all share the

---

[38] *The Nature of the Church*, ed. R. N. Flew, p. 161.   [39] *Worship*, p. 302.
[40] *The Nature of the Church*, ed. R. N. Flew, p. 162.   [41] Ibid. p. 166.

responsibilities which that experience places upon them. 'The worship, preaching, sacramental observances, fellowship and witness are all congregational acts of the whole Church in which each member shares responsibility, for all are held to be of equal standing in Christ, though there is a diversity of gifts and a difference of functions.'[42] We must remember that the Church Covenant brings the individual Church into being just as Believers' Baptism is the sign of a personal covenant which brings the individual Christian into being. Many of these Church Covenants are still extant, and we shall refer to one of them. The following is typical of them all:

'The Covenant to be the Lord's People and to walk after the Lord, signed by the Church of Christ under the Pastoral care of Joseph Jacob, a servant of Christ Crucified.'[43] The Covenant is divided into two parts, the first part refers to the people's relationship to God. They covenant themselves:

> To avouch Jehovah alone for our God.
> To chuse His written word for our only rule.
> To walk blameless in all His ordinances.
> To discharge our several relative duties.

Secondly, they covenant to discharge their duty to the whole Church, jointly as a body of Christians, in the fervent words:

> To be holy to the Lord in all manner of conversation.
> To stand together in defence of the truth.
> To keep the unity of the Spirit in the bond of peace.
> To press forward on our heavenly course.

Alongside the Church Covenant and closely linked with it as the basis of Baptist Belief is the doctrine of the priesthood of all believers.

(1) *The Priesthood of all Believers explains the Baptist doctrine of the Church and the Ministry*

It is the whole Church that is active in all Christian ministrations. The Baptist Union Statement of March 1948 says:[44] 'It is the Church which preaches the Word and celebrates the Sacraments, and it is the Church which, through pastoral oversight,

---

[42] Ibid. p. 163.   [43] See Duncan Coomer, *English Dissent*, pp. 17-18.
[44] *The Nature of the Church*, ed. R. N. Flew, p. 164.

feeds the flock and ministers to the world. It normally does these things through the person of its minister, but not solely through him. Any member of the Church may be authorized by it, on occasion, to exercise the functions of the ministry, in accordance with the principle of the priesthood of all believers, to preach the Word, to administer Baptism, to preside at the Lord's table, to visit, and comfort or rebuke members of the fellowship.' A similar conception of the Ministry is to be found in the Baptist reply to the Lambeth Appeal: 'Our doctrine of the Church determines our doctrine of the Ministry. We hold firmly to the priesthood of all believers, and therefore we have no separated order of priests. The ministry is for us a gift of the Spirit to the Church, and is an office involving both an inward call of God and the commission of the Church. We can discover no ground for believing that such a commission can be given only through an episcopate, and we hold that the individual Church is competent to confer it. For us there is no more exalted office than a ministry charged with the preaching of the Word of God and with the care of souls. Yet any full description of the ministerial functions exercised among us must take account of other believers who, at the call of the Church, may preside at the observance of the Lord's Supper or fulfil any other duties which the Church assigns to them.'[45] Here again as in the Lutheran tradition the proclamation of the Word has a central place. The sermon in Nonconformity is not regarded as an interruption but as a culmination. Preaching is an 'act of God', or, to use Barth's phrase, 'an event'. Alexander Maclaren (1826-1910) declared to the Baptist Union in 1875: 'If we had to offer to the world a Gospel of rites, the form of our ministry would be sacerdotal. If we had to offer a Gospel of thoughts, it would be professional and didactic. But we have a Gospel of fact, and therefore we preach.'[46]

(2) *The Priesthood of all Believers explains the Baptist position in relation to the State*

'The distinctive contribution of Baptists to "the Church universal" is to be found in their insistence on the individual soul in relation to God, without human mediation of parent, priest,

---

[45] A. C. Underwood, *A History of English Baptists*, p. 262.
[46] Quoted in J. W. Grant, *English Free Churches*, p. 33.

church, or sacrament, and in the conception of the entire ecclesiastical autonomy of the church. Their root belief and life principle has been and remains individualism and voluntarism in religious experience, relation and responsibility. They believe that the entire Gospel and programme of God in human history are based on the conception that God intends the individual to be the unit of His relation to mankind and deals immediately with every soul. Out of this basic principle grows their insistence on voluntariness in ecclesiastical relation, without external restraint or compulsion, or interference with the individual or the Church. Out of this understanding grows also the distinct Baptist contribution . . . of the entire separation of Church and State, complete independence of the two institutions, with mutual helpfulness between the two in the social order.'[47]

(3) *The Priesthood of all Believers explains Baptist teaching on Holy Communion*

It is a spiritual act. 'The Lord's Supper is, and is intended to be, first and last, spiritual. It lays no claim to any magic formula, nor do its benefits depend on any privileged class who alone can mediate the grace of God. That grace and the gift of Christ's presence in the heart are regarded as the gift of God to every willing, contrite spirit, needing no intermediary priest nor any special ritual.'[48]

When believers meet for this act of spiritual communion with their Lord they are all one. In the spiritual priesthood there can be no gradations of rank and no distinctions. All are equal in the succession of believers. 'One by one grateful believers make their contribution of prayer and devotion; but together they gather as a fellowship of the Church, for the supreme act of worship in which all human distinctions are forgotten in that community of faith and experience which makes them truly one.'[49] This emphasis on fellowship is prominent in Baptist teaching on Holy Communion. For this reason laymen have a part in the service. Sometimes the whole service is conducted by the minister, but more often than not the prayers are said by deacons. Always the deacons receive the Bread and Wine from the Minister and distribute them to the members of the congregation.

[47] W. O. Carver, in *The Nature of the Church*, ed. R. Newton Flew, p. 297.
[48] F. Townley Lord, in *Holy Communion*, ed. Hugh Martin, p. 97.   [49] Ibid.

Sometimes, however, a layman may preside at the celebration of the Lord's Supper, for as Dr Townley Lord says: 'The attitude of the two denominations (Baptists and Congregationalists) on this point is, of course, greatly influenced by the Lutheran principle that all Christians are priests, and by the view that when there is a celebration of the Lord's Supper it is really the Church, and not any man, which celebrates.'[50] The two denominations may also be linked together in our next observation. They do not normally practise private Baptism or private Communions, on the ground that the Baptismal Service and the Holy Communion Service are expressions of the corporate priesthood of the whole People of God.

Above all, the Lord's Supper is a further assertion of the Crown Rights of the Redeemer. Neither State nor Hierarchy, indeed nothing must be permitted to challenge His imperial claims. This truth has been effectively stated by P. J. Forsyth: 'The rite ... reflects Him as essentially Saviour, and not incidentally so. It is a fellowship, but more—*a redeeming royalty* that we experience. It is the Kingdom. It is the Lordship of the *Priest*, it is Christ as Redeemer.'[51] It is as King and Priest that we meet Him; as the Giver of all grace and the Ruler of all life. Therefore, we do not only partake in a sacred rite, we are clothed with a sacred rank, for we participate in His Kingship and Priesthood. It will be seen, then, that the doctrine of the priesthood of believers is not incidental but central in Baptist Theology. It was stated at the beginning of the seventeenth century by John Smyth and it has been expounded, confirmed, and implemented by his followers ever since.

It is of more than passing importance that the Baptists who have so much in common with other Nonconformists should find it impossible to join the Congregationalists, Methodists, and Presbyterians who united with the Anglicans to form the Church of South India in 1947. As far as the Baptists were concerned, there were three major issues: Believers' Baptism, which was expected to provide a difficult problem; the question of Church organization; and Ordination. Regarding the second problem it was said at one of the preliminary meetings: 'Every company of believers united together according to the laws of Christ is

---

[50] Op. cit. p. 93.   [51] *The Church and the Sacraments*, p. 240.

wholly independent of every other. Every such Church is perfectly capable of self-government. No Church recognizes any higher authority, under Christ, than itself.'[52] There is, of course, no simple answer to these problems, but they raise certain vital questions.

For instance, is it permissible to jeopardize the unity of the universal Church by insisting on the autonomy of a single congregation? Dr Manley does not appear to ascribe to the universal Church any realistic existence. It seems that the only real unit is the autonomous, self-sufficient, local Church. Baptists and Congregationalists are in danger of overlooking the '*all*' in the priesthood of all believers; they forget the universal aspect of the doctrine. The same point is called into question by Dr T. W. Manson, who disagrees with some words spoken at an Ordination service by no less an authority than Bernard Manning. Addressing the members of the local Church, Professor Manning said: 'You have conferred on him all that the holy Catholic Church can confer. . . . It is you who ordain. Other ministers present here merely represent you.'[53] In spite of this undue authority which is ascribed to the local Church, the following words are included: 'He is a minister not of this but of the universal Church.' Commenting on this passage, Dr Manson says: 'I confess myself puzzled. For it seems to me that to state the matter thus comes perilously near to claiming for the local congregation rights which we very properly deny when they are claimed for the Papacy. In this account of the matter the universal Church is an intellectual abstraction.' It seems clear that those Churches which emphasize the local or gathered church are in danger of neglecting the universal significance of the Church. But there is a further criticism to be made against Professor Manning's interpretation: In every case, the pronoun 'you' should be replaced by the word 'Christ'. The primary action in Ordination is always that of God and not man. If it is said that the local church is emphasized because the covenant is made with the local community, the answer is that the original covenant was not limited in such a way. 'I will establish my covenant between me and thee and thy seed after thee throughout their generations'

---

[52] T. P. Manley, *Lutheran Baptists and the Church of South India* (1948 Report), p. 27.
[53] *The Church's Ministry*, p. 92.

(Gen 17⁷). What the Baptists and Congregationalists do not appear to have noticed is that it is just as dangerous to invest too much authority in a particular congregation as it is to invest it in a particular person. The arguments which hold good against a priestly hierarchy are equally appropriate against a priestly oligarchy.

It was partly because Baptist churches are separate, autonomous entities that they were not able to join the Church of South India as a united body. 'Would it be possible for Baptist churches to join the Church of South India without doing violence to the Baptist concept of the nature of the Church?' asks Dr Manley.[54] Whatever may be the answer to that question, there is certainly little hope of union in existing circumstances. All the same, it is strange that a Church which for three hundred years has steadfastly refused to be bound by questions of credal form, external organization, and ritualistic practice, should now make these factors within her own communion the barrier to a wider union. We must remember that we proclaim the priesthood of *all* believers, and shape our deeds as if the words were true.

Referring to Ordination, Dr Manley says: 'Our concept in this begins and ends with the august sentence of the C.S.I. Basis of Union: "The ordainer and consecrator is God." Any group of people duly organized as a Church may set apart one of their number to the Gospel ministry if he shows credible evidence of divine appointment. The so-called ordination is purely a form of recognition of the divine call, and *it is not essential that any previously ordained person participate in the service*.' Does not the implication that laymen are essential at an ordination, whereas ministers are not, involve the very error which the Baptists are seeking to avoid? The stipulation mentioned above means that ordained persons do not belong to the universal priesthood, which surely cannot be what is meant.

The following statement which was made by Dr Ernest Payne, the Baptist historian, to the Free Church Annual Congress in 1953 sums up the case not only for the Baptist Church but for all the Free Churches. Dr Payne refers to six insights which he claims are supported by a three-fold appeal—an appeal to the New Testament, an appeal to Christian theology, and an appeal to Church History. It is, however, the last three

[54] *Lutheran Baptists and the Church of South India*, p. 27.

insights which are of particular interest for our present study.

'(1) We make a serious and sustained appeal to Scripture.

'(2) We are clear that membership of the Church must be based on personal faith, conviction and profession.

'(3) The Church should be free from secular control.

'(4) We believe that the freedom of the Christian man involves freedom within the Church from any priestly caste of hierarchy standing between the individual and his Maker and controlling the channels of God's grace; freedom from any uniform pattern of organization, however ancient. . . . We agree with Dr Walter Horton that "The only strictly necessary requirements for a Christian Church are two: some means of historical continuity with the Incarnate Lord, and some means of communion with the Living Lord". (*Ecumenical Review* (1949), p. 381.)

'(5) Because we believe in the priesthood of all believers—and also in what Dr Wheeler Robinson called "the prophethood of all believers"—we believe that an evangelistic responsibility rests on every Christian. There are varieties of spiritual gifts. There are varied offices within the Church. But we see danger in any rigid distinction between clergy and laity, partly because it seems inevitably to obscure the duties of believers, individually and corporately, to witness to others by lip and by life, and partly because it seems to deny the power of the Spirit to reveal the things of Christ to all who have faith in Him.

'(6) While we would sharply separate Church and State, we distrust any rigid distinction between sacred and secular. The Church is to be an instrument of the rule of God on the earth. From within its fellowship men and women go out armed for the battle against evil. The Gospel must be applied to the ordinary daily life of men and nations and to the whole of life. . . . The Gospel must be preached to all men everywhere without distinction of race, nationality and class. The proclamation of the Gospel is the concern of the whole Church.'[55]

The last three emphases—religious liberty, evangelistic responsibility, and the corporate vocation of the whole Church—are vital and essential truths, and they are seen in their proper context when they are seen to arise out of the doctrine of the priesthood of all believers.

[55] *Free Church Report* (1953), pp. 11-13.

VII. DEVELOPMENTS IN CONGREGATIONALISM

(1) *The Principle applied in the Congregational idea of Church Government*

The Independents who fled to Holland at the beginning of the seventeenth century were soon faced with two major doctrinal problems: first, in answer to the question: Who are believers? John Smyth insisted that they were those who had been baptized. Johnson would not accept this view and Smyth parted company with him and became the minister of a separate Church in Amsterdam. Second, in answer to the question: To whom is entrusted the government of the Church? Johnson answered that it was the duty of the Presbyters, while Smyth and Ainsworth held that such powers were entrusted to all believers. Horton Davies has put his finger upon the real issue when he says: 'Meanwhile, Johnson in the other Church (in Amsterdam) was claiming almost tyrannical and inquisitorial powers for the eldership over the commonalty of the Church. Ainsworth, pleading the priesthood of all believers, disagreed and withdrew, accompanied by thirty associates, to form the third Congregational Church in Amsterdam.'[56] It will be seen, then, that the doctrine of the priesthood of believers became a central issue early in the history of Independency. The fortunes of the doctrine have varied however in this particular branch of the Church. It has been most clearly enunciated and at the same time more frequently misunderstood in the Independent tradition than in any other. One of the greatest exponents of the doctrine in Congregationalism was Dr A. M. Fairbairn. Writing on the meaning of Congregational polity Dr Fairbairn says: 'The first thing to be noticed is this, the polity was the complete negation of what we have called sacerdotalism, with its political and religious bases. It signified the affirmation that religion was altogether spiritual, and real only as it was realized in the spirit and in the truth (John 4^{23-4}). The priesthood of all believers is the only priesthood Independency knows (1 Pet 2^{5-9}, Rev 5^{10}); its only sacrifices are those of spiritual service (Rom 12^1, Phil 4^{18}). It will allow no official person to stand between the soul and God; they two must meet each other face to face. The man who leads it is the teacher and preacher, not the priest but the prophet,

---

[56] *The English Free Church*, p. 55.

able to exercise his office only by right of a divine vocation, with no right to it unless the call be manifestly of God. . . . Faith is the first thing demanded from every man; on personal conviction alone can a real religious experience be built.'[57] It is sometimes supposed that Dr Fairbairn's statements on this subject are individualistic and negative. Yet it is true that the soul's relationship to God is, in the last analysis, an individual matter, and the individual's responsibility cannot be shifted on to the shoulders of any other, not even a priest's. Further, Dr Fairbairn's denunciatory statements on any subject are expressed with great power, but so are his more constructive and positive declarations, and we must be careful not to discount the strength of his arguments because of a dislike of his style. At all events, Dr Fairbairn's assertion that religion is spiritual, that experience is based on faith, that the Church is a priesthood of all believers, and that its sacrifice is service, are truths which any Protestant will endorse.

The question of authority in the Congregational Church is linked with this idea that every member is directly responsible to God. Indeed, this question has become the focal point of Congregationalism and in practice has resulted in much more significance being attached to the individual member than is afforded in other denominations. As K. L. Carrick Smith observes: 'The great contention of Congregationalism is not that every Christian has a *right* to share in the government of the Church, but that every Christian is directly responsible to Christ for maintaining His authority in the Church. . . . This makes the Church meeting among Congregationalists and Baptists take a far more important place than it holds in the life of other churches. The underlying principle is not democratic but theocratic, for the meeting is the means whereby the members find *God's* will *together*.'[58]

The important question is not whether or not the Church should be organized, for we may all assume that some kind of organization is essential. As Dr Flew rightly says: 'In this world of space and time Christianity must always take form as a visible community, and therefore the idea of the Church is essential to Christian theology.'[59] The vital question is: What is the

---

[57] *Studies in Religion and Theology*, p. 297.
[58] K. L. Carrick Smith, *The Church and the Churches*, p. 109.
[59] *Jesus and His Church*, p. 23.

determining principle of the Church? Oman answers this question and also points out where true succession is to be found: 'To the Catholic the determining principle is in the institution—its priesthood, bishops, councils, Pope; to the Protestant it is in the fellowship, in all that is involved in the two or three met in the name of Christ, in the succession of believers, in the bond of love.'[60] But if the Church is a fellowship of believers united to their Lord and to one another, it is a divine society rather than an earthly institution. This has been stated by many Congregationalist writers but by none more effectively than the eminent scholar—Bernard Manning: 'On the one hand Congregationalists have outdone all other Christians in the emphasis they have laid on the visible Church and on the supreme importance of continual personal exercise in it by every individual. On the other hand, Congregationalists have clearly understood, frankly confessed, and effectually lived by the truth that this all-important visible Church is a divine spiritual society, not an earthly historic society, that it depends wholly on grace, not at all on law. From this double truth comes the possibility of a virile churchmanship utterly untouched by Judaic legal clericalism.'[61] The Church, therefore, is a visible fellowship of believers, whose members are directly and individually responsible to Christ.

(2) *The Principle applied in the Congregational idea of the Ministry*

All this affects the Independent view of the Ministry. If the Congregationalists attached so much importance to the congregation it is partly because spiritual gifts and order, and even the office of ministry are given to the whole Church and function through it. 'Congregationalists believe that the gifts of Ministry and the orders and offices in the Church are given not to individuals to exercise in the Church, but to the Church to be exercised by individuals. Thus while the ordained minister is almost invariably what in other Church orders would be called the "celebrant", in Congregationalism it is the whole Church which celebrates the Sacraments and offers worship. It is at this point that the words of 1 Peter are applied to the whole Church, we are "a holy priesthood".'[62]

---

[60] *The Church and the Divine Order*, p. 207.   [61] *Essays in Orthodox Dissent*, p. 164.
[62] Dr J. Marsh, in *Ways of Worship Report* (1951), p. 156.

Congregationalists oppose most strongly the view of episcopal succession not because it is an inadequate form of Church government but because it is an inadequate form of God's government. Such a view, they hold, misrepresents and limits the activities of a gracious God. They regard the view that the ministry is the *peculiar channel* of God's grace as untenable. It will be noticed that their objection is not on grounds of ecclesiastical order but on a point of doctrine. Bernard Manning speaks for all Congregationalists when he says: 'Their opposition to the claims put forward for the "historic" episcopate is made in no factious spirit. It is made because episcopacy has come to symbolize the contention that Christianity is still living under the Old Dispensation, that grace is given on legal terms by legal methods, that the Gospel needs Judaic machinery. As long as, and only as long as, episcopacy menaces the doctrine of free grace Congregationalists will be relentless about it.'[63]

In recent years many attempts have been made to re-emphasize the churchmanship of Congregationalism, and in this respect the works of Forsyth, Oman, Manning and Micklem have wielded a tremendous influence. Although Forsyth's works were lightly regarded by his contemporaries, they have received in this generation the attention they deserve. His aim was to remind the Church of her chief task which was to affirm the Lordship of Christ. If his words had been heeded he would have done for his generation what Dr Karl Barth has done for ours. Forsyth's work is summed up by Dr J. W. Grant: 'One cannot understand Forsyth apart from his intense conviction that religious experience, Christian freedom, and theological progress are all meaningless abstractions unless seen in relation to the Word that was in Christ Jesus. This insistence led to his criticism of Nonconformist churchmanship and gave it its incisiveness. Forsyth regarded the recognition of a sacrificing priesthood and the doctrine of the Mass as grave errors, but he could forgive them when set in the life of a supernatural Church. He could not abide the frame of mind that regards Churches as embodiments of human aspiration, ministers as laymen with more than average competence in the running of boys' clubs and women's guilds, and sacraments as impressive media of religious education.'[64] How far the Churches

---

[63] *Essays in Orthodox Dissent*, p. 170.
[64] *Free Churchmanship in England, 1870-1940*, p. 245.

have allowed themselves to be deflected from their true course is only too plainly implied in those words. It is very true of course that a Church which has lost the Gospel and Sacraments has lost its soul and is no longer a Church. Any amount of commendable clubs and social activities cannot save a spiritually impoverished Church from death. We may say then that Forsyth succeeded in so far as he reminded the Church of her true mission.

The main function of the Ministry remains for the Congregationalists, as for the other Churches in the Reformed Tradition, the preaching of the Word, the re-creating act of God. There is a good reason for this belief. 'When some insignificant little man is raised up out of the dust to speak God's Word, he is God's own minister, God's very lieutenant. The preaching of the Word of God is the Word of God.'[65] It is for this reason that Congregationalists believe that the Sacraments are in the service of the Word.

'Grace is supremely mediated in the Word. Thus the Sacraments do not *add* anything to the message of the Word about Christ's finished work; they do but movingly reiterate it.'[66] In such assertions Congregationalists are striving for the priority and centrality of the Evangel. The 'enacted Word' as well as the 'proclaimed Word' are only secondary to the Evangel which is prior to both. In both of them God's action is manifested and not the priest's. Both point to God's act of redemption. Indeed, the preaching of the Word is the proclamation of God's redemptive act as well as the anticipation of human response. Out of these two emerges a new creation—the Church. Dr Whale emphasizes this in the following passage: 'The Church . . . is the whole company of the elect that have been, are, or shall be, on earth and in heaven; one body whose sole head is Christ. The utter supremacy of God's gift in redemption is the fundamental fact which initiates and includes man's believing response, and on which the priesthood of all believers is built.'[67]

(3) *The Principle applied in the Congregational idea of Proclamation*

Proclamation is the business of the whole Church, however, and not only of a few representatives of it. 'The preaching of the

---

[65] J. S. Whale, *Christian Doctrine*, p. 153.
[66] Grant, *Free Churchmanship in England, 1870-1940*, p. 337.
[67] *The Ministry and the Sacraments*, ed. R. Dunkerley, p. 212.

Word, and the celebration of the Sacraments are, therefore, acts of the *whole Church*. Preaching is not merely (what in some churches it is said to be) the expression of the prophetic gift by individuals: it is the Church declaring the faith.'[68] How closely Bernard Manning is following in the steps of Dr Forsyth will be seen from the following passage: 'The one great preacher in history, I would contend, is the Church. And the first business of the individual preacher is to enable the Church to preach. He is to preach to the Church from the Gospel so that with the Church he may preach the Gospel to the world. . . . That is to say, he must be a sacrament to the Church, that with the Church he may become a missionary to the world. . . . The preacher's place in the Church is sacramental. It is not sacerdotal, but it is sacramental. He mediates the Word to the Church from faith to faith, from his faith to theirs, from one stage of their common faith to another.'[69]

If preaching is sacramental, and if a layman is permitted to preach, what reason can there be for debarring him from fulfilling other sacramental functions also? The importance of this lies not in the fact that the Congregationalists answered this question in the way they did, but in the fact that they asked the question at all. Dr Grant has pointed out that things were moving in that direction in the middle of the nineteenth century. 'There had been a trend in this direction for some time, Alfred Rooke having assumed in 1866 that the deacon "may administer the sacraments whenever the necessity arises, just because he shares in the priesthood of Christ and the consecration that sanctifies every believer".'[70] To regard this movement as a revolt of the laity is to miss the point entirely; for the leader of it was Dr Dale.[71] In order to give added significance to his contention he requested the Church Meeting at Carr's Lane to appoint a layman once a year to celebrate the sacrament of Holy Communion as a reminder of the priesthood of all Christians.

'Few would have argued at this time that a layman should dispense the Sacraments when an ordained minister was available. The way was opened, however, for the theory, familiar to modern Congregationalists although unknown to their ancestors, that the

---

[68] B. L. Manning, *Essays in Orthodox Dissent*, p. 165.
[69] P. T. Forsyth, *Positive Preaching and the Modern Mind*, pp. 79-80.
[70] *Free Churchmanship in England, 1870-1940*, p. 79.
[71] See Horton M. Davies, *The English Free Churches*, p. 164.

ministry has no single function that cannot and may not be discharged by any Church member.'[72] The Congregationalists were, of course, right in asserting the principle of the priesthood of all believers, but there were times when they adopted some odd methods of applying the principle. For instance, is it really permissible to practice lay celebration with complete disregard for questions of personal character and prior authorization? Again, does the rejection of ministerial dress and the adoption of lay attire really affect the ministerial office in any sense whatsoever? And does not the idea that clerical dress makes a minister, indicate a very impoverished doctrine of the ministry? The truth is that the doctrine of the priesthood of all believers has nothing whatever to do with form of dress, and any such idea reduces the whole matter to absurdity. What is important is to discover what Dale and his associates were trying to do. As Grant says, 'Dale's intention was to spiritualize the laity rather than secularize the clergy', but at the same time it seemed sometimes as if the latter intention was predominant. Their real aim was to relate the ministry to the active life of the world, to set the ministry in the midst of the hurly-burly of the life of the community. This is a worthy aim but it is no part of its realization for ministers to become as unlike priests as possible.

During the past half-century Nonconformists have been mainly on the defensive, and this circumstance has had unfortunate repercussions in the sphere of doctrine. Doctrine, therefore, has succumbed to the psychology of the opposition. This has certainly affected the Nonconformist attitude to the Church and Ministry. Commenting on this development Grant says: 'In practice the result was to call in question the supernatural life of the Church, to abandon the Church's priestliness along with the *sacerdos*, and to substitute for the prophet with a message from God the man of spiritual insight with an inspiring message of his own.'[73]

The approach of the early Separatists, however, was very different. If they rejected one form of ministry, they substituted for it the priesthood of all believers. It was not their intention to banish the priest but to assert the priesthood of all Christians. Modern Independents will do well to learn from them. A theological doctrine does not need defending upon social or

[72] J. W. Grant, *Free Churchmanship in England, 1870-1940*, p. 80.
[73] Ibid. p. 389.

political grounds. The priesthood of believers is the natural corollary of the believers' relationship to God; it is expressed in the corporate worship and witness of the Church; and far from being anti-ministerial, it sets the ministerial priesthood within the context of the universal priesthood. The Church is not a collection of individuals claiming their rights, but a kingdom of priests—a united spiritual society exercising in various ways that priesthood which is common to all believers. This is another way of saying that ministers and laity are necessary to the true worship, witness, and service of the Church. One thing is certain: no one can study the history of the Independents without realizing what an important place is given to the doctrine of the priesthood of believers, and we may be sure that it will be the determinative principle in any reassessment which Congregationalists make of their distinctive witness.

VIII. THE SOCIETY OF FRIENDS

No study of the historical development of the Church and the Ministry can be regarded as complete which does not find room for a movement which has deviated to a considerable extent from the orthodox teaching of the Churches. Moreover, it is impossible to understand the doctrinal position of Quakerism without first understanding the spiritual experience of George Fox. Fox was an ardent seeker after Truth, but he did not find an answer to his need in the various Churches of the Commonwealth. Oppressed by the spiritual malaise, legalistic outlook, and ineffectual witness of the Church, he was determined to find not only the cause of this mental and spiritual torpor but also its cure. Turning away from the gloom which surrounded him, he found a clear light shining within his own soul. This is how he tells the story of the great discovery which he made in September 1643.

'As I had forsaken all the priests, so I left the separate preachers also, and those esteemed the most experienced people.... And when all my hopes in them and in all men were gone, so that I had nothing outwardly to help me, nor could tell what to do, then, O then I heard a voice which said, "There is one, even Christ Jesus, that can speak to thy condition," and when I heard it, my heart did leap for joy.... Then the Lord let me see why there was none upon the earth that could speak to my condition, namely, that I might give Him all the glory.... Thus when God doth work, who shall hinder it? and *this I knew experimentally*. My desire after the Lord grew stronger, and zeal after the pure knowledge of God, and of Christ alone, without the help of any man, book, or writing. For though I read the Scriptures which spoke of Christ and of God, yet I knew Him not but by revelation, as He who hath the key did open, and as the Father of Life drew me to His Son by His Spirit.'[74]

Historically George Fox appears between Luther and Wesley, and it is not without significance that the spiritual experiences of these great Protestant leaders were very similar. Luther's words (1516) were: 'I found that neither Baptism nor Monkery could help me. There is a faith which believes what is said of God is true; there is a faith which throws itself on God.' So Luther, failing to find any help whatsoever in man, was compelled to find all in God. Wesley's words (1738) after his soul-transforming experience in Aldersgate Street, were: 'I felt I did trust in Christ, Christ alone, for salvation; and an assurance was given me that He had taken away *my* sins, even *mine*, and saved *me* from the law of sin and death.' Indeed Wesley's exposition of the doctrine of Assurance is simply an exemplification of George Fox's striking words: 'This I knew experimentally.' Out of this remarkable experience of 1643, three important truths emerged which were to shape subsequent Quaker belief.

(1) Fox claimed to have rediscovered the living Christ. Luther, Fox and Wesley sing in unison across the centuries: 'Christ alone, Christ alone.' This concept was determinative for Fox's theology. He was not interested in what others had heard or said or written about Christ, but in Christ Himself. For him, personal encounter was more important than an inherited faith or mature understanding. He had found 'Christ alone, without the help of any man, book, or writing'. 'He had never had any doubts about the historical Christ. All that the Christians of his time believed *about* Christ, he, too, believed. His long search had not been to find out something *about* Christ, but to find *Him*.'[75] It is very important that we should understand this clearly because it colours the whole of Quaker doctrine. It explains the throwing away of the crutches, the discarded symbols, and the rejected Sacraments. 'I had not', says Fox, 'fellowship with any people,

---

[74] *George Fox: An Autobiography*, ed. R. M. Jones, pp. 82-3.
[75] Ibid. p. 28.

priests or professors, or any sort of separated people, but with Christ who hath the key, and opened the door of light and Life unto me. . . . My living faith was raised, that I saw *all was done by Christ* the life, and my belief was in Him.'[76]

In spite of the various theologies and theories which were abroad in the seventeenth century, the Quakers were by no means convinced that men were in contact with the Living Christ. Their simple yet all-important claim was that they had transformed Christianity from a theological formula into an experimental reality. A. N. Brayshaw has shown how this aspect of Quaker doctrine is centred on New Testament teaching: 'It may without presumption be said that they had rediscovered the central truth of the Christian religion set forth in the Pauline and Johannine writings, but largely overlooked by the teachers of their day—that Jesus Christ, *the Word of God*, is no mere theological conception or fading figure of the past, but a living and present reality, continuing and reproducing His own life in the souls of His followers, revealing to them in actual experience at once the character of God "whom no man hath seen nor can see", and the lives that God would have them live.'[77] If the Quakers tended to pay little attention to the Man of Galilee and Jerusalem, it was really due to their eagerness to emphasize that the source of all new life is the 'Christ within'.

They did not think it sufficient to say that Christ lived and died and rose again for men, unless He was known to live in men's lives today. The historical events ensure that Christ lives in the world now. In short, the Quakers hold that present experience is more important than history, and to be 'in Christ' is more vital than correctness of belief. E. Grubb states the same truth as follows: 'Its (Quakerism's) primary emphasis was inward and ethical. Salvation it regarded as essentially a work to be wrought *in* man, and not merely *for* him; as a transforming experience to be known in the soul here and now, and not merely as a means of escaping penalty in the world to come.'[78]

(2) The second principle which arose out of Fox's spiritual experience is closely related to the first. 'Man', as used in the above paragraph, is a generic term. The rediscovery of the living Christ is not the monopoly of the privileged few but the true

---

[76] *George Fox: An Autobiography*, ed. R. M. Jones, pp. 83-4.
[77] *The Quakers*, p. 53.   [78] *The Historical and Inward Christ*, Preface.

inheritance of all men. Rufus Jones sees in the exposition of this universal principle the original contribution of Quakerism: 'The larger truth involved in his (George Fox's) experience soon became plain to him, namely, that he found a universal principle that the Spirit of God reaches every man. He finds this divine human relationship taught everywhere in Scripture, but he challenges everybody to find the primary evidence of it in his own consciousness.'[79]

We come, therefore, to three main characteristics of the doctrine of the Inner Light. This Light is universal because it is *for* all men; it is inward because it is *in* all men; and it carries social implications because it shines *through* men to others.

'(a) The belief in the inner light presupposed the capacity of all men to recognize and respond to God's revelation of love, and was a direct denial that this ability was limited, as Calvinism taught, to the elect, who alone were assisted by prevenient grace.

'(b) The inner light is also the description of man's interior and experimental knowledge of God. The doctrine and experience had, as its consequences, the conviction that communion with God cannot be restricted to time or place, to a priestly caste or sacrament, or to a Bible, indispensable guide as that is.

'(c) This belief that all men were capable of receiving revelation provided the basis of a universal philanthropy and a complete democracy. The Quakers were religious levellers, and their mysticism was social in character and influence.'[80]

(3) The third principle which arose out of Fox's spiritual experience is one that is frequently overlooked in estimating the permanent value of the Quaker method of worship. If it is true that the Living Christ, by the Spirit, reaches every man, it is also true that Christ may only do the work He has to do in human life if the mind is disciplined and the soul prepared. Fox could not forget how carefully his own heart and mind had been prepared even from childhood for his life-work: 'That all may know the dealings of the Lord with me, in order to prepare and fit me for the work unto which He appointed me, and may thereby be drawn to admire and glorify His definite wisdom and goodness, I think fit (before I proceed to set forth my public travels in the service of Truth) briefly to mention how it was

[79] *George Fox: An Autobiography*, ed. R. M. Jones, p. 28.
[80] Horton M. Davies, *The English Free Churches*, p. 109.

THE PURITAN TRADITION

with me in my youth, and how the work of the Lord was begun, and gradually carried on in me, even from my childhood.'[81]

Quakerism has nothing in common with a lazy Quietism which seeks to create a mental vacuum. It is not mysticism in the commonly accepted sense of that term, for it does not seek a sort of spiritual Nirvana by the process of negation. In Quaker teaching an empty mind is not a condition of divine guidance. On the contrary, it is to the alert mind and the waiting soul that God speaks. Moreover, the necessity of spiritual responsiveness is always paramount. The distinctiveness of Quakerism lies in this confident and expectant waiting before God in an atmosphere of spiritual responsiveness. Braithwaite maintains that the Quaker disposition has resulted from this condition of spiritual responsiveness. 'The result has been to produce . . . the man or woman who goes through life endeavouring to decide every question as it arises, not by passion or prejudice, nor mainly by the conclusions of human reason, but chiefly by reference to the light of God that shines in the *prepared soul*.'[82]

Silent worship does not mean inactive worship. Indeed, worship is spiritual action, and Quakers believe that the Spirit leads the dedicated worshipper. 'God speaks His message through the prepared and disciplined mind, but not through the inactive one; the secret lies in the dedication of each worshipper's will to Him, and not in the abdication of that will from its true responsibility.'[83]

We must inquire how far these principles have influenced Quaker ideas on Worship and the Ministry.

The Quaker idea of Worship

George Fox had discovered that direct communion with Christ was a glorious possibility which was not dependent upon any intermediary. Nor had he found that this experience was impossible apart from sign, symbol, or sacrament. If silence was the characteristic of an early Quaker Meeting, it was the silence of great power. It was this sense of spiritual power which impressed Robert Barclay, the Quaker theologian, when he first entered the Meeting House. 'When I came into the silent assemblies of God's people, I felt a secret power among them that

---
[81] *George Fox: An Autobiography*, ed. R. M. Jones, p. 65.
[82] *Spiritual Guidance in Quaker Experience*, pp. 31-2.
[83] R. Howe, in *Holy Communion*, p. 106.

touched my heart.' They considered that the other churches had the shell but not the kernel, the body but not the soul, the temple but not the Spirit. But the Quakers were concerned mainly about the kernel of the Christian Faith; soul and spirit meant everything to them. This is why they appear to be so different from their contemporaries. Grubb has drawn attention to the difference in practice between Fox and the religious leaders of his time: 'He was prepared to *trust* the direct and personal experience of the Spirit's immediate presence and guidance to such an extent as to base his whole church policy upon it and therefore to sweep away all outward safeguards which had been built up in the hope of maintaining order and unity in the Church: an ordained ministry, with sacraments and set forms of worship....'[84] In fact, however, the idea that Quakerism 'sweeps away sacraments and set forms of worship' is somewhat misleading. They did not banish the sacraments. In the light of their direct contact with God, all symbols seemed unnecessary and therefore dropped away. As Stephen Hobhouse correctly says: 'It was their intense conviction of the immediate contact of God with the soul, to be realized at all times and in all places, that led to the depreciation of sacramental rites by George Fox and the first Quakers. They believed that they had the substance; the symbols were not needed and just dropped away.'[85]

This new attitude to worship was a spontaneous reaction rather than an organized campaign. It was in Quakerism that the change from liturgical to spontaneous worship, and from sacramental embodiments of spiritual action to pure inwardness took place. Worship consisted in the quiet gathering together of souls to share fellowship with God, and in corporate silence which ensured the freedom of the Spirit's course in each individual soul. Thus the basic assumption of their theology is that God speaks and that He must be heard. This idea could not be better expressed than in the lines of Frances Ridley Havergal:

I am listening, Lord, for Thee,
What hast Thou to say to me?

God's word is more important than man's and therefore it is more important for man to listen rather than speak. This is why

[84] *What Is Quakerism*, ed. Grubb, p. 27.
[85] *William Law and Eighteenth-century Quakerism*, p. 196.

the Quaker views with suspicion the idea of premeditated and prepared worship. He does not appreciate the idea of prepared prayers, hymns and sermons. He will allow the necessity for a disciplined mind and a responsive heart, but he does not understand the over-careful organization of what *man* is going to say to God. It is God's Word addressed to man that gives life. Yet man seems to place undue emphasis upon the manner in which he addresses God. Miss K. L. Carrick Smith has pointed out that their worship is centred on God and not on man. 'It is hardly overstating the position to say that it seems to them fantastic that when the children of God gather together to worship Him they should come prepared themselves to speak, in prayer or hymn, almost continuously. When Friends gather together in their "Meeting for Worship", they do so in the expectation that the communion and communication will come from God's side, and His people come to listen. "The Lord is in His holy temple; let all the earth keep silence before Him" (Hab 2^{20}).'[86]

No Quaker will agree to the statement that the Society of Friends do not observe the Sacraments. Although they do not observe them outwardly, they sincerely believe that they do so inwardly. They maintain that by rejecting the outward ceremony they lay greater stress on the inward and real meaning of the Sacrament. This, of course, is consistent with their whole attitude to worship. An official statement on this subject says: 'Our manner of worship springs from our experience of God and gives expression to it. Friends do not use the altar and the symbols of sacrifice in order to reach God, because it is an outstanding fact of our knowledge of Him that He is at hand, waiting to enter the heart that is opened to Him. . . . Worship finds its natural expression not in ritual acts but in the service of all God's children.'[87]

'In holding that outward rites are unnecessary and contrary to their understanding of the nature of God, Friends only insist the more strongly that the whole of life is sacramental. . . . The life of saintliness, the life which is based on prayer is a continual offering to God, is itself the true sacrament.'[88]

There have been times when the ideal of a Quaker Meeting

---

[86] *The Church and the Churches*, pp. 73-4.
[87] Ronald Howe on Society of Friends, in *Holy Communion*, p. 101.
[88] Ibid. pp. 101-2.

and its realization in practice have been very far apart, but Quakers have at least remained true to the ideal. There have been times of spiritual famine when the silence has been oppressive; when someone has spoken out of desperation rather than out of inspiration. Fox himself, whilst calling attention to those who outran their Guide in speaking uncalled-for words, laid stress on the harm done by others withholding what they ought to share. Yet they have consistently borne witness to the pure spirituality of worship, and they have given an entirely new interpretation to the doctrine of the priesthood of all believers. In their teaching on the responsibility and capacity of each soul; in the universality of the doctrine of the Inner Light; in the general call to sanctity; and in the freedom of all to take part in the Meeting as guided, they have applied in practice the doctrine of the priesthood of believers.

The Quaker idea of the Ministry

(a) Quakers claim that their idea of Ministry is based on the New Testament. They believe that their idea of Testimony or Ministry is in accordance with New Testament teaching. They are convinced that in the New Testament there is no sign of any specially holy times, places, or persons, and that the only priesthood which existed then was the priesthood of all believers. They believe that God's people are His temple and His altar is set up in their hearts. Upon this subject a Quaker scholar has this comment to make:

'The Ministry practised in the earliest Christian churches is fully recorded for us, in a way that admits of no mistake, in the First Epistle to the Corinthians. Each one had a song, or an exhortation, a revelation, or a piece of instruction. The Ministry was exercised so freely by so many members of the congregation that it was necessary to specify that only one was to speak at once, and caution had to be given against supposing that everyone could possess the more showy gifts. There is, therefore, no difficulty in seeing that the earliest Christian form of worship was, in manner and form, a Friends' meeting of the early enthusiastic type.'[89]

It is not difficult to see that the Quakers find their prototype in 1 Corinthians 14; what is difficult to understand is that while

[89] John W. Graham, *The Faith of a Quaker*, p. 188.

paying careful attention to the type of worship delineated in Chapter 14, the Quakers should completely disregard the Eucharistic worship which is equally plainly stated in Chapter 11. Moreover, if the Quakers are eager to emulate the customs of the early Church, ought they not more seriously to consider the congregational form of the Communion Service of which details are given by many early Fathers but especially by Clement of Rome and Justin Martyr?

(*b*) A Quaker Meeting is an exemplification of the priesthood of all believers.

To be really effective a Quaker Meeting presupposes a deep sense of spiritual fellowship. Mutual trust is essential; not just trust in one leader but in every person present. Everyone is capable of conveying the divine Word to all the others. There must therefore be no limitation of the Spirit's activity. 'This note of *one another* shows the conception of the divine Word as coming to the individual not only direct from the Holy Spirit, but also as mediated through the fellowship, even in silence.'[90] This idea that the word is mediated through the fellowship and not merely through an individual leader is characteristic of Quakerism. In their eyes it would be a limitation of the Holy Spirit if only a Minister was permitted to speak, to the exclusion of all others. Men or women may offer a prayer or give forth a message as it is committed to them. True worship consists in the living silence and the living ministry which together form a complete whole. Ministry, therefore, is exercised by all believers, for, as Brayshaw puts it: 'The ministry comes from men and women of all ages and of all stations of life, from farmers, merchants and shopkeepers, from scholars and professional men, from those whose speech may, as Penn said of the speech of Fox, "sound uncouth and unfashionable to nice ears", but who, out of the furnace of life, bring a message which cannot be spared.'[91]

In the light of the above consideration, it cannot be maintained that the Quakers do not believe in ministry. To be sure, they do not recognize any such *office*, but they do believe that the spiritual gift of ministry is vouchsafed to all. In other words, they believe that the exercise of spiritual gifts and the various functions of ministry are a shared responsibility rather than an exclusive one.

---

[90] A. N. Brayshaw, *The Quakers*, p. 211.
[91] Ibid. pp. 81-2.

'Of all conceptions of ministry, the simplest and most comprehensive is to be found in the Society of Friends. Christians of other communions who have once or twice attended a "Meeting for Worship" sometimes leap to the conclusion that there is no ministry in the Society; for Friends simply sit together, for the most part in silence, "centred upon" the God who is in their midst, and any member of the gathering may speak a few words of reflection, exhortation or prayer. But the truth is that in this meeting there is no laity. The "priesthood of all believers" means, in the Society of Friends, that no one is in any way set apart to minister to his fellows but the responsibility for exhorting one another and building one another up in love is shared by all.'[92]

According to Dr Rufus Jones two important principles which arose out of Fox's own experience were: The Spirit is universal, and the Priesthood is universal.

'God is not far off. He needs no vicar, no person of any sort between Himself and the worshipper. Grace no more needs a special channel than the dew does. There is no special holy place, as though God were more *there* than *here*. He does not come from somewhere else. He is Spirit, and needs only a responsive soul, an open heart, to be *found*. . . . With his usual optimism, he believed that all men and women were capable of this stupendous attainment. He threw away all crutches at the start and called upon everybody to walk in the Spirit, to live in the Light.'[93]

The universality of the Spirit presupposes a universal priesthood. Priesthood in this sense means discovering God, appreciating God, and serving God, and as these privileges are open to all, priesthood is said to be universal. So in Quaker worship, 'there was no priestly mitre, because each member of the true Church was to be a priest unto God. . . . From beginning to end worship was the immediate appreciation of God, and the appropriate activity of the whole being in response to Him. . . . As fast and as far as any man discovers God it becomes his business to make him known to others. His ability to do this effectively is a gift from God, and makes him a minister.'[94]

It follows, then, that in Quaker teaching the doctrine of the priesthood of believers is not a theory, but a fact, not an idea but a reality, not a doctrine but an experience. As all may discover

---
[92] K. L. Carrick Smith, *The Church and the Churches*, p. 48.
[93] R. M. Jones, *George Fox*, p. 38.   [94] Ibid. p. 39.

God, so all may use and indeed must use the gifts He bestows. Quakers are not mistaken when they maintain that the distinctiveness of their teaching lies in this very point: 'In the Society which he (Fox) founded there was no distinction of clergy and laity. He undertook the difficult task of organizing a Christian body in which the priesthood of believers should be *an actual fact*, and in which the ordinary religious exercises of the Church should be under the directing and controlling power of the Holy Spirit manifesting itself through the congregation.'[95] This was undoubtedly a unique achievement and therefore Trevelyan's opinion is not exaggerated when he says that Fox, 'made at least the most original contribution to the history of religion of any Englishman'.[96]

It cannot be denied, however, that as far as Quaker teaching is concerned, the doctrine of the priesthood of all believers needs clarification and elucidation at various points. For instance, what is the relation between the inner Light and the universal priesthood? Again, has the doctrine been fully worked out in relation to Quaker worship, and have the evangelistic implications of the doctrine been given sufficient attention?

Regarding the first of these: what is the Inner Light? In referring to it as a universal factor, Fox himself says that it was a divine principle in Nebuchadnezzar which caused him to say: 'Blessed be the Lord God of Shadrach, Meshach, and Abed-nego.' This light is said to shine in the hearts of the heathen even if they have never heard of Christ. But if the Light shines automatically in the life of Christian and Pagan alike, it cannot have much relationship with the priesthood of all *believers*. We have noticed that initiation into the Royal Priesthood is sometimes through Baptism, or Confirmation, or admission to Church membership, or Regeneration.[97] But none of these is applicable in the case of Quakerism. We cannot say that membership in the Royal Priesthood equals possession of the Inner Light because unbelievers are included in Fox's classification of those who possess the Light. Sometimes he and the early Quakers identified this principle with Christ. This, however, only adds to the confusion, for if Christ is to be identified with the Light-principle, then the

---

[95] R. M. Jones, *George Fox*, p. 40.
[96] E. Payne, quoted in *Free Church Tradition*, p. 52.
[97] In previous chapters.

question of conscious acceptance enters in, for to maintain that pagans, materialists, and the adherents of other religions are indiscriminately and unconsciously in possession of Christ is an assumption that is theologically untenable. Even Barclay, the ablest of Quaker theologians is not sure of his ground on this question, for he identifies the Light with the Trinity, with a 'seed' in all men, and with the spiritual body of Christ.[98] If the Inner Light is Christ, then we cannot say that it shines in all men everywhere irrespective of their response; on the other hand, if the Inner Light is a universal principle dwelling in all men, then it is to be identified with the '*imago dei*' or with the idea of prevenient grace. In either case it has no connexion with the priesthood of all believers. The two notions are clearly quite separate.

Whatever may be the reason for it, there is no doubt that the Quakers have become mainly exclusive, isolated groups with a keen social conscience but lacking that passionate evangelistic fervour which characterized their early leaders. In the early days they were eminently conscious of their mission: 'As fast as any man discovers God it becomes his business to make Him known to others.'[99] This is an aspect of the universal priesthood which should not be overlooked. But whatever may be said in regard to the doctrinal shortcomings of Quakerism, it has shown that the priesthood of believers is not to be confined to the realm of doctrine, but is to be translated into the life, practice, and worship of believers. In insisting that the whole worshipping Congregation is a Priesthood to which each member is subject, and in affording the opportunity for each member to participate actively in worship, as well as in stressing that true priesthood is only to be realized in relation to others by serving the community, by instituting social reforms, and by ceaseless endeavours in the cause of universal peace, Quakers have made a unique contribution to the history of religion.

---

[98] See discussion in Neibuhr, *Nature and Destiny of Man*, pp. 175-87.
[99] R. M. Jones, *George Fox*, p. 38.

5

Methodism

1. THE THEOLOGY OF EXPERIENCE

It has often been maintained that Wesley's theology is incurably subjective, but this verdict has frequently been pronounced after an inadequate and one-sided examination of his views. It is important that we should know what Wesley did not mean by religious experience. Certainly Methodism was and is concerned with the subjectivity of direct feeling and inward experience, but it must be emphasized that this is very different from the subjectivity of the practical intellect as shown in Socinianism, or the subjectivity of self-effort as shown in Pelagianism. Wesley was convinced that religion had been too long preoccupied with the practical intellect on the one hand, and with the efficacy of human effort on the other, and his firm resolve 'to direct sinners away from all else whatsoever to Christ' was in the true Reformation tradition, for it shifted the emphasis from an anthropocentric to a theocentric theology.

It is also true that the religion which Wesley preached was something which took place *in man*, but it was not *of man*, and because it was not of man no work of man affected the issue. Indeed everything that is 'only of human appointment' is doomed to failure. Sometimes the Church has given the impression that religion was of man, and whenever this happens faith has to be buttressed by irrelevant factors and external forms. Wesley firmly rejected the view that religion consisted in outward observances, and he went so far as to say that even if outward forms and ceremonies were appointed by God Himself (as in the case of the Jews) yet, 'true religion does not principally consist therein'.[1] 'How much more', he cries, 'must this hold concerning rites and forms as are only of human appointment! The religion of Christ rises infinitely higher, and lies immensely deeper, than all these.'[2]

[1] *Sermon* VII.1.4. [2] Ibid.

The truth is that outward actions, however noble, point to a religion of works.

If true religion was not to be found in rites and ceremonies, neither was it to be found in orthodoxy and right opinions. 'For these', says Wesley, 'are not in the heart but in the understanding.' All the same, the notion that Wesley substituted the faith and feeling of the individual for the conception of religion as pure doctrine and outward obedience does not tell the whole truth. Wesley was anxious to remove the wedge which had been driven between God's saving act and man's appropriation of its results. Out of His infinite love God has taken action in the interests of man's salvation, and without that divine act, all the faith in the world is futile. But if that divine act is not only to reveal God's love but also to redeem man, then faith is a necessity. The difference is between what God has done for us and what He does in us. Apart from faith God's act remains impersonal and unrelated. God's act is an effective means of salvation *for* all mankind, but if it is to be a reality *in* me, faith is indispensable. In the end it is faith in God's act which banishes our alienation. Staupitz's words to Luther are pertinent here: 'You are right, Brother Martin, in contrasting God's holiness with your sinfulness, but you are wrong in keeping these two permanently apart.' Again the dialogue in Charles Wesley's hymn clarifies the matter: We say,

> *Cause us the record to receive,*
> *Speak and the tokens show—*

Our Lord answers:

> *O be not faithless, but believe*
> *In Me, who died for you!*

Wesley asserted salvation by faith alone not against a version of Christianity which interpreted man's salvation as an objective act of God, but against one in which salvation was offered as a reward for human effort and on terms which made its ultimate attainment a matter of uncertainty. He dealt with the first by proclaiming that salvation was by faith alone, and with the second by expounding the doctrine of an inner certainty born of faith and effected by the witness of the Spirit in the believer. In each case he appealed to experience, and by this is meant the reign of God in the soul of man. 'This holiness and happiness . . . is termed "the kingdom of God", because it is the immediate fruit of God's reigning in the soul.'²

How does God reign in the soul? In other words: What is the meaning of religious experience? Various theories were prevalent in Wesley's day. Before Wesley died one of the Hallensian Pietists, Schleiermacher, was studying scientifically the whole question of religious experience. Its object was said to be the perception of the infinite scattered throughout the universe, and it was described as a faculty which assumes conscious dimensions in all men. It was, in fact, a religion which relied solely on postulates of self-knowledge. This is not what Wesley meant by religious experience. Later, William James in America had much to say on this question but in his view religious experience was no more than Utilitarian Pragmatism. On this view religion is to be judged solely by the standards of practical utility. Far too often religious experience has been interpreted in terms of an enlightened conscience, but Maximin Piette has given an adequate answer to such a view: 'The state of a man's conscience, should anyone wish to entrap it for microscopic examination, can no more portray living religious experience than a vessel of water taken from the river can give an idea of the flowing current.'⁴ Wesley would have had little sympathy with Schleiermacher's equation of religious experience and postulates of self-knowledge. He would, however, have agreed with Schleiermacher in his insistence upon man's absolute dependence, but in accordance with the whole trend of his theology he would have wanted to ask: 'Dependence upon whom?' In other words, Schleiermacher's exclusive subjectivism was as abhorrent to Wesley as the cloud-cuckoo-land of rationalist objectivism.

Wesley stressed the ethical implications as firmly as did William James but he did not maintain that religion was to be judged only by its utilitarian value. No single concept has led to greater error, for it assumes that religion is summed up in the phrase 'doing good'. 'Being good' is a more adequate definition but only when it is understood as the appropriation through faith of God's goodness whereby He is glorified.

In rejecting the view that religious experience is to be interpreted along the lines of an enlightened conscience, Wesley says

³ *Sermon* VII.1.12.   ⁴ *John Wesley in the Evolution of Protestantism*, p. 479.

that conscience is 'of an indifferent nature', and the Word of God is 'the whole and sole outward rule whereby his [man's] conscience is to be directed in all things'.[5]

Although Wesley's views on religious experience differed from those which were prevalent in his day, he never appealed to experience alone. In the New Testament the argument from experience is always placed alongside other arguments. Inward certainty is connected with an appeal to Scripture: 'For what saith the Scripture?' (Rom 4³). Sometimes this inward certainty is linked with the great fact on which it is based—the Resurrection: 'If Christ hath not been raised, your faith is vain' (1 Cor 15¹⁷). Again, he relates experience to the witness of the Holy Spirit: 'The Spirit Himself beareth witness with our spirits' (Rom 8¹⁶). This inward certainty is also connected with the results manifested in the outward life—the 'fruits of the Spirit', for these 'fruits' are the evidence that the Spirit has been received (Gal 5³²).

It may therefore be stated emphatically that it is no part of Wesley's theology to maintain that experience alone, unsupported by anything else, is sufficient to prove a doctrine. His argument is as follows: (*a*) Experience is sufficient to *confirm* a doctrine which is already *grounded* in Scripture.

(*b*) Experience is confirmed by an inward and outward witness. To the Corinthians who sought a proof that Christ was speaking in him, Paul appealed to an indirect outward witness, 'In the mouth of two or three witnesses shall every word be established', and to a direct inward witness, 'Know ye not your own selves, how that Jesus Christ is in you' (2 Cor 13¹, ⁵).

(*c*) Experience is confirmed 'by its fruit, "love, peace, joy", not indeed preceding, but following it'.[6]

Experience, therefore, is to be checked by Scripture, the outward witness of believers, the inward witness of the Spirit, and by outward holiness. There is abundant support for Lindström's observation 'that Christian experience played a most important role in his (Wesley's) theology'.[7] Bett goes much farther than this when he says: 'Methodism shifted the ultimate authority in religion to the last and the right place—to religious experience.'[8]

What then did Wesley teach about religious experience? His

---

[5] *Sermon* XII.6.   [6] *Sermon* XI.v.2.
[7] Lindström, *Wesley and Sanctification*, p. 5.
[8] Bett, *The Spirit of Methodism*, p. 93.

doctrine was based on his own experience which, in turn, was founded on the bed-rock of saving-faith. His experience led to certain especial insights, namely, that a man may be saved by individual faith alone, that a man may be absolutely sure of his salvation, and that every man may be blessed with this certain knowledge. We must now explain how these insights were revealed to him.

When John Wesley was on his way to Georgia he noted in his *Journal*, '... a new book (*Pietas Hallensis*, by A. H. Francke) is begun with Charles and company'; then he adds what appears to be an irrelevant remark—'a storm breaks'.[9] It is not, however, as irrelevant as it may seem, for Wesley's first contact with the continental Pietists meant that a storm was brewing in the sphere of theology and evangelical Christianity. Certainly a storm was needed in the religious life of England in the eighteenth century, and although it did not break until two years later (1738), there can be no doubt that it was imminent from the moment he met the Moravians.

The religion of the Moravians was characterized by a gay confidence, hope and peace, and Wesley was quick to notice the sharp difference between their buoyant faith and his own bondage to ecclesiastical law and to a rigid system which did not leave much room for 'the freedom of the Spirit'. To be told by others that he possessed faith was a very feeble guarantee where so much was at stake, and Wesley refused to listen to such comfort, preferring to wait till he was inwardly convinced of his salvation by the inward working of the Holy Spirit. The gay confidence of the Moravians was due to an inner certainty which Wesley did not possess. The assurance which was given by others of his own salvation did not fit in with his theology even at that early stage. 'If it is said that I have faith (for many such things have I heard from many miserable comforters), I answer, so have the devils—a sort of faith; but still they are strangers to the covenant of promise.... The faith I want is a sure trust and confidence in God, that, through the merits of Christ, my sins are forgiven, and I reconciled to the favour of God. I want the faith which St Paul recommends to all the world, that faith which enables everyone that has it to cry out, "I live, yet not I, but Christ liveth in me, and the life that I now live in the flesh, I

[9] *The Journal of John Wesley* (Standard edn), III.116.

live by the faith of the Son of God who loved me and gave Himself for me".'[10] Piette endeavours to prove that Wesley's conversion was not so much a receiving of saving faith as a discovery of the love of God after the Catholic pattern.[11] He has a hard task because Wesley's personal history before Aldersgate Street was marked by the most commendable good works and labours of love, by which he sought to win salvation. He had turned away from self-love and tried to love God in purity, but he did not realize that no man can love God in purity until he realizes that God has first loved him and this is impossible apart from faith, which, again, is divinely bestowed. Previously Wesley had thought of salvation as the gradual unfolding of God's purpose of love, but the cry at Aldersgate Street, 'An assurance was given me that He had taken away *my* sins, even *mine*, and saved *me* from the law of sin and death', was not so much the silent unfolding of a flower as a thunder-clap which arrested him and revolutionized his whole existence. As Luther trudged up the stairs of the Scala Santa he heard words which he never forgot: 'The just shall live by faith.' The words which Wesley heard were different, but the experience is the same: 'I felt I did trust in Christ, Christ alone for salvation.'

The question which had previously occupied Wesley's mind was: 'Can an individual soul be the channel of divine grace and know it?' After the remarkable experience on 24th May 1738 he was compelled to ask another question: 'Can *every* individual soul be a channel of divine grace and know it?' There was little doubt about the answer which Charles Wesley later put into song:

> *The grace through every vessel flows*
> *In purest streams of love.*

Divine grace operative in and through the experience of every believer was not a new Gospel but it was a forgotten one, and salvation by faith as proclaimed by Wesley was an emphatic declaration in favour of the religion of experience. Dr Rigg has pointed out that this grasp of the doctrine of salvation by grace through faith, coloured the whole of his theology, and formed the basis of his message: 'Until Wesley learned the doctrine of salvation by grace through faith, not of ourselves but as the gift

---

[10] *The Journal of John Wesley* (Standard edn), III.116.
[11] See Maximin Piette, *John Wesley in the Evolution of Protestantism*.

of God, he had been a ritualist, and it had been his doctrine that salvation was secured by moral and ritual conformity to what the Church requires.'[12] He turned his attention from the requirements of the Church to the requirements of God and this was a vital step in his career. He did not cease to be a ritualist, but he claimed that ritual and Church requirements generally were no longer necessary to salvation. Dr Rigg shows great skill in touching upon the truth which changed Wesley's entire religious outlook—the merging of the priestly office with the prophetic function: 'He was not to be a priest, observing, enforcing, carrying out a ritual; but, like the Baptist, whose priestly office was merged in his great prophetic function, he was to be a herald and a witness whose one vocation was to direct sinners away from himself, from the Church, from all else whatsoever, *to Christ*, as "the Lamb of God which taketh away the sins of the world".' 'Faith henceforth was to be his doctrine; he was to teach that men are saved by faith. But "faith cometh by hearing, and hearing by the word of God".'[13]

Certain definite conclusions emerge from these considerations, and they must now be elucidated.

(1) *The Author and Giver of Faith is God alone*

It is essential that man should recognize the divine revelation and receive the benefits of Christ's Passion, and this can only be done through faith. The authority of experience is therefore the authority of living faith. If this faith is the work of man, the criticism of those who regard it as subjective would be valid. Upon no other single truth is Wesley so definite and persistent as upon the fact that faith is God-given. Indeed, this faith can only operate in human experience when all other attempts to reach the righteousness of God are set at nought. It has been said that Bishop Butler used every argument in favour of religion except the argument from experience. He was ploughing in the sand. The fact that it was possible for an apologetic to be written which almost entirely disregarded the fact of individual experience is a significant commentary upon the religion of that century. It was Wesley's view that faith possessed an imperious authority because by faith alone does the righteousness of God become a fact of individual experience. This is something more

[12] Rigg, *The Living Wesley*, pp. 115-16.   [13] Ibid. pp. 116-17.

than an appreciation of divine revelation. In the eighteenth century revelation was regarded as a 'kindly light' which shed its gentle rays upon natural religion. That this notion persisted even in the nineteenth century is evidenced by the suggestion in Newman's hymn that Christ is no more than a light shining in the gloom as man continues his never-ending search for God. Charles Wesley's words are far removed from that insipid glorification of natural religion:

> *Believe in Him that died for thee,*
> *And, sure as He hath died,*
> *Thy debt is paid, thy soul is free,*
> *And thou art justified.* (MHB 372[2])

Revelation does not mean shedding a little light but revealing the nature of One who redeems. Further, it means that in the act of revelation something is offered to man whereby he might grasp the meaning of what is revealed to him. God and not man is the Author of all that is good. The Author of faith and salvation is God alone. It is He that works in us both to will and to do. He is the sole giver of every good gift, and the sole author of every good work. 'God gives this faith; in that moment we are accepted of God: and yet, not for the sake of that faith, but for what Christ has done and suffered for us.'[14]

(2) *Faith is the sole condition of salvation*

We may now take Wesley's argument a step farther. Man's capacity to believe in God is the gift of God. This faith saves, and nothing else does. In Wesley's words: 'Faith, therefore, is the *necessary* condition of justification; yea, and the *only necessary* condition thereof . . . the very moment God giveth faith (for *it is the gift of God*) to the "ungodly" that "worketh not", that "faith is counted to him for righteousness". He hath no righteousness at all, antecedent to this, not so much as negative righteousness, or innocence.'[15] Again he says: '. . . the covenant of *grace* doth not require us to *do* anything at all, as absolutely and indispensably necessary in order to our justification; but only to *believe* in Him who . . . "justifieth the ungodly that worketh not", and imputes his faith to him for righteousness.'[16]

---

[14] *Sermon* XX.II.13.   [15] Ibid. V.iv.5.   [16] Ibid. VI.i.8.

Now it is an undeniable fact that the Christian religion began as a revelation of God in Christ which became a spiritual experience in the lives of the first disciples. But how did this come to pass? It certainly did not come to pass through an organized priesthood. Dr Bett sums up the position thus: 'Early Christianity knew nothing of priesthood, except the completely spiritualized conception of Christ as the one great High Priest, and of all believers as a holy priesthood; nothing of sacrifice except the completely spiritualized conception of the Cross as the one perfect sacrifice for the sins of men, and of the devoted lives of believers as a living sacrifice from day to day.'[17] The revelation of God in Christ becomes a spiritual experience in the lives of believers not through the medium of an organized priesthood but by faith. Other means may be helpful but not essential; in any case they are nothing without faith. 'Do you, at all opportunities, partake of the Lord's Supper? use public and private prayers? fast often? hear and search the Scriptures, and meditate thereon? These things, likewise, ought you to have done, from the time you first set your faith toward heaven. Yet these things also are nothing, being alone.'[18] Then Wesley mentions the essential things which they had overlooked, 'Those you have forgotten: At least, you *experience* them not—Faith, mercy, and the love of God; holiness of heart; heaven opened in the soul.'[19] In this observation Wesley shows both sides of the coin of our salvation: on the one side, the mercy and love of God; on the other, faith, and holiness of heart. We must now show how intricately these two sides are related.

(3) *Faith in relation to the Righteousness of God*

Righteousness is the cause of God's action, the result of God's action, and the action itself. Let us notice how Wesley links all these together. 'Righteousness is the fruit of God's reigning in the heart; it is God's sole dominion over us; it is God's free gift for Christ's sake.' Commenting on the epistle to the Romans, Wesley says that ignorance of God's righteousness had grave results. It meant not only that they were ignorant of that holiness of heart which is, in fact, God's righteousness, but it meant that

---

[17] *The Spirit of Methodism*, p. 103.
[18] *Sermon* XXXIII.iii.3.   [19] Ibid.

they 'went about to establish their own righteousness'. This was a grave offence and held dire consequences. Seeking their own righteousness 'they hardened themselves against that *faith* whereby alone it was possible to attain it'. It was not simply that they did not seek God's righteousness; it was worse, they presumed to establish their own.

Yet this righteousness which God makes possible is known only to faith; it is not known by unbelievers. There is no ambiguity in Wesley's words on this point: 'When they believe: In that very hour the righteousness of Christ is theirs. It is imputed to every one that believes, as soon as he believes: Faith and the righteousness of Christ are inseparable. . . . There is no true faith, that is, justifying faith, which hath not the righteousness of Christ for its object.' 'To all believers the righteousness of Christ is imputed; to unbelievers it is not.'[20]

Modern biblical scholarship confirms this point of view. Commenting on Romans 1[17] Dr Anderson Scott says: 'ἀποκαλύπτεται means not "is being revealed" but "communicated" and the sense of the verse is "the righteousness of God is taking effect in the experience of men; it is an experience being gone through". ἐκ πίστεως εἰς πίστιν thereby receives its natural meaning. The righteousness of God is communicated to men "on the ground of faith to faith, faith being at once the ground on which justification is conferred and the faculty which receives it.'[21] That this experience is factual is stressed by Dr Vincent Taylor: 'For St Paul it is axiomatic that the work of God in Christ must, on the one hand, be fully in harmony with His essential righteousness, and on the other hand, must give a righteous status, which is no fiction to the man who enters into fellowship with Himself.'[22] We may now claim that two important truths have been established: that faith is the key to an understanding of Wesley's spiritual experience as it is also the key to an understanding of his theology. From these truths there emerges what can only be described as a systematic treatment of the doctrine of the priesthood of all believers. Using the same key we shall now endeavour to open the door to a fuller appreciation of this doctrine.

[20] Sermon XX.II.1.
[21] *Christianity according to St Paul*, p. 63.
[22] *Atonement in New Testament Teaching*, p. 111.

II. THE PRIESTHOOD OF ALL BELIEVERS

(1) *Faith as the Christian's Priestly Office*

In regard to this particular doctrine Luther and Wesley are one. In renouncing Dr Dorner's theory that Reformation theology is to be understood in the light of the formal and material principles, Dr Lindsay makes the following statement: 'What have been called the formal and the material principles of the Reformation are united in and spring out of this simpler but deeper impulse —the right of entrance into God's very presence. The *one principle* of the Reformation is the Priesthood of all Believers—the right of every living man and woman, whether lay or cleric, to go to God directly. . . . It was this thought—that God's presence is free to the faithful seeker—that lay at the basis of the whole round of Reformation theology.'[23] All this is true, but it is not the whole truth. When considering this doctrine we discover that the privilege of direct access to God is but one side of a many-sided gem. Our aim is to examine it from every angle.

For Luther and Wesley the ground of the priesthood of all believers is the primary authority of faith, not as excluding all other authority but as transcending it. It may justly be said that while Lutheranism has relaxed her hold upon this vital truth, Methodism has reaffirmed it both in doctrine and practice. Hildebrandt, himself of Lutheran origin, supports this view. ' "Draw near with faith" is the call of Christ; but we seem to be content with the knowledge that the door is open without ever troubling to "step in". There is a close connexion between the two Reformation doctrines of assurance and of the common priesthood of believers; and it is not incidental that both have been denied by the Roman Church and both been allowed to lapse in the history of Lutheranism. Now is the time to rediscover "the new and living way, which He hath consecrated for us" (Heb 10^{20}) and to revive the sense of our common priestly vocation. If Lutherans have sometimes been in danger of finishing their reading of Romans with the last verse of Chapter 11, the function of Wesley would be to remind them of what follows immediately in the "paraenetical" part beginning with Chapter 12.'[24]

[23] *The Reformation* (1882), pp. 185-6. [24] *From Luther to Wesley*, p. 131.

What then has Wesley to teach us? He teaches us, first, that a line of demarcation must be drawn between those who possess faith and those who do not. He refers to those who only imagine that they are Christians, but he shows that they are not really 'kings and priests'; they have the name without understanding the true experience of a Christian: 'They have been *called* so ever since they can remember; they were *christened* many years ago; they use Christian *modes of worship*; they live what is called a good Christian life, as the rest of their neighbours do.' Wesley goes on to question whether all these things make men Christians: 'And who shall presume to think or say that these men are not Christians?—though without one grain of true faith in Christ, or of real, inward holiness; without ever having tasted the love of God, or been "made partakers of the Holy Ghost"! Ah poor self-deceivers! Christians ye are not.'[25] There was much to commend them, but they had not true faith in Christ, and true faith in Christ constitutes men Kings and priests unto God. Not all the other commendable factors can accomplish this for faith alone is the Christian's priestly office and inward holiness the true mark of priesthood. Wesley had no room for the view that faith is a sober trust, or a set of opinions, or a mood of intellectual assent. 'A string of opinions', he cried, 'is no more Christian faith than a string of beads is Christian holiness.'

There is another reason why faith is regarded as the Christian's priestly office: it is faith which enables the believer to draw near to God, to pierce the veil and to see Him who is invisible. 'Faith is a kind of spiritual *light* exhibited to the soul, and a supernatural *sight* or perception thereof. . . . We have a prospect of the invisible things of God; we see the *spiritual* world, which is all round about us, and yet no more discerned by our natural faculties than if it had no being.'[26]

But if faith enables man to draw near to God, it also makes it possible for the divine revelation to pass directly from God to the believing soul. So whether we consider the matter from the manward direction or the Godward direction faith is the sole indispensable factor. '(Faith) is the internal evidence of Christianity, a perpetual revelation, equally strong, equally new, through all the centuries, which have elapsed since the Incarnation, and passing now even as it has done from the beginning, directly

---

[25] *Sermon* XXXVII.16-17.   [26] *Sermon* XLIII.II.1.

from God into the believing soul.' A proper understanding of this definition implies a revolution in religion. The keenly critical intellect of Coleridge noted its significance: 'I venture to avow it as my conviction that either Christian faith is what Wesley here describes, or there is no meaning in the word.'[27]

Faith relationship implies a direct relationship. Wesley never tired of asserting that all the ways of the grace of God act directly from the spirit of God on the secret springs of motive and will. This view has important consequences for theology. Where faith is paramount, everything else must be secondary. The view that worthiness, merit, spiritual fitness, and validity of orders must be taken into account before grace can be bestowed upon the believer, cannot be maintained. It is not to be supposed that grace is not bestowed by these means but rather that they can never be the conditions of its bestowal. Indeed, when Wesley considers the various functions of the priest, he emphatically declares that all these may be fulfilled through faith which is God's gift. It is the peculiar work of the priest to perceive God, to discern the will of God, and to lift the veil which lies on the hearts of men, yet all this is to be accomplished through faith alone. That is why faith is the Christian's priestly office.

(2) *Christ as the great High Priest*

We shall now see how the Christian's priestly office is dependent upon and closely related to the Priesthood of Christ. Ultimately all priesthood derives from Christ. Wesley had much to say on the threefold office of Christ. We must first consider what he said about it, and then discuss the interpretation which is to be placed upon his words. The message which Wesley had been called to proclaim may be summed up on the word 'Christ'. 'It is our part', he writes, 'thus to preach Christ by preaching all things whatsoever he hath revealed.' It is interesting to notice that when Wesley delineates the threefold office, it is Christ as High Priest that takes the first place. He emphasizes three important truths about Christ's priesthood:

(*a*) He is taken from among men and ordained for men, in things pertaining to God.

---

[27] W. H. Fitchett, *Wesley and His Century*, p. 427.

(b) He reconciles us to God by His blood.
(c) He ever lives to make intercession for us.[28]

In explaining the Priesthood of Christ, Wesley is at the same time propounding the three vital doctrines of the Christian religion of which Christ alone is centre—the Incarnation, the Atonement and the Ascension. 'He is taken from among men.' It was necessary for Him to 'become like unto his brethren' (Heb 2^{11-13}) in order that He might be ordained for them in things pertaining to God. The purpose of the Incarnation was the Atonement, and the great High Priest offers Himself as the only perfect Sacrifice in order to reconcile us to God. Having ascended on high, our High Priest is engaged in a continuous activity of intercession, so that day by day His presence and power and prayer are made available to us. Christ, therefore, belongs to us altogether, as the incarnate Lord, the crucified Lord, and the ascended Lord.

He is Prophet as well as Priest.
As Prophet He helps us in two ways:

(a) He is made unto us wisdom.
(b) By His word and Spirit He is with us always, guiding us into all truth.

Christ is also King as well as Priest and Prophet. What does His kingship mean?

(a) He gives laws to all whom He has bought with His blood.
(b) He restores to the image of God those whom He has first reinstated in His favour.
(c) He reigns in all believing hearts until He has 'subdued all things to Himself'.

Christ then is Priest, Prophet and King, and in these offices the people share.

As soon as we understand the meaning of these words we will know the meaning of His office, work and dignity. Early was our Lord's kingship asserted, for the wise men sought a king. When the prophets spoke of the coming of the Messiah, they always used the expression: 'Behold thy king cometh unto thee.'

---

[28] See *Sermon* XXXVI.1.6.

Christ revealed Himself as a king when he stood before Pilate even though He admitted that His Kingdom was not of this world. Indeed, He rejected the sort of kingship which was envisaged by the Jews (Jn 6^{15}), and it is just when He stands before His judge that we speak of Him as King. He is the King of the outcast, the captive, the sinner, and He reigns through suffering. This is a different kind of kingship. Judgement, suffering and death assert rather than deny His kingship. Moreover, it is the suffering King who is the ruler at the last day (1 Cor 15^{24}). If, therefore, Christ delivers up the kingdom to God at the end, He must be king *now*. His office does not change, and the One who is King at the end must also be King now. This truth, surely, is not in doubt; what is in doubt is the ability of man to understand it and his willingness to recognize it. Christ is the king for all eternity—that is the simple truth.

Psalm 110^4 says, 'Thou art a priest for ever after the order of Melchisedec', and Psalm 2^7 says: 'Thou art my son, this day have I begotten thee.' The letter to the Hebrews joins together the ideas in these two Psalms (5^{5-6}) where the exact words are quoted. This means that the dignity of Jesus as the Son seems to include His priestly office. This is important because it shows that Christ did not put Himself in this office but was chosen of God (Heb 5^4). It is because of His priestly sufferings that He gains the kingly glory at God's right hand. As the Son, He comes from God; as Priest He is 'taken from among men', and there is no contradiction between the two. Now if there is one word which is used more than any other to describe a believer in the New Testament it is the word 'son', and is this a privilege which involves no responsibility or commitment or obligation? Does not our sonship include our priestly office as in the case of our Lord? Surely, this must be so. To speak of Christians as priests and kings is not to emphasize the circumference but the very centre of the Christian message.

Wesley is fond of saying that faith appropriates the 'whole Christ', by which he means that there is no way other than faith whereby we may receive more, and that we receive Christ in all His offices. This is important because it implies that nothing is outside the range of living faith. It strikes at the heart of the belief that there are other blessings to be received in other ways. No other way exists. 'It is of faith (whether we term it the *essence* or rather a *property* thereof) that we receive Christ; that we receive Him in all His offices, as our Prophet, Priest and King. It is by this that He is made unto us wisdom and righteousness, and sanctification and redemption.'[29] Or again: '. . . a deep conviction of our utter *helplessness*, of our total inability to retain anything we have received, . . . teaches us truly to live upon Christ by faith, not only as our Priest, but as our King. Hereby we are brought to "magnify him", indeed; to "give him all the glory of his grace"; to "make him a whole Christ, an entire Saviour; and truly to set the crown upon his head".'

(3) *Succession as the Christian's Priestly Heritage*

An understanding of this phrase involves the investigation of the Methodist doctrine of the Ministry. Methodism recognizes the need for an order of ministry in the Church, but resists most strenuously the notion that any single system can guarantee the validity of the Ministry. If this were possible, it would mean that the system surpassed in importance the truth it was meant to safeguard. Any such theory breaks the second commandment, for the worship of a system is idolatry.

Further, Methodism does not accept the view that episcopacy and apostolic succession are synonymous terms. Modern Methodists have little sympathy with Charles Wesley's gibe:

> *How easily are bishops made*
> *By man or woman's whim!*
> *Wesley his hands on Coke hath laid,*
> *But who laid hands on him?*

John gave an effective reply: 'I firmly believe that I am a Scriptural *episcopos* as much as any man in England or Europe.'[30] The adjective is significant because Methodism starts with Scripture in its interpretation of episcopacy. How, then, does Methodism interpret the word '*episcopé*'? It asserts that *episcope* includes the pastoral oversight of the flock—teaching, preaching, the care of souls, and other functions essential to the ordering of a Christian society. In the *Methodist Principles of Church Order*, it is affirmed: 'Episcopy, in the broader definition . . . comes little short of being the complete ministry of service of the Church, both to those

---

[29] *Sermon* XIV.III.4.
[30] Townsend and Workman, *New History of Methodism*, I.231.

within and to those that are without. The first principle on which Methodism has laid emphasis is that Episcopy, *in its fullness or perfection belongs to the whole Church*, so that all its functions will be duly exercised only if every member of the Church is bearing his part and doing his duty. The ideal Church does not consist of an active few—the ordained clergy and the passive many, the laity who are just content to be recipients of benefits from their clergy: all are called to *serve* in the Church of Christ.'[31]

This idea that only the whole Church may express ideally and perfectly the true meaning of Episcopy does not imply that Methodism leaves no room for a separated ministry. On the contrary, the Methodist Catechism asserts that Christ fulfils His purpose through faithful members—through ministry and laity alike. In answer to the questions: 'What is the Ministry of the Church?' the Catechism states: 'The ministry of the Church is the continuation of Christ's own ministry *through the whole membership of the Church* . . . exercised by all those ordained to the care of souls, the preaching of the Word, and the administration of the sacraments, by those fulfilling particular functions in the ordered life of the Church, *and* by all members in their worship and service.'

The true relation of the universal priesthood to the ministry is laid down in the Deed of Union: 'Christ's Ministers in the Church are Stewards in the household of God and Shepherds of His flock. Some are called and ordained to this sole occupation and have a principal and directing part in these great duties but they hold no priesthood differing in kind from that which is common to the Lord's people, and they have no exclusive title to the preaching of the Gospel or the care of souls. These ministries are shared with them by others to whom also the Spirit divides His gifts severally as He wills.'[32]

This statement continues: 'The Methodist Church holds the doctrine of the priesthood of all believers and consequently believes that no priesthood exists which belongs exclusively to a particular order or class of men but in the exercise of its corporate life and worship special qualifications for the discharge of special duties are required and thus the principle of representative selection is recognized.'[33] The emphasis, therefore, is on the succession of believers which Methodism believes to be truly apostolic.

[31] Pp. 5-6.   [32] Pp. 22-3.   [33] Ibid.

'Methodism has maintained its witness to the Apostolic Faith in worship, doctrine, sacraments, personal life, and fellowship. While it recognizes the place of "order" in the preservation of unity and continuity of the Church, its main emphasis is upon the succession of believers who have answered the call of God in Jesus Christ and who rejoice and share what they have found with others. Such a nexus of Christian believers, all learning the secret of God's personal dealing with us through Jesus Christ and passing it on to others, is in the true succession from the apostles and is within the one Church.'[34] It is within the context of a universal fellowship of believers that Methodism understands and interprets the nature and mission of the Church. 'Our spiritual ancestry goes back through a multitude of saints which no man can number. . . . Behind each believer of today there stretches a long chain, each link a Christian man or woman, till we find ourselves with the first disciples, in the company of the Lord Himself. Through such a succession of believers Methodists may echo the confession of one of the early Apologists: 'Christians trace their genealogy from the Lord Jesus Christ.' In these genealogies there is no distinction between laymen and ministers, men and women. Indeed, all Christians may be priests in this holy Office.'[35]

Aristides (A.D. 125), however, not only stated the fact of the Christian's spiritual genealogy but he also emphasized the plain obligation which is laid on all believers and which was gladly accepted by the twelve disciples: 'Christians trace their genealogy from the Lord Jesus Christ, who had twelve disciples who went out into all the world and discoursed on his majesty.' The Methodist doctrine of apostolic succession begins here: twelve men believed the truth and went forth to proclaim it. Faith and proclamation are intimately united. Acceptance of the Faith involves its proclamation in life and word, witness and worship, sacrament and vocation. True continuity depends upon fidelity to apostolic truth and this is to be found in the faith and experience of believers.

(4) *Prayer as the Christian's Priestly Privilege*

All Christians are priests in virtue of their access to God. This

---

[34] *Message and Mission of Methodism*, p. 17. (Conference, 1943).
[35] *The Nature of the Church according to the Methodists*, p. 32 (Conference, 1937).

means that there is no caste with the exclusive right to this approach. Anglicans, Congregationalists, Presbyterians and Methodists of South India speak with one voice upon this truth, for the following statement was incorporated in the constitution of the Church of South India: 'All members of the Church have equal access to God. All, according to their measure, share the heavenly High Priesthood of the risen and ascended Christ from which alone the Church derives its character as a royal priesthood. All alike are called to continue upon earth the priestly work of Christ by showing forth in life and word the glory of the redeeming power of God in Him. No individual and no one order in the Church can claim exclusive possession of this heavenly priesthood.'[36] In the words of Dr G. G. Findlay: 'Those who share Peter's faith share his power. Each confessor of the Son of God is empowered to open to the penitent, so far as human hands may, that gate of faith through which he himself has passed.'[37] Dr Whale considers that this is not only a privilege but a bounden duty: 'All of us have our inalienable priesthood as believers; unless we are ambassadors for the faith we are not holding the faith.'[38]

Our Lord's priesthood involves continual intercession for His people. The organization of Methodism leaves room for meetings for corporate prayer. Here all believers exercise their ministry of intercession which is their high privilege. The Church must ever seek to identify itself in true sympathy with men and women in their need, standing beside them, suffering with them, sharing their burdens, and as the world's representative before God, interceding for the world and offering its life to God on behalf of all. This is the Christian's priesthood, and every Christian ought to pray in the words of the great high priestly prayer: 'For their sakes I sanctify myself.' Less than this is not enough. Our Lord, 'ever liveth to make intercession' for us, and this is regarded as the privilege of one who sits at the right hand of God. This is the privilege granted to One who said, 'I am come to do Thy will, O God', and fulfilled these words in every aspect of His life. It was His perfect obedience to God which made possible the continual ministry of intercession. Our obedience to the Father's

---

[36] *Scheme for Church Union in South India*, p. 29.
[37] *Nature of the Church according to the Methodists*, p. 21.
[38] Whale, *What is a Living Church?*, p. 62.

will opens up to us inestimable privileges so that we also may share the intercession of Christ which is going on all the time; this is the priesthood which all believers share with their Lord. Hence Charles Wesley's hymn, quoted in his brother's sermon on 'The Repentance of Believers'.

> *He ever lives above,*
> *For me to intercede.*

(5) *Ministry as the Christian's Priestly Service*

Universal priesthood implies a plurality of ministries, for the New Testament words 'minister' and 'ministry' are applied widely to the most varied types of Christian service.[39] In 1 Corinthians the ministries are described as apostles, prophets, teachers, miracles, gifts of healing, helps, governments, diverse kinds of tongues; in the Epistle to the Ephesians, as apostles, prophets, evangelists, pastors, teachers. These lists testify to the rich variety of the ministries exercised in the early Church. This view is confirmed by Protestants generally: 'Every single Christian has a ministry bestowed upon him by Christ.'[40] Since the gift of the Holy Spirit is given to all Christians each has a definite ministry to fulfil. 'While thus maintaining the Ministry as an office, we do not limit the ministries of the New Testament to those who are thus ordained but affirm the priesthood of all believers and the obligation resting upon them to fulfil their vocation according to the gift bestowed upon them by the Holy Spirit.'[41] This is what Protestants mean when they say with Whale: 'We stand in the apostolic succession of all believers.'[42] Another Protestant, Dr Fairbairn, has put this truth in memorable words: 'Over against their official priesthood, let us place the spiritual priesthood, the office and the function at once common and sacred to all believers. . . . Let us feel, every man of us, that we are priests, standing before God for men, before men for God. Let us create in our Churches the feeling that they are priestly bodies, where every man by watching and prayer, by personal communion with God and loving intercourse with men, can help to work

---

[39] *The Nature of the Church according to the Methodists*, p. 21.
[40] *The Catholicity of Protestantism*, p. 104.
[41] Ibid. p. 35.
[42] *What is a Living Church?*, p. 52.

the reconciliation of humanity and God. Over against their organized sacerdotal society, let us place our Christian brotherhood, our commonwealth of saints, where every man is free to exercise all his rights and bound to fulfil his every duty. And finally, over against their theory of the continuity of the apostolic succession, let us set our faith in the continuity of religious life, which makes us possess the truth and hold communion with the saints of all the churches, share in and sympathize with all the good of all ages.'[43] This is no mean doctrine of the function of the Church. To labour by every possible means for the reconciliation of humanity to God; to seek the realization of a universal fellowship, and in a spirit of broad toleration, to recognize and appreciate the saints in all churches and in all ages, are aims and ideals which we cannot afford to ignore, and which are vital aspects of our common priesthood. Not only in St Paul's letters (Rom 12^{4-7}, 1 Cor 12^{4-28}) but in 1 Pet 4^{10} we find that the possession of any gift was regarded as implying a debt to others, the discharge of which would be a ministry. There were vital implications in this for the future of religion in England and even farther afield. If religion was not infallibly based upon the activity of any recognized apostle, or upon any humanly contrived system, or upon any outward authority, but upon personal allegiance to Christ as Head, and upon the belief that the 'Spirit bloweth where it listeth', it follows that any man who is truly dedicated to Christ may be moved by the Holy Spirit and thereby called to serve one or other of the various ministries of the Church. The most thoroughgoing application of these basic principles that has ever been attempted in the history of Christendom was undertaken by John Wesley, and it is to his credit that the doctrine of the universal priesthood, often misunderstood and sometimes forgotten, passed from the realm of theological speculation into the very constitution and day-to-day practice of the Church. He was unaware of the tremendous consequences of the revolution in theology and practice which his work was sure to effect, but some of the consequences were very clear indeed. One of these was the firm belief that the idea of the succession of believers inevitably led to the view that Christians were the 'servants of mankind'. In Von Hugel's words: 'Spiritual experiences are like a great living Cloth of Gold with not only the woof going from

---

[43] Fairbairn, *Studies in Religion and Theology*, p. 138.

God to Man and from Man to God, but also the warp going from man to man.'[44] Methodism has always been mindful of the horizontal as well as the vertical dimension of priesthood.

(6) *Mission as the Christian's Priestly Obligation*

Christians, then, should view their priesthood in the light of their Lord's. Just as Christ is sent into the world, ordained of God to fulfil a special *mission* for mankind, so also the Christian is commissioned to fulfil the mission with which he is entrusted. Indeed, it is only in the light of Christ's vocation, Christ's priesthood, that we rightly understand the true meaning of the Church's vocation. Obviously, Jesus possesses a unique vocation, being taken from among men and ordained of God. He revealed God. It is also true that God chose Israel (the people of God's possession) to be, in fact, His own people. God has a special purpose for them—they must show the people of the earth who He is. Now the priests of the Old Testament were the liaison between God and the people, and the High Priests wore the names of the tribes of Israel on their breasts. When, therefore, the Lord promises that Israel will become a Royal Priesthood and a holy people, this means that Israel will be the means in God's hands of fulfilling the priestly service on behalf of all the people. The choice of Israel does not imply the rejection of other nations; on the contrary, it implies their acceptance, for immediately before they were called 'a kingdom of priests' (Ex 19^6), they were told, 'for all the earth is mine' (Ex 19^5). It was the duty of Israel to bring home this truth to all nations, and it is in this sense that she was pre-eminently the servant of God. The fact that Israel was chosen of God does not mean that she will be specially protected, but rather that her responsibility is increased, for it is the measure of her inestimable privilege. Israel is regarded as holy unto the Lord only as she is conscious of the mission to which she is committed. The same is true of the New Israel. Mission is the Christian's priestly obligation. But in referring to the similarity between the Old and New Israel, we must not overlook the contrast.

Priesthood implies holiness unto the Lord. There is another aspect of Wesley's teaching which is relevant. In ancient times the Jewish priest drew near with a sacrifice, and in the new

[44] Quoted in H. B. Workman, *Place of Methodism in the Catholic Church*, p. 86.

priesthood the believer draws near to sacrifice every part of his life to God. This spiritual surrender is the token of perfect love. In the early days it was fatal to draw too near to God; now it is a crime to stay away. So the Christian makes his offering not out of fear, but because he loves God with all his heart and soul and mind and strength. 'A pure and holy heart is a sacrifice with which he [God] is always well pleased. But he is always well pleased with all that outward service which arises from the heart; with the sacrifice of our prayers (whether public or private), of our praise and thanksgivings; with the sacrifice of our goods, humbly devoted to him, and employed wholly to his glory; and with that of our bodies, which he peculiarly claims, which the Apostle beseeches us, "by the mercies of God, to present unto him, a living sacrifice, holy and acceptable unto God".'[45] Hence the Christian sings with Charles Wesley:

> *Take me, whom Thyself hast bought,*
> *Bring into captivity*
> *Every high aspiring thought*
> *That would not stoop to Thee.*

Yet this offering is incomplete and inadequate unless it involves a priestly service toward all mankind. The mission of Methodism is universal and turns its members into 'servants of mankind'. Methodism declares that this priestly service is only fulfilled if evangelism becomes the concern of every Church member. It is not any Order in the Church but the whole Church which gladly embraces this responsibility and sings:

> *My heart is full of Christ, and longs*
> *Its glorious matter to declare!*
> *Of Him I make my loftier songs,*
> *I cannot from His praise forbear.*

Bready's observation rings true: 'To the Second Reformation . . . the priesthood of all believers bore a vital significance, for was not every convert a mediator and missionary of the cause of Christ? And one of its marked manifestations was its capacity for creating "lay saints" to whom prayer and spiritual meditation became instinctive, and to whom Christian altruism became the necessary concomitant of Christian faith.'[46]

---
[45] *Sermon* XXIV.III.I.   [46] W. Bready, *Before and After Wesley*, p. 297.

Wesley's two famous maxims have been indelibly impressed upon all true evangelical tradition:

(a) The Gospel of Christ knows no religion but social, no holiness but social holiness.
(b) I look upon the whole world as my parish.

Concerning the first, Wesley himself said: 'Christianity is essentially a social religion; and . . . to turn it into a solitary religion, is indeed to destroy it. . . . When I say: This is essentially a social religion, I mean not only that it cannot subsist so well, but that it cannot subsist at all, without society—without living and conversing with other men.'[47] Religion is both inward and social, and these two elements are always present in Wesley's writings. No doubt this is why Wesley always spoke of 'The People called Methodists'. There is nothing individualistic or sectarian implied in this phrase. Indeed, far from stressing an individualistic subjectivism, the Methodist conception of the Church as the People of God, or as the Society of Believers, is so deep-rooted that many people see in it the very ethos of Methodism. Such is Dr Workman's view: 'In his system of class meetings the basal principle of individual experience was saved from excess by the correction given through the experience of others, as well as the spiritual obedience demanded by the whole congregation and framework of his societies. . . . In an effective practical fashion the experience of the whole Church is brought to bear upon the isolated feelings of the separate member. In the working of Methodism the appeal to individual experience is ever checked and balanced by the appeal to collective experience.'[48] For Methodism, therefore, the priesthood of all believers is not simply a catch phrase or loosely held theory, but a practical reality and a necessary element in the day-to-day life and witness of the Church.

We must now consider the second maxim. What was the doctrine which inspired and became the driving force of this world-wide evangelistic activity? Bready gives the answer: 'The Priesthood of all believers, once more, as in Apostolic days, constrained every faithful convert to become a missionary.'[49]

---

[47] *Sermon* XXIV.I.I.
[48] Townsend and Workman, *New History of Methodism*, I.29.
[49] Bready, *Before and After Wesley*, p. 448.

Following in the steps of Spener, Methodism placed the responsibility for Christian witness and instruction upon the lay Christian. So Spener and Wesley realized that if they were to fulfil the vital mission committed to them, they could only do so by harnessing and marshalling all their resources in a single, overriding and all-important task. They knew that this could only be done by strengthening the priestly service and prophetic testimony of the whole Christian community, and both of them were swift to notice that the theological basis of their work was the same for them as it was for Luther—the universal priesthood.

(7) *Praise as the Christian's Priestly Offering*

By faith the believer draws near to God (Rom 5^{1-2}), and apart from faith there is no way to God. By faith he inherits the promises (Heb 6^{12}). By faith he receives the salvation of his soul (1 Pet 1^9). All who accept Christ through faith are partakers in the new priesthood. The Mosaic barrier between the High Priest and the people is broken down and Christ as our forerunner (Heb 6^{20}), invites us with 'boldness to enter into the holiest' (Heb 10^{19}). This new priesthood of which we partake through faith constitutes, in Wesley's words, 'a congregation ... of *faithful men* ... men endued with *living faith*',[50] Christ shares all things with those who believe in Him. As He is Son, Heir and Priest, so His followers are sons, heirs and priests. Being a priest, then, is the same as believing in Christ or being a Christian, though for Luther's 'We are all priests by Baptism', we prefer to substitute, 'We are all priests by Regeneration', which is Wesley's view. Through faith comes the new birth which consecrates each individual as a priest of Christ, for he is one who partakes of the redeeming grace of Christ and will be set in God's kingdom. There is ample evidence for this in the 1739 edition of Wesley's hymns. In Hymn 642 the Christian's priesthood is synonymous with regeneration:

> *O that all were taught of God,*
> *All anointed by Thy grace,*
> *Kings and priests redeemed with blood,*
> *Born again to sound Thy praise.*

[50] *Sermon* LXXIV.16.

The same connexion of ideas is also to be found in Hymn 16:

> *O what an age of golden days!*
> *O what a choice peculiar race!*
> *Wash'd in the Lamb's all-cleansing blood,*
> *Anointed kings and priests to God.*

The blessings of salvation are applied to the hearts of believers by the Holy Ghost as is clearly stated in this verse:

> *We, through the Holy Ghost, can witness better things,*
> *For He, whose blood is all our boast,*
> *Hath made us Priests and Kings.*

It will be noticed that in each verse Christians are anointed as Priests and Kings by the merits of the Sacrifice of the great High Priest, which means that our priesthood does not exist independently of His.

If on the basis of His Priesthood we are priests, also on the basis of His kingship we share the reign of Christ on earth. This also is linked with our regeneration: we share the kingship of Christ on account of our New Birth.

> *On all the kings of earth*
> *With pity we look down;*
> *And claim, in virtue of our birth,*
> *A never-fading crown.*

Upon this verse Dr Flew makes the apt comment: 'Our connexion with Christ makes us truly imperial.'[51]

It is in the central act of the Church's worship—the Lord's Supper—that every member of the Royal Priesthood is called to take his part in the priestly service of the whole Church. This being so, there is little wonder that in the mind of Charles Wesley the Royal Priesthood is closely connected with the Lord's Supper. Indeed, nowhere is the universal priesthood of all believers stated more explicitly than in the following Eucharistic hymn:

> *Ye royal priests of Jesus rise,*
> *And join the daily sacrifice;*
> *Join all believers in His name*
> *To offer up the spotless Lamb.* (No. 177.)

---

[51] R. N. Flew, *Jesus and His Church*, p. 235.

Two points are of particular importance in this verse: firstly, the phrases 'royal priests' and 'all believers' are found in it—a very rare occurrence indeed. Secondly, it shows that Wesley believed (and throughout his turbulent career there is no evidence that this belief was modified) that the Eucharist meant an offering up of the spotless Lamb. At the same time it must be noticed that the offering was not made by a priest of a particular line but by all believers. This, it must be confessed, was very significant indeed for a man of Charles Wesley's churchmanship. But the words are clear: 'Join all believers in His name.' Whether we consider this central act of the Church as a re-presentation of Christ's Sacrifice or as a representation of it, it is most important to remember that it is the sacrament of the Royal Priesthood. While Methodists in no sense under-rate the significance of Holy Communion, it is perhaps fair to say that the last line of the verse quoted, 'To offer up the spotless Lamb', cannot be regarded as characteristic of Methodist doctrine on this subject today. Most Methodists would probably be happier with another verse of Wesley's where the emphasis is rightly upon what Christ has already done for us rather than upon anything that we can do:

> *We need not now go up to heaven,*
>   *To bring the long-sought Saviour down;*
> *Thou art to all already given,*
>   *Thou dost e'en now Thy banquet crown:*
> *To every faithful soul appear,*
> *And show Thy real presence here.*

The penultimate line may serve to introduce another of Charles's hymns which contains a curious phrase.

> *How richly is the table stored*
> *Of Jesus, our redeeming Lord!*
> *Melchisedec and Aaron join*
> *To furnish out the feast Divine. . . .*
>
> *'Tis here He meets the faithful line,*
> *Sustains us with the bread and wine;*
> *We feel the double grace is given,*
> *And gladly urge our way to heaven.*[52]

[52] J. E. Rattenbury, *Eucharistic Hymn of John and Charles Wesley*, pp. 209-10.

Dr Rattenbury points to the difficulty in the following words: 'The problem is whether "the faithful line" can be identified with the outward successive priesthood or with the Church in its priestly character as expressed in the phrase "the priesthood of all believers".' Dr Rattenbury himself accepts the first interpretation and Dr Ryder Smith the second. There are two reasons for supporting the second interpretation: the first is that the context suggests it, and the second is that it is more in accordance with the idea of Melchisedean priesthood.

(1) The context must be decisive. This is where the words of a previous hymn shed some light.

> *To every faithful soul appear,*
> *And show Thy real presence here.*

As far as believers are concerned much depends upon the reality of the experience implied in those words. Are these words confirmed in the experience of believers? Does Christ in reality appear to every faithful soul? We sing, 'All may of Thee partake', and by this we mean that Jesus meets not only chosen representatives but all who draw near with faith. This being so, we must affirm that 'The faithful line' refers to all believers.

(2) Further, it must be remembered that Abraham, the ancestor of Israel, was blessed by Melchisedec and paid tithes to him, and therefore Melchisedec's claims were higher than those of the regular Aaronic or Levitical ministry. In the words of Milligan: '*He* (Melchisedec) belonged to a more spiritual and universal economy than that in which Israel had been placed. . . . He belonged to a date when he could discharge the duties of a priesthood wide as the world, and when no member of the human family was excluded from the benefits of his priestly rule.'[53] The Epistle to the Hebrews makes it clear that the priesthood of Melchisedec is spiritual, universal, and royal. We may assume that while Aaron represents the narrower Judaistic priesthood, Melchisedec represents the wider universal priesthood of all believers.

The universal aspect of this priesthood is referred to in another hymn which speaks of 'A heaven-born race of priests', which is strikingly reminiscent of Justin Martyr's reference to Christians as 'A true high-priestly race'.

[53] W. Milligan, *The Ascension and Heavenly Priesthood of Our Lord*, pp. 8ff.

> *O God let all my life declare*
> *How happy all Thy servants are;*
> *How far above these earthly things,*
> *How intimately one with God,*
> *A heaven-born race of priests and kings.*

Charles Wesley has much to say on the continuing High Priesthood of Christ after His Ascension, but he looks backward as well as forward and finds in the Old Testament as well as the New the Christ of whom both bear witness. Christ, the Priest, is the substance of which the shadows only are to be seen in the Old Testament. Doubtless Charles Wesley would have endorsed the sentiments of one of his contemporaries who wrote:

> *Teach me to love Thy sacred word,*
> *And view my Saviour there.*[54]

Indeed, the activity of Jesus in saving His people and working through them was manifest from the beginning:

> *Two shadows of one substance see!*
> *The Lord who sets His people free,*
> *Persists to save the ransomed race;*
> *Jesus doth all the work alone,*
> *Our Captain and High Priest in one,*
> *In Joshua fights, in Moses prays.*

Yet it is upon the continuing priesthood of Christ that he loves to dwell.

> *Entered the holy place above,*
> *Covered with meritorious scars,*
> *The tokens of His dying love*
> *Our great High-priest in glory bears.*

There is neither need nor room for any merit of ours in the light of His 'meritorious scars'.

Having stated that our Lord has entered heaven, Wesley goes on to explain the reason why He ascended and the work which He continues to do:

[54] Anne Steele (1716-78).

> *He ever lives above,*
> *For me to intercede.*

Even in 'that holy happy place above' it is still the Sacrificed Lamb who pleads for us all:

> *O Thou eternal Victim, slain*
> *A sacrifice for guilty man,*
> *By the eternal Spirit made*
> *An offering in the sinner's stead;*
> *Our everlasting Priest art Thou,*
> *And plead'st Thy death for sinners now.*

If our Lord is the Sacrificed Lamb, He is also the victorious Priest and in that victory His followers share. The promises given to 'him that overcometh' in Revelation 2^{17} and 3^{12} are to be linked with the victorious declaration of 20^6 that 'they shall be kings and priests unto God'. Charles Wesley had the first two passages in mind when he wrote:

> *Thy nature, gracious Lord, impart;*
>   *Come quickly from above;*
> *Write Thy new name upon my heart,*
>   *Thy new, best name of love.* (*MHB* 550.)

Those who thus overcome and upon whose heart is written the new name share Christ's reign while they are yet in the world. They are conquerors of the world (Rom 8^{37}) and sit in heavenly places (Eph 2^6):

> *By the Spirit of our Head,*
> *Anointed priests and kings,*
> *Conquerors of the world, we tread*
> *On all created things;*
> *Sit in heavenly places down,*
> *While yet we in the flesh remain*
> *Now partakers of Thy throne,*
> *Before the Father reign.*

Nor can Wesley's characteristic teaching on Christian Perfection be separated from the doctrine of the priesthood of believers. To be sure, Charles did not always agree with his brother that

Christian Perfection was an experience possible in this life, yet it was Charles who wrote:

> *O glorious hope of perfect love!*
> *It lifts me to the things above,*
>   *It bears on eagles' wings;*
> *It gives my ravished soul a taste,*
> *And makes me for some moments feast*
>   *With Jesu's priests and kings.*

There is in many of Wesley's hymns a pervading reference to the sacredness of all secular tasks, for these are hallowed if they are linked, as in some sense they must be, to His Sacrifice. Thus he sings:

> *Jesus this mean oblation join*
> *To Thy great Sacrifice.*

Indeed, it is only when every work and word proclaims the goodness of God, and when 'holiness unto the Lord' is written not only on the High Priest's robes but on every heart, that the priesthood of all believers is truly expressed.

> *O that every work and word*
>   *Might proclaim how good Thou art,*
> *Holiness unto the Lord*
>   *Still be written on our heart!*

We do not find that the world-wide mission of the Church is specifically named as a function of the Royal Priesthood, yet it is surely significant that immediately after his commission to preach every Methodist preacher hears the strains of Monsell's hymn:

> *As labourers in Thy vineyard,*
>   *Lord, send them out to be,*
> *Content to bear the burden*
>   *Of weary days for Thee. . . .*
>
> *Make them a Royal Priesthood,*
>   *Thee rightly to adore,*
> *And fill them with Thy fullness*
>   *Now and for evermore.*

Perhaps no verse sums up the universal mission of Methodism more effectively than Annie Matheson's missionary hymn:

> *Tell every man on earth,*
> *The greatest and the least,*
> *Love called him from his birth,*
> *To be a king and priest.*

So, waiting and hurrying, the Church goes forth to meet her great High Priest, for the End of things is the day when all men are conscious of the priesthood which is theirs in Christ.

> *See where our great High-Priest*
> *Before the Lord appears,*
> *And on His loving breast*
> *The tribes of Israel bears,*
> *Never without His people seen,*
> *The Head of all believing men.*

In him all priesthood inheres, and the Priest is never seen without the Church which is a priesthood.

(8) *Experience as the Christian's Priestly Authority*

The stress upon the individual experience of the believer is not a denial of the collective experience of the Church. It is a false antithesis which separates them. In fact, one is the complement of the other. Charles Wesley does not see any real problem here:

> *Joined to the hidden Church unknown,*
> *In this sure bond of perfectness,*
> *Obscurely safe, I dwell alone,*
> *And glory in th' uniting grace,*
> *To me, to each believer given,*
> *To all thy saints in earth and heaven.*[55]

The current controversy which is related to this very point was initiated by the authors of *Catholicity*, who state: 'Hence it is a distortion of apostolic doctrine to say that men are *first* united to Christ through faith, within an invisible society of the truly faithful, and *then* find admission to the visible Church. The right order is not: Christ—faithful individuals—the Church; but:

[55] *The Poetical Works of John and Charles Wesley*, VI.71.

Christ—the Church—faithful individuals.'[56] This view is based on a sermon by Archbishop Frederick Temple in which he states: 'The Church takes its origin, not in the will of man, but in the will of the Lord Jesus Christ. . . . Everywhere men are called in: they do not come in and make the Church by coming.' Protestants generally will have little quarrel with this statement, but they will not all agree that the statement made by the authors of *Catholicity* follows from it. The doubtful theology of a well-known hymn sets the problem in perspective:

> *Rise up, O men of God!*
> *The Church for you doth wait,*
> *Her strength unequal to her task;*
> *Rise up and make her great.*

Of course, men do not make the Church great; the Church is the Lord's; and the rising up of a thousand men will not make the Church greater, nor enhance the majesty of Christ. On the other hand, men are not called into the Church but into fellowship with Christ. Nor are they called *en masse* unless we are prepared to sacrifice the primary meaning of the sacrament of Baptism.

Bishop Aulén, however, asserts categorically that modern Lutheranism fully agrees with the time-sequence suggested by the authors of *Catholicity*. 'Obviously the accusation of a want of catholicity is based on the idea that Lutheranism has an individualistic view of the relation between the individual Christian and the Church. However, according to a well-known utterance of Luther, the Church is "the Mother who gives birth to and fosters every individual Christian". That is no casual remark: on the contrary, it expresses clearly what Luther really thought. If the Church is the Mother who gives birth to every Christian, the individual cannot possibly be prior to the Church. Luther's statement emphasizes the dependence of the individual on the Church, and the antecedence of the Church in reference to the individual. Therefore the order must be precisely the order that *Catholicity* describes as catholic: Christ—the visible Church—the individual Christian.'[57]

On the other hand, the authors of *The Catholicity of Protestantism*

---
[56] Op. cit. p. 13.   [57] *World Lutheranism Today*, p. 4.

give a different answer: 'We agree without hesitation that in order of time, "Christ—faithful individuals—the Church", repudiated by the Archbishop and the authors of *Catholicity*, is entirely false. But the order which they substitute for it, "Christ —the Church—faithful individuals", is just as false. It is indefensible to erect a temporal sequence as though the Church came first and Christians after. It seems to depend on the erroneous identification of the Kingdom and the Church. The truth is that the Church is there at Pentecost because the Spirit promised for the last days has entered the lives of those who have faith in the person and promise of Christ. From henceforth there cannot be faithful individuals before there is a Church, nor a Church before there are faithful individuals. The Church is the New Israel, the community of the last days, and that community is now a visible community in abiding union with the divine life.'[58]

Set in the context of Pentecost, it is difficult to see how the Church and the individual Christian may be separated, for although the Spirit was poured out upon all flesh (Acts 2^{17}), 'it sat upon each of them' (Acts 2^3). Nor can it be doubted that the Spirit came upon them that believed; 'All that believed were together.' In fact, Pentecost gave birth both to the individual believer and the Church, and therefore the individual and communal aspects of the experience of Pentecost are inextricably joined.

The truth is to be found in Charles Wesley's lines:

> *Christ, from whom all blessings flow,*
> *Perfecting the saints below,*
> *Hear us, who Thy nature share,*
> *Who Thy mystic body are.*

This is the true relationship: Christ perfects the saints below, who are, in fact, His mystic body, the Church. Although the members are closely related to the Body, it is a mistake to treat them as identical. Important as is the metaphor of the Church as the Body of Christ in New Testament theology, it must be remembered that it is not the only metaphor, and it holds serious dangers when it is regarded as an exclusive and a conclusive argument. Often in Catholic thought and sometimes even in Pro-

---

[58] Op. cit. p. 22.

testant theology, the idea of the Church as an extension or a continuation of the Incarnation has been prominent. This tendency has often resulted in a reduced Christology. The idea that Christ is reincarnate in the life of the Church is plain heresy. The Church is not and cannot be a substitute for Christ. The idea of the Church as a continuation of the Incarnation is based upon the view that grace operates mechanically in the institution. Individual faith becomes redundant and the question of the integrity of the Church's representatives becomes irrelevant. The consequence of all this is that the idea of the Church as a company of pardoned sinners is forgotten.

The medieval Church was a vast ecclesiastical corporation through which salvation was offered to man. The inexorable corporation was everything, the individual was nothing. Faber makes this clear out of his own experience: 'In the Roman Church the individual realized the peace which passes all understanding as he thus escaped from the burden of his individuality, and found rest from storm and passion in the consciousness of his oneness with an innumerable company of others, holier, wiser, stronger than himself.' Dr Torrance's view that 'the expression "priesthood of all believers" is an unfortunate one as it carries with it a ruinous individualism'[59] may be a timely warning, but the phrase must be considered in the light of the historical circumstances. Luther as well as Wesley was faced with an equally ruinous transcendentalism, a sort of 'saving' machine, an infallible corporation, and this conception could only be countered by stressing the paramount importance of the inner life of the individual. 'For whatever else justification by faith may mean, it stands for the claim that between the individual and his Saviour no corporation, no priest, no sacrament, no saints may intervene.'[60] It is not the verdict of history that this view is 'ruinous'. History rather confirms that in asserting the Crown Rights of the Redeemer as well as the spiritual privileges of the individual believer, Luther and Wesley were not mistaken.

All the same, it is when we try to define more closely the individual's relation to God that difficulties arise. There is a case for the view that Methodism completed the work of the Reformation. In answer to the vital question: 'Where does authority

---

[59] T. F. Torrance, *Royal Priesthood*, p. 35 note.
[60] *A New History of Methodism*, I.9.

lie?' Luther often gives the impression that it lies with the individual. At other times he asserts the authority of the Bible. Sometimes he seems to conclude that authority rests with the State, and he is not inconsistent in holding this view since he believed that the Princes in all their dealings were exercising their priestly function as members of the Royal Priesthood. All the same, it seemed very much like the rule of law, and in this sense it was an appeal to an objective and external authority. This most certainly implied a weakening of the original stress upon the need of individual faith.

On the other hand, when the Dutch Church declared the Netherland Confession as an infallible symbol, authority, again, was regarded as wholly external. Zwingli flatly rejects the idea that authority lies with Rome and takes the view that it rests with an inerrant Church. 'The true Church', he says, 'is certainly inerrant because it does nothing in accordance with its own desires, but always what the Holy Spirit ordains. The Gospel which is proclaimed in the Church was dictated by the Holy Spirit and therefore cannot err.' If these statements by Zwingli were beyond dispute, the question of authority would be solved forthwith. If the Church is comprised, as Zwingli thinks, of individuals who cannot err, their status as individuals of independent judgement is instantly brought into question, and the question also arises as to the difference between a Roman infallible Church and Zwingli's inerrant Church.

In this matter Calvin does not greatly help us. Salvation, according to his view, depends no longer upon the act of the individual, but upon immutable decrees. Yet if all human actions are limited and conditioned before all time by a sovereign decree, what, we may well ask, becomes of the individual? Apparently, the individual is eliminated altogether. Calvin did not, of course, aim at this conclusion, but it was the only one that was left as the logical outcome of his reasoning.

The Methodist emphasis upon the necessity of individual living faith does not in any sense minimize the value of the corporate experience of the Church. The Church is not a collection of isolated individuals, it is a priesthood of believers. Priesthood expresses the corporate experience and function of the Church, while the term 'believers' refers, as it says, to those who believe, and expresses the living faith which is the basis of any spiritual experience individual or corporate. As Dr Griffith Thomas has observed:

'The truth, therefore, is that Christianity *is*, not *has*, a priesthood.⁶¹' The distinction made here is of the utmost importance. The Church as a whole is a corporate body, and the fact that it *is* a priesthood is the only indisputable warrant for its spiritual and organic unity, whereas the statement that the Church *has* a priesthood may easily militate against that sense of unity which is envisaged here. The idea that the Church has a priesthood, may easily lead to the thought that it is something which may be lost, or that it may be dispensed with, or possibly outgrown. The statement that the Church *is* a priesthood, however, does not leave any room for doubt about the matter; it is a final and irrevocable fact. It is only by the indwelling of the Spirit in believers that the Church becomes a spiritual house, wherein are offered up 'spiritual sacrifices acceptable to God through Jesus Christ'. This unity in Christ lifts personal religion to a higher plane. 'The whole life of Christ is given to the Church *in solidum:* the Spirit, the New Life, the Priesthood, everything, belongs to each as it belongs to all.'⁶²

III. SERVANTS OF MANKIND

Having considered the various ways in which the doctrine of the Priesthood of all Believers has been emphasized in Methodist theology, we must now endeavour to show its practical outworking in the everyday life and witness of the Church. The doctrine has been implemented in three different directions: in the proclamation of the Gospel, in the layman's acceptance of pastoral responsibility, and in a strong sense of the universal mission of the Church.

(i) *In the Service of the Word*

If the claim that is made in the *New History of Methodism*, namely that 'Wesley renounced the apostolic succession and reasserted the priesthood of all believers',⁶³ how did this fact influence his subsequent actions? He saw more clearly than any of his contemporaries that the root of religion was not to be found in

---

[61] Griffith Thomas, The Catholic Faith (Intro).
[62] J. A. T. Robinson, *The Historic Episcopate*, p. 14.
[63] Op. cit. I.228.

form and system but in dynamic spiritual experience. He saw, as did Luther before him, that the phrase, 'the liberty of the Christian man', must become a reality and not simply a pious hope or a meaningless shibboleth. Yet in the eighteenth century the Law dominated the Gospel, and obedience to canon Law had once again superseded obedience to Christ. Cold philosophic maxims were substituted for the living flame of the Evangel. The true Gospel seemed strange even to those who had been commissioned to proclaim it. Wesley's message was not recognized as truth in a world which had already forgotten the vital issues of the Reformation. Theologically, Wesley's task was a simple one—it was to reassert the principles of the Reformation; in practice, it was formidable because the orthodox method of proclaiming them was denied him. On the whole, Anglicanism had failed, and was as unconscious of its failure as was the Roman Church in the sixteenth century. The blind, it seemed, were leading the blind, and twice in two centuries all had been in danger of falling into the ditch of apathy and unbelief. Wesley's doctrines which held at least part of the answer to the confused moral and spiritual ideas of the age, were unacceptable, and consequently, the doors of the established Church were closed both to him and his followers. Yet those very followers, especially Bowers, Nelson, Maxfield, Mather and Olivers were preaching the Gospel with power and with signs following.

For a high Churchman of Wesley's sort all this presented a grave problem: was he justified in permitting these men to preach? Although at first he was genuinely baffled, he was wise enough to see in this new development the solution of an even greater problem. He knew that great good may be accomplished for the kingdom of God through the help of these dedicated men. They were often criticized. 'But they are uneducated', said the Archbishop of Armagh. 'Some are,' replied Charles Wesley, 'and so the dumb ass rebukes the prophet.'[64] Their lack of education did not prevent them from becoming instruments of divine power. Ultimately Wesley grew weary of the unreasonable and vitriolic attacks upon his helpers: 'Soul-damning clergymen', he cried, 'lay me under more difficulties than soul-saving laymen.'[65] Then he made a statement which shocked Christendom as it had not been shocked since Luther married the nun Catherine von Bora

[64] *New History of Methodism*, I.293. [65] Ibid. I.321.

in 1525. In a letter to Alexander Mather, he wrote: 'Give me one hundred preachers who fear nothing but sin, and desire nothing but God, and *I care not a straw whether they be clergy or laymen, such alone will shake the gates of hell and set up the kingdom of heaven upon earth.*'[66] Yet Wesley was greatly exercised in mind concerning the question of the 'call'. Were the lay preachers inwardly and individually called or not? Were the dangers of acknowledging this insuperable? The preachers of the established Church did not help Wesley to make up his mind. 'Now, that many of the clergy, though called of man, are not called of God to preach the Gospel is undeniable. First, because they themselves utterly disclaim, nay, ridicule the inward call; secondly because they do not know what the Gospel is; of consequence they do not and cannot preach it. That I have not gone too far yet, I know, but whether I have gone far enough, I am extremely doubtful.'[67] Even these remaining doubts were banished when he heard his mother's opinion upon the matter. In 1741 Wesley had hurried from Bristol to London when he had heard that Thomas Maxfield had been preaching. This was nothing short of a scandal and Wesley was about to censure him. His mother, who had heard Maxfield, quietly advised him: 'Take care what you do with respect to that young man, for he is as surely called of God to preach as you are. Examine what have been the fruits of his preaching, and hear him also yourself.'[68] Susanna did not realize that this statement was to bring about a revolution in John's thinking, not because her words rendered ordination unnecessary but because the emphasis was shifted in such a way as to place the inward call and the fruits of preaching *before* ordination. In Methodism it has remained so ever since. Wesley returned to this question of the fruits of preaching in a sermon entitled: 'A Caution against Bigotry.' If a man shows fruits for his preaching, if devils are cast out and lives transformed—

1. Do not forbid him because he is not of our party. There is an echo of his mother's words in what follows: 'Beware how you attempt to hinder him, either by your authority, or arguments, or persuasions. Do not in anywise strive to prevent his using all the

---

[66] *The Letters of John Wesley*, VI.271-2.
[67] *New History of Methodism*, I.321.
[68] Simon, *John Wesley and the Methodist Societies*, p. 25.

power which God has given him. If you have *authority* with him, do not use that authority to stop the work of God.[69]

2. Do not forbid him because he is a layman. Wesley asks: 'But what, if he be only a layman, who casts out devils! Ought I not to forbid him then? ... Is there reasonable proof that this man has or does cast out devils? If there is, forbid him not; no, not at the peril of your soul. Shall not God work by whom he will work? No man can do these works unless God is with him? unless God hath sent him *for this very thing*. ... If you must needs acknowledge "that a notable miracle hath been wrought"; then with what conscience, with what face, can you charge him whom God hath sent, "not to speak any more in His name"?'[70]

3. Do not forbid him because he possesses no outward authority. 'I allow, that it is highly expedient, whoever preaches in his name should have an outward as well as an inward call; but that it is *absolutely necessary*, I deny.' Then Wesley poses two questions which call for an answer: what are we to understand by the text: 'No man taketh this honour unto himself, but he that is called of God, as was Aaron' (Heb 5⁴). Wesley holds that when used in relation to preaching, the quotation is unfortunate, for 'Aaron was not called to preach at all; he was called "to offer gifts and sacrifices for sin".'[71] This problem must be viewed in the light of Wesley's age. He was not contending that an outward commission was unnecessary, but stressing the fact that refusal by the religious authorities to recognize a preacher's inward call, and consequently their refusal to ordain him, did not invalidate the preacher's call.

The second question was: 'What was the practice of the apostolic age?' Wesley quotes Acts 8²: 'There was a great persecution against the church which was at Jerusalem; and they were all scattered abroad throughout the regions of Judea and Samaria, *except the Apostles*.' His keen insight swiftly grasped the significance of the last three words. Verse four states not only that they were scattered but also what they did: 'Therefore they that were scatted abroad went everywhere preaching the word.' 'Now were all these,' asks Wesley, 'outwardly called to preach? No man in his senses can think so. Here then is an undeniable proof, what was the practice of the apostolic age. Here you see

---

[69] *Sermon* XXXVIII.iii.4.   [70] Ibid. iii.5-6.   [71] Ibid. iii.7.

not one, but a multitude of Lay Preachers, men that were only sent of God.'[72]

It would be a serious mistake to assume from these facts that Wesley was a fanatical anti-clerical revolutionary. Nothing is farther from the truth. A man less like a fanatic has never been born. Deep and eternal truths were at stake and Wesley summoned all his powers to fight for them. After 1738 he had little room for the sacerdotalism which had meant so much to him. He was prepared to fight to the death the view that the Church had gained power over God. When someone told him that it was sacrilege to preach the saving Gospel outside the churches, he replied: 'Church or no Church, we must save souls.' The Church, the sacraments, preaching, teaching, neighbourly love, were means whereby God's grace was made available for man: for in all these the love of God could be seen in action. But the means must not be elevated to a place higher than grace, nor must the means be regarded as possessing power in themselves. Wesley is explicit upon this truth and it is questionable whether the implications of his statement have ever been fully appreciated. 'Before you use any means, let it be deeply impressed upon your soul—there is no *power* in this. It is, in itself, a poor, dead, empty thing; separate from God, it is a dry leaf, a shadow. Neither is there any *merit* in my using this, nothing intrinsically pleasing to God; nothing whereby I deserve any favour at his hands. . . . But, because God bids, therefore I do.'[73]

The priestly and prophetic offices are not separate in Wesley's thought. Preaching is an expression of the Christian's priestly office. Preaching is eternal truth expressed through finite means. This priestly-prophetic office may be exercised either by a minister or a layman. Wesley maintains that our Lord's ministry, properly understood, is that of the Priest-Prophet, and this is why he stresses that Christ must be proclaimed in all His offices. 'To preach Christ, as a workman that needeth not to be ashamed, is to preach him, not only as our great High Priest, . . . but likewise as the Prophet of the Lord.'[74] Methodism is not alone in seeing the close connexion between these two offices. Dr Payne has shown that the offices of priesthood and prophecy are connected in all

---

[72] *Sermon* XXXVIII. para. 8. [73] *Sermon* XVI.v.4.
[74] *Sermon* XXXVI.1.6.

the Free Churches: 'This belief in the freedom of the Church under the guidance of the Spirit has led to an emphasis of the priesthood of all believers. The Free Church has constantly insisted on the responsibilities of all the Church members, and has been ready to make the fullest use of the leadership of "lay" men. . . . There is to be linked with this the emphasis on preaching—on the proclamation of the Gospel—and on evangelism—the constant and sustained attempt, shared in by all believers, to spread the knowledge of the Gospel by every means in their power.'[75]

One of the responsibilities laid upon the Church is that of the proclamation of the Gospel, and in the Free Churches preaching has been regarded as a function of the common priesthood. In Presbyterianism, however, few laymen exercise this gift. In Congregationalism and in Baptist Churches there are more lay preachers than in Presbyterianism, but it must be clearly affirmed that it is one thing to accept the principle of lay preaching but an entirely different thing to apply that principle by permitting 25,000 persons to exercise that ministry as is the case in modern Methodism. Nor is there anything haphazard in the manner of their appointment. They are men and women who are conscious of an inward call and whose call is confirmed by the Church. They are examined in Scripture and Theology and undergo intensive training for this high task. John Wesley's test of the 'fruits of preaching' is applied to each one, and they are publicly recognized in the presence of the whole congregation as preachers of the Gospel. Their office is recognized in the following words: 'We give you the right hand of fellowship in token of welcome by the Church and in recognition of your *place* and *office* as preachers therein.'[76] In their hands is placed the true and final authority of every preacher: 'Take now, at our hands, this Holy Bible; and may He who gave the Word give you grace, wisdom and power to proclaim truth even as truth is in Jesus.'

It will undoubtedly be noticed that Methodism has advanced an important step beyond the English Reformers in that it has not only accepted the principle of lay-preaching, but has appointed and recognized an Order of Lay Preachers whose

---

[75] *The Free Church Tradition in the Life of England*, p. 145.
[76] 'Order of Service for the Public Recognition of Local Preachers', *Methodist Book of Offices*.

METHODISM 225

services are employed and gratefully acknowledged week by week.

Luther also connects the priesthood of all believers with the call to preach. He asserts that it is this doctrine which is the basis of the Christian's right to preach. There has never been, however, as far as preaching is concerned, a thoroughgoing application of the doctrine among the laity of Lutheranism. There seem to be two reasons for this: (i) The Lutherans distinguish between the Apostle of the early Church and the modern Apostle. (ii) The doctrine of the priesthood of believers has tended to remain in the sphere of dogma and has not become a practical factor in the life of the Church.

The truth of the first of these is effectively stated by Hildebrandt. Having stated that God's people 'limited the Holy One of Israel', he continues: 'This limitation has again in Lutheranism taken one particular turn of fateful importance. The Reformers are very emphatic in their assertion that the believer, preacher or layman, is not an apostle; our vocation is not like theirs, immediate, but mediated through the written Word; our discipleship in following Christ is of a different, secondary kind; our "succession" cannot in the same direct way lay claim to the privileges and powers which Christ gave to those who were His early companions.'[77] Methodism knows no such limitation of the term 'apostle', for the gift at Pentecost enabled all to become apostles. 'If Protestants have been eager to point out that the power conferred upon Peter (Mt 16[16]) was not confined to him, but applied equally to the other apostles (Mt 18[18]) they also ought to notice that this "breathing of the Spirit" takes place upon all the disciples, not only the twelve, and that the sphere of His direct "influence" is no more restricted in time than it is in space. What right have we to pick and choose the "general" promises in the New Testament from the "special" ones reserved for the Apostles without once more committing the sin of "limiting the Holy One of Israel?"'[78]

> *Lord, we believe to us and ours*
> *The apostolic promise given.* (*MHB* 274[1])

This being the case, Methodism not only goes one step beyond the English Reformers but also a step farther than the Continental Reformers, not only in banishing once and for all the false dis-

[77] *From Luther to Wesley*, pp. 140-3.   [78] Ibid. p. 143.

tinction between 'early' and 'modern' apostles, but also in calling upon the Churches to exercise their apostleship and *be* apostles. The opportunity is given to all. Christians may exercise their apostleship by using the gifts which God bestows upon them and by obeying the command: 'Go ye into all the world and preach the Gospel.' Though all are not called to preach, all *may* be called.

(2) *In the service of the Church*

Preaching, however, is not the only sphere wherein spiritual gifts may be exercised. It was Wesley's view that service in the Church was service for mankind. Large numbers of people who had embraced the Faith were waiting to be encouraged, instructed and nurtured in the truths of the Gospel. How was this to be done? There is no doubt whatever that in answering this question Wesley learned much from Zinzendorf at Herrnhut. Zinzendorf owed much to Luther. Zinzendorf saw that it was the Cross alone which made the Gospel the power of God unto Salvation. Even the oft-abused 'blood and wounds' theology leads straight back to all that followed from Luther's acceptance of Staupitz's advice: 'Begin from the wounds of Christ.'

The influence of Spener and Franke also is clearly seen in the whole pattern of the teaching of the Renewer of the Church of the United Brethren. Zinzendorf embodies the true prophetic-evangelical type of piety characteristic of German Protestantism. Of these special characteristics there are four:

(1) The instinct of homely colloquy with God.
(2) The Preaching of the Word.
(3) The simple converse and spiritual exercises in company with like-minded souls.
(4) The warm and cheerful devotion to Jesus the Lord and Saviour.

The absorbing passion of Zinzendorf's life was to promote fellowship among all believers. 'The only ground for the existence of a Church is that it may create and promote fellowship among souls who live in a state of ardent love and obedience to the Saviour.'[79] Again he says: 'I appoint you as your rendezvous the

---

[79] W. G. Addison, *The Renewed Church of the United Brethren*, p. 24.

heart of our Saviour, and for guide, his holy life.' There were two potential hindrances to fellowship—ignorance of spiritual things and autocracy. Zinzendorf contrived to offset these dangers by forming classes for instruction, and by asserting once for all the source of true authority. The danger that the Chief Elder might become 'a Protestant Pope' in his own community was averted by the famous decision on 16th September 1741 in Red Lion Street, London: 'That the office of General Elder be abolished and be transferred to the Saviour.'[80]

For the purpose of instruction and fellowship, Classes and Bands were formed. These were not identical. The Bands were free unions open to the more earnest souls seeking a richer fellowship. They were usually a small group of three to seven people who met to 'converse heartily and kindly over their whole hearts with one another . . . for more complete nurture in the Lord'. On the other hand the Classes were *compulsory* groupings based on sex and age and usually consisted of seven to eleven persons. In general the Classes were for the training of those who were new in the Faith—for their instruction and edification; the members of the Bands were engaged in advanced Bible Study and in seeking to apply the truths they learned to the theological and pastoral problems in the life of the community. The members of the Band were like a General Staff on the battle-field: 'Watchful and careful they viewed all parts of the battle array and endeavoured to fix their field dispositions so as to throw back the enemy. . . . By virtue of their Band organization, they marked which individuals the enemy sought to alienate from their fellowship. At these points they focused their cares in prayer, exhortation and punishment and thus very often gave timely assistance to the weaker brother and sister.'[81]

Wesley was sufficiently familiar with the good fruits of this system which he had personally witnessed at Halle and Herrnhut to be convinced of its many possibilities, and he was determined to make the fullest use of these principles which were thoroughly suited to the nascent Methodist organization. At present Classes are often known by another name but their purpose is the same. There is little doubt that as a training-school for new converts, as a battle-school of evangelism, as an opportunity for thorough

[80] W. G. Addison, *The Renewed Church of the United Brethren*, p. 55.
[81] Ibid. pp. 24-5.

biblical study, and as a means of intimate Christian fellowship after the apostolic pattern, the Class and Band system is still unrivalled.

There was another reason why Wesley laid much stress upon the necessity of these groups for fellowship. It was not only that he had seen it work in Germany, but he had noticed, in the same country what happened when such a system was absent. Of his visits to some of the Roman Churches in Germany he writes: 'I was a little surprised to observe that neither in this (Cologne), nor in any other of the Roman Churches where I have been, is there, properly speaking, any such thing as joint worship; but one prays at one shrine or altar, and another at another, without any regard to or communication with one another.'[82] Of course there is room for private worship but it surely holds many perils if it is regarded as a substitute for corporate worship. John had definite ideas about fellowship and Charles turned them into song:

> *Why hast Thou cast our lot*
> *In the same age and place,*
> *And why together brought*
> *To see each other's face;*
> *To join with loving sympathy,*
> *And mix our friendly souls in Thee? (MHB 716²)*

Let us now examine Wesley's idea of spiritual fellowship.

Anglican Religious Societies and Methodist Fellowship

These meetings for spiritual fellowship and edification in the Faith were not new. Such meetings began at Pentecost, and they have never been entirely absent from the Church since those early days. The Friends of God, the Little Brothers of St Francis, the Religious Societies in the Anglican Church of the eighteenth century, the Pietists of Halle and Herrnhut, were formed with the same general purpose in view—to deepen faith, to effect instruction, and to strengthen the bonds of fellowship. Indeed the Anglican Religious Societies were known as classes for 'practical divinity'. Wesley's distinct contribution was that he equated the 'fellowship of believers' with the Church. Classes were not regarded as isolated groups meeting independently of the Church,

[82] *Journal*, II.8.

they *were* the Church. The sum of all the Classes was the Church, and each class was an epitome of the fellowship of the whole. No single word more adequately describes Methodism than the word 'fellowship'.

The difference, then, between the aforementioned movements and Methodism is inescapable. The Franciscans became an Order; Pietism waned after the death of Spener and Franke, not because its principles were faulty but because no leader emerged who was able to integrate those principles into the life of the Lutheran Church as a whole; the Religious Societies failed, partly through faulty aims and partly as a result of failure in fellowship on the part of the Anglican Church, which missed an opportunity of the greatest moment. 'The children were come to birth and there was no strength to bring them forth.' Methodism became not an Order or a Sect, but a Church.

It may be asked: 'Did not the layman play a prominent part in the Religious Societies?' The answer is in the affirmative but the main reason why he did so was because of the difficulty of finding clergy who were interested in religion as 'the life of God in the soul of man'. It was a different matter in Methodism. Laymen became members and even leaders of the Methodist Classes not because the ministers were indifferent but because the priesthood of all believers entitled laymen also to lead and teach and exercise spiritual oversight within the Society. Christ was the Head of the fellowship by whom they were drawn together, and in such a gathering all distinctions vanished. No wonder the opening hymn was almost always:

> *Love, like death, hath all destroyed,*
> *Rendered all distinctions void;*
> *Names, and sects, and parties fall:*
> *Thou, O Christ, art all in all.*

So Wesley laid down one of the basic principles of Methodism: 'The necessity of a living fellowship in the realities of Christian experience, in order to nourish the life of God in the soul and to enrich the Body of Christ.'[83] Further, 'Christianity is essentially a social religion and to turn it into a solitary one is to destroy it. . . . It cannot subsist at all without society,—without living

---

[83] *Rules for the People called Methodists.*

and conversing with other men.'[84] The example of the Moravians and his own study of Scriptural doctrine, led Wesley to this exclusive emphasis upon the fact of spiritual fellowship as the basis of religion. That this emphasis was not misplaced was borne out by Wesley's colleague and friend, George Whitfield, who commented near the close of his life: 'My brother Wesley acted wisely. The souls that were awakened under his ministry he joined in class, and thus preserved the fruit of his labour. This I neglected and my people are a rope of sand.'[85]

The truth is, however, that it was not Whitfield's lack of organization only but also defective theology which brought about this failure, since the doctrine of absolute divine sovereignty with its corollary of immutable decrees deprives a man of the stimulus to seek fellowship, and tends rather to promote indifference and sloth. Fellowship could not, by the very nature of Calvinistic theology, mean the same to Whitfield as it meant to Wesley.

To the ecclesiastical mind the danger of Bands and Classes was that they could exist without priestly direction and control. But this fact was the glory, not the bane, of Methodism. It did not mean that the authority of the minister was surrendered, but that the laymen being 'priests unto God' were able voluntarily to share the work to which the minister was committed in a life-long vocation. Dr Rattenbury has noticed the importance of this: 'No Church system, while liberating the minister for an independent response to his vocation, has given better opportunities to laymen for the service of God and their fellows.'[86] It should also be remembered that the gifts of 'teaching' and 'helps' were given to believers in addition to the gift of 'prophecy', so Wesley had New Testament sanction for marshalling the powers of laymen in the service of the fellowship classes of the Church. The call to pastoral responsibility was added to the call to preach.

In fact, the leader of the class was generally a layman. In the words of Dr Workman: 'The open fellowship of believers in prayer, meditation and praise, is of none the less value (than personal testimony) both for the building up of the Church and for maintenance of the more public worship. Over every class

---

[84] *Sermon* XXIV.v.1. [85] Quoted by W. B. Brash, *Methodism*, p. 54.
[86] *Wesley's Legacy to the World*, p. 141.

there was a leader, generally a layman, who, though not ordained for this office is solemnly and deliberately chosen.'[87]

The Classes and Collective Experience

The Class system has sometimes been criticized on the ground that it led to individualism, introspection, and developed into exclusive holiness sects. No movement is without its dangers but the charge of individualism is odd. Dr Bett has stated the position with characteristic vigour: 'There has probably never been in the whole history of the Church of Christ, any community where religious fellowship was quite so real or so deep as it has been in Methodism, and, in the face of such a fact, to accuse the movement of excessive individualism seems a little queer.'[88] The truth is that the class meetings were not organized for individual experience but for collective experience, and indeed, collective experience was only possible in the orientation of such fellowships. It may even be claimed that Wesley's teaching and institutions flourished because they held the balance between individualism and collectivism in religion. It was Wesley's strong sense of the corporate experience of the Church which held his allegiance to the Anglican Church to the end of his life. As Dr J. E. Rattenbury truly remarks: 'One of the reasons why Wesley never failed to insist on the Ancient Services and Sacraments of the Church was that they embodied the collective experience of centuries. Wesley believed that experience was no less experience because it happened to be corporate.'[89]

From all this we may conclude that the priesthood of all believers is the very ethos of the class meeting. First, the leadership was open to all believers—ministers or laymen. Second, each member was permitted to exercise his priesthood by taking an active part in prayer, praise and testimony, and, finally, the testimony of each member was strengthened and confirmed by the whole believing community.

(3) *In the service of the World—*
Service to one's neighbour

We have seen how Methodism calls all believers into the service of the Word (the call to preach); and into the service of the

[87] *A New History of Methodism*, I.120.   [88] *The Spirit of Methodism*, p. 90.
[89] *Wesley's Legacy to the World*, p. 1.

Church (the call to pastoral responsibility); we must now consider in what sense all believers are called into the service of the World (i.e. the service of neighbourly love).

Man was created to enjoy fellowship with God. It is only in God that he may find peace, satisfaction and happiness. It is Wesley's view that God is the sole object of human love. All else becomes a means to this end. After 1738 Wesley began to work out how this view affected love to our neighbours. The proper order is: God's love to man—man's love to God—neighbourly love. Even in works of piety or works of charity man's sole intention must be the glory of God. They will, of course, increase the happiness of man, but that is their secondary and not their primary motive.

There is a wide difference between Wesley's conception of love and that of William Law, the mystic. Love, according to the mystics, was often equated with drastic asceticisms, and this involved a frequent preoccupation with self. Law writes: 'The immediate, essential, necessary means of uniting men to God are prayer, mortification and self-denial.' Wesley thought of love in a social context and as something which was offered to God in the service of one's neighbour. Lindström has pointed out that Wesley thought of neighbourly love as operating in three concentric circles which are:[90]

(1) Love within the Christian congregation.
(2) Love within the universal Church.
(3) The Love which embraces all mankind.

(1) *Love within the Christian congregation*

The Christian in the first circle is described by Wesley as follows: 'He is fixed in his congregation as well as his principles. He is united to one, not only in spirit, but by all the outward ties of Christian fellowship. There he partakes of all the ordinances of God. There he receives the supper of the Lord. There he pours out his soul in public prayer, and joins in public praise and thanksgiving. There he rejoices to hear the word of reconciliation, the Gospel of the grace of God. With these his nearest, his best-loved brethren, on solemn occasions, he seeks God by fasting. These particularly he watches over in love, as they do over his

[90] See Lindström, *Wesley and Sanctification*.

soul; admonishing, exhorting, comforting, reproving, and every way building up each other in the faith. These he regards as his own household.'[91] This view of the visible Church represented by the fellowship of believers in the local congregation held wide consequences which, if Wesley saw them, he did not feel the time was ripe to apply them. The single mark of the Church is holiness. The fellowship of believers is the place where God is active by the Holy Spirit, where faith responds and holiness is the outcome. These factors—the activity of the Spirit of God and the response of faith do not only function among a small section of men who happen to be religious although they undoubtedly find their driving force there. It is in this fellowship of believers, this congregation of saints, that these important functions take place consistently and without hindrance. It is not so much in the community at large that this interaction of the divine Spirit and human response takes place, but in the fellowship of believers. Now the fellowship of believers must always be distinguished from non-believers. In fact, this distinction is only possible in a Free Church. Perhaps Wesley knew this, but even if he did, he was not prepared to carry this view to its logical conclusion. It was left to his followers to work out in practice what he had set out for them in doctrine. If we allow Wesley's basic premise—that the Church is a fellowship of believers, we cannot avoid the conclusion that a Free Church was the only possible outcome. The opposite view is to believe that the Church becomes the nation in its totality which means an equation of State and Church—a view which has resulted in confusion and compromise wherever it has been turned into a fact. The mark of the visible fellowship of the Church was always the same—holiness.

(2) *Love within the universal Church*

Neighbourly love, however, must not be confined to the small circle in which the Christian worships and finds the most intimate spiritual fellowship, it must be wider. So another circle is drawn which embraces all who love God through Christ: 'Love me', says Wesley, '. . . not only as thou lovest all mankind; not only as thou lovest thine enemies, . . . not only as a stranger; . . . love me with a very tender affection, as a friend that is closer than a

---

[91] *Sermon* XXXIX.III.3.

brother; as a brother in Christ, a fellow-citizen of the New Jerusalem, a fellow-soldier engaged in the same warfare, under the same Captain of our salvation. Love me as a companion in the kingdom and patience of Jesus, and a joint-heir of His glory.'[92] This second circle must of necessity cross the boundaries of race, colour and language. The fellowship of *all* believers means what it says—the fellowship of believers throughout the world. It does not simply refer to a visible fellowship. If Methodists require Wesley's warrant for their keen interest in the ecumenical movement, it is to be found here. The experience of God's love to man, resulting in sanctification, becomes the foundation of the unity of Christians. The fellowship of all Christians is based on love as the fruit of faith. This ecumenical feature is seen soon after 1738. In *The Character of a Methodist* (1742) he writes: 'By these marks, these fruits of a living faith, do we labour to distinguish ourselves from the unbelieving world, from all those whose minds or lives are not according to the Gospel of Christ. But from real Christians, of whatsoever denomination they be, we earnestly desire not to be distinguished at all, not from any who sincerely desire to follow after what they know they have not attained. No. "Whosoever doeth the will of my Father which is in heaven, the same is my brother, and sister and mother." And I beseech you brethren that we be in no wise divided among ourselves. Is thy heart right as my heart is with thine? I ask no further question. If it be, give me thy hand. For opinions, or terms, let us not destroy the work of God. Dost thou love and serve God? It is enough. I give thee the right hand of fellowship.' The second circle, then, means that Christian fellowship is based on neighbourly love between all Christians.

(3) *The Love which embraces all mankind*

There is another circle that is wider still, for it embraces all men everywhere. It encircles not only race, colour and language, but creed also. A Christian may love the brethren in the local congregation because they are visible to him, and he may love his Christian brethren throughout the world because of the unseen spiritual bonds which make them one, but does his love reach out

[92] Sermon XXXIX.II.3.

to all mankind? In this as in all things the Lord must be his pattern:

> *The arms of love that compass me*
> *Would all mankind embrace.*

The Christian's love to God is demonstrated by his neighbourly service to all mankind. Every conceivable obstacle is swept away by the mighty love which living faith has brought into his heart. 'The Christian's heart', as Wesley, puts it, 'is full of love to all mankind.'[93] Every man may look forward to spiritual liberation.

> *Since the Son hath made me free,*
> *Let me taste my liberty. (MHB 568.)*

Yet all the freedom he has is the freedom to give, love and live, and the real criterion of his spiritual freedom is his capacity to become a servant of mankind. Charles expresses this in sublime verse:

> *Not in the tombs we pine to dwell,*
> *Not in the dark monastic cell,*
>   *By vows and grates confined;*
> *Freely to all ourselves we give,*
> *Constrained by Jesu's love to live*
>   *The servants of mankind.*

Indeed the 'altogether Christian' is one who has learned to love his neighbour. 'If any man ask, "Who is my neighbour?" we reply, Every man in the world; every child of His who is the Father of the spirits of all flesh. Nor may we in anywise except our enemies, or the enemies of God and their own souls. But every Christian loveth these also as himself, "as Christ loved us".'[94]

Wesley develops the full meaning of Catholic love when he says: 'His (the Christian's) heart is enlarged toward all mankind, those he knows and those he does not; he embraces with strong and cordial affection neighbours and strangers, friends and enemies. This is catholic or universal love. And he that has this is of a catholic spirit. For love alone gives the title to this character: catholic love is a catholic spirit.'[95]

Neighbourly love is the priestly service which man renders to

---

[93] Wesley's *Description of a True Methodist*.   [94] *Sermon* II.II.2.
[95] *Sermon* XXXIX.III.4.

God. Not in this way does man attain salvation, but rather in this way does he express the love which God has given. No man may take unto himself any glory for this service. No, as the Apostle puts it: 'It is God who is at work within you, giving you the will and the power to achieve His purpose' (Phil 2^{12}; Phillip's Trans.).

Thus Wesley called the Methodist people to share with him the pressing obligations of neighbourly service. Only disinterested Christian love can turn the world into the kingdom. It is the Christian's high privilege to employ in God's service every gift of God and above all, to love with all his heart and soul and strength, which is, in fact, what Wesley meant by Perfect Love. Living faith is the key to man's relationship with God; disinterested love is the key to the Christian's relationship with man.

How far Wesley was influenced by Luther in his teaching on this particular subject we do not know, but the close harmony of their views may be noted from the following words of Luther: 'In so far as the Christian is free, he requires to do nothing. In so far as he is a servant, he must do everything.'[96] 'All that we do must be designed for the benefit of our neighbour, because each one has sufficient for himself in his faith. Other deeds or another kind of life are unnecessary to himself, and so he may serve his neighbour out of unconstrained love.... To my neighbour, I will be as a Christian, what Christ has become to me, and do just what I see is needful, helpful or acceptable to him, for I have enough in Christ for my faith.'[97] Commenting on Luther's doctrine of neighbourly love, Dr Whale makes the apt remark: 'All is of God and all is for God, but the divine $\dot{\alpha}\gamma\dot{\alpha}\pi\eta$ comes down from the eternities as a parabolic curve which returns thither by way of human priesthood; the priesthood of all believers one to another.'[98] Upon this question Luther and Wesley speak with one voice, and we are nearest to New Testament teaching when we are nearest theirs.

We may summarize our findings as follows: Beginning with the assumption that Methodist theology is essentially empirical, we discovered that Wesley followed Luther in stressing the primacy of Faith. We also found that Faith was the basis of Wesley's interpretation of the doctrine of the priesthood of all believers,

---

[96] Lee Woolf, *Reformation Writings*, p. 369. [97] Ibid. p. 375.
[98] *The Protestant Tradition*, p. 98.

which is clearly enunciated both in the sermons of John and the hymns of Charles. Further, we noticed that the practical out-working of the doctrine is to be seen in the proclamation of the Gospel, in Church organization, and in that sense of universal mission which has always been a predominant characteristic of Methodism. Thus in the service of the Word, in the service of the Church and in the service of the World, the priesthood of all believers is fulfilled.

6

Conclusions and Reinterpretation

FROM THIS historical survey we may draw the following conclusions:

(1) No single Church has been able to express in its worship, work, and witness, the full richness of this doctrine.

(2) The doctrine has been a living issue in each century since the Reformation.

(3) It is a unitive, positive, and comprehensive principle which springs directly from the Evangelical concept of 'free grace'.

(4) It affirms that the divine Revelation is more important than the means which God uses to mediate it.

(5) It is an assertion that God's justifying activity is proclaimed in the lives of all believers.

(6) It is intrinsically related to the High Priesthood of Christ.

(7) It is significant for an understanding of the word 'ministry'.

(8) It is significant for current Ecumenical studies.

(9) The truths inherent in the doctrine should be incorporated in the worshipping life of the Church.

(10) It anticipates the full participation of all Christians in the evangelistic action of the Church.

(11) It leads to a fuller understanding of the doctrine of divine vocation.

(12) The Eschatological significance of the doctrine.

We shall now explain and amplify these conclusions and show how they are related to the present situation in the Christian Church.

(1) *No single church has been able to express in its worship, work, and witness, the full richness of this doctrine.*

The Anglican Church has unquestionably emphasized the importance of expressing the universal priesthood in the liturgical

CONCLUSIONS AND REINTERPRETATION 239

life of the Church, but has been prevented from giving complete expression to it by two factors. These are the idea of lineal succession, and the very limited place which has been afforded to the service of the laity.

Nonconformists, on the other hand, have preserved its ethical and evangelistic emphasis, but have been prevented from giving complete expression to it by three factors: (i) They have never successfully developed the corporate aspect of worship; (ii) they have never fully grasped the idea that the two Sacraments of Baptism and the Lord's Supper are pre-eminently Sacraments of the universal priesthood and are expressions of it; and (iii) they have not, until our own day, given sufficient attention to the doctrine of divine vocation. It is strange that the liturgical wing which gives an almost mystical value to personal priesthood asks from the universal priesthood of the congregation an increasing share in worship through responses and chants, while those who chiefly stress the universal priesthood reduce the congregational part in worship to a minimum. The Churches of the Independent Tradition are unable to give complete expression to the universal priesthood because their assertion of the independence of the local congregation has led to the neglect of the universal concept. Certainly they would acknowledge their utter dependence upon Christ, but, are not all Churches *interdependent* in the sense that they share a common faith, a common succession, and a common message?

The Eastern Orthodox Church expresses conciliatory ideas with regard to the universal priesthood. They tend, however, to minimize the achievement of the Reformation on the grounds that the doctrine was already firmly established in their own theology. But to affirm that the organic conception of the Church implies the priestly prerogative of the whole Christian community, and that the Sacrament of Confirmation means a consecration of *all* the faithful, and that the hierarchy itself is only a special organization of the universal priesthood, is not to explain the priesthood of all believers but to explain it away. It is purely an example of Orthodox latitudinarianism.

There is no doubt that the Roman Church has proclaimed the doctrine, but it is doubtful whether it has ever seriously accepted it. The elevation to a dogma of the Bodily Assumption of the Virgin Mary militates against the idea of the universal priesthood. Since the Virgin Mary is the symbol of the celibate priesthood, her bodily assumption into heaven carries with it what amounts to a deification of the priesthood. This separates Rome more sharply than ever from the idea of the priesthood of believers. Further, the intransigent attitude of the Roman curia to the attempt of the French worker-priests to implement the doctrine of the priesthood of believers cannot be overlooked.

While it is true that no single Church has given complete expression to the doctrine under review, it is also true that in general the circumstances are more favourable than they have ever been for a more adequate application of it in the life of the Churches. The Bible is now available in the native tongue of many nations. The work of Dr Laubach has served to raise the standard of literacy in the nations of the East. Church architecture no longer accentuates the barrier between priest and people. A revived interest in the doctrine of divine vocation has considerably minimized the sharp distinction between the 'religious' and 'secular' vocations. The raising of the general level of education has resulted in an awakened sense of responsibility and a desire to examine the theological foundations upon which our Faith rests. The inauguration of the Church of South India has proved that the question of 'Orders' need not prove a permanent obstacle to the reunion of the churches; and the Ecumenical Movement has brought riches, spiritual and liturgical, to the whole Church of God. This examination of the doctrine of the priesthood of all believers in the light of the new situation which the aforementioned factors have created, may at least simplify, to some extent, the task of the Church as she seeks to incorporate its vital truths into her life and witness. At any rate, it is a challenge which the Church cannot afford to ignore.

(2) *The doctrine has been a living issue in each century since the Reformation.*

It has attracted the attention of theologians of every denomination, and it is deeply significant that lively discussion upon it has coincided with times of spiritual awakening. We have seen that independent investigations were made by Luther, Calvin, Cartwright, Robert Browne, George Fox, Spener, and Wesley, and that the doctrine of the priesthood of all believers was decisive and determinative in the exposition of their message and in shaping the course of their respective movements. While it is true that the great minds of the Church have not always emphasized the same aspects of the doctrine, or stated it in identical form, there is no doubt that it has formed the basis of their thought and action. Luther looked upon it as the basis of spiritual liberty.[1] Cranmer grasped its significance for the worshipping life of the Church, Browne interpreted it as the guiding principle of Church government, and Spener and Wesley showed that it was essential to the practical life and witness of the Church as well as to its doctrine. The History of the Reformation, the History of Puritanism, and the History of the Evangelical Revival, are the story of the extent to which Christians have understood and applied the doctrine of the priesthood of all believers.

(3) *The doctrine is a unitive, positive, and comprehensive principle which springs directly from the Evangelical concept of 'free grace'.*

Protestantism is based upon three major emphases: (i) *sola scriptura*; (ii) *sola fides*; (iii) *sola gratia*. As the Reformers expounded these three truths they found themselves proclaiming the doctrine of the priesthood of all believers. They reacted against the Catholic doctrine of Scripture *and* Tradition, because they did not believe that any authority should be on an equality with Scripture. The emphasis upon Tradition had led to developments which had no warrant in Scripture. Hence the Reformers appeal to *sola scriptura*. Moreover, the Reformers did not, as is frequently supposed, argue against the Church and Sacraments. They simply wished to stress the fact that where individual faith was lacking, multiple satisfactions, rites and ceremonies were of no avail as a means of salvation. Hence their assertion of *sola fides*. The emphasis upon *sola gratia* was determined by their conception of God. Luther's discovery of the gracious God had taught him that salvation was not dependent upon any work of man however noble, but solely upon the grace of God. These three specifically Protestant emphases lie behind the doctrine of the priesthood of all believers. The doctrine has three important characteristics.

(a) *It is Unitive*. Therefore, it is not anti-clerical. Both Luther and Calvin set the Ministry *within* the universal priesthood. There is no suggestion of an antithesis between them. No branch

[1] See 'The Liberty of the Christian Man' in *Reformation Writings*, Vol. I, Lee Woolf.

R

of Puritanism opposed the idea of a separated Ministry, yet all of them fervently proclaimed the universal priesthood. Wesley was emphatic upon the subject of the functions of the laity, but in none of his writings does he make this view the ground of anti-clerical sentiments. Any notion of discarding the idea of a separated Ministry would have been unthinkable to Wesley who lived and died a true Anglican. We assert, therefore, that far from being a dividing factor, the doctrine of the priesthood of believers, properly understood, transcends the distinction between clergy and laity, and, while allowing difference of function, unites them in the exercise of a priesthood which is common to all.

(*b*) *It is Positive*. The doctrine has sometimes been represented as possessing a purely negative meaning. This is a false idea, and arises out of the fallacy that Protestantism in general is essentially negative. But, as we have seen, the word 'protest' means 'speaking as a witness' or 'making a declaration'. Protestantism bears witness to certain truths by declaring them; it is, properly speaking, a proclamation rather than an objection. It is a proclamation of the primacy as well as the finality of faith. There are two reasons for refuting the view that the doctrine of the universal priesthood is negative. First, the divine origin of the People of God, who were conscious of a divinely appointed corporate mission which could only be fulfilled in terms of sacrificial service, was, as we have noticed, an affirmation long before the period of the great controversies of the Church arrived. It does not depend upon opposition for its intrinsic value. It was the proclamation of a divine revelation. Second, we have expounded the view that the universal priesthood was the only priesthood that was known to the New Testament and to the Church of the first two centuries. When the New Testament writers spoke of the Royal Priesthood they were not setting it over against an established doctrine, they were asserting that it was the fulfilment of the purpose of God which was made known to the Old Israel but which only culminated in the coming of Christ and in the creation of the New Israel. Moreover, when the Early Fathers spoke of the universal priesthood they were not opposing a doctrine which already existed, for that was the only doctrine of priesthood they knew. If there was a protest, it must be attributed to Cyprian, not Luther. The doctrine of the priesthood of all believers is, therefore, positive.

(c) *It is Comprehensive*. It is not to be regarded as a purely individualistic interpretation of religion. It cannot be limited, for instance, to the idea of private judgement. It is true, as Luther affirmed, that the absolute necessity of individual faith in man's relationship with God is included in its meaning, but this truth does not exhaust its meaning. On the contrary, it was Luther who made it abundantly clear that the doctrine was determinative for an understanding of the seven 'marks' of the true Church. Indeed, the greatest single lesson which we may learn from our study of the works of Luther is the comprehensiveness of the doctrine of the priesthood of all believers. This, then, is our second general conclusion: the doctrine is a unitive, positive, and comprehensive principle which springs directly from the evangelical concept of 'free grace'.

(4) *The doctrine affirms that the divine Revelation is more important than the means which God uses to mediate it.*

We have noticed repeatedly that there has been a tendency to confuse the means of God's revelation with the Revelation itself. Whenever this has happened there has been a tendency to divert attention from the God of Grace to the means whereby He is revealed. Again and again attention has been focused exclusively upon the divinely appointed means to the neglect of the Revelation of grace. Sometimes the Nation has been regarded as an 'end', sometimes Tradition or Canon Law, at other times human Reason has been regarded as an 'end', and sometimes a particular ecclesiastical structure, or even the Written Word. We must now assert that no single means must ever be regarded as the Revelation itself, and this is the vital lesson which successive generations have had to learn afresh. Therefore, from time to time a stern corrective has been necessary. In order to administer this corrective God has raised up here a Jeremiah, there a Wyclif, here a Luther, there a Calvin, here a John Owen, there a Wesley, lest at any time man should gaze indefinitely upon the imperfect means and miss the perfect Revelation. Each of these leaders has proclaimed with varying emphases the same theme, namely, that the Revelation is supreme and transcends all the means whereby it may be known. Faith alone is the one thing needful, and without this the appointed means are of little worth. The doctrine which has served as a corrective from the sixteenth to the twentieth centuries is the priesthood of all believers.

(5) *The doctrine is an assertion that God's justifying activity is proclaimed in the lives of all believers.*

The vital question is: How may we mediate Christ's justifying activity to the world? In our study of Cranmer's teaching we came to the conclusion that there were three important aspects to be remembered: (i) This justifying activity is essentially the work of the Holy Spirit; (ii) it ensures the survival of the Church; and (iii) it is operative by the Spirit in every member. It is clearly the duty of all Christians to mediate the justifying activity of God, and it is in the fulfilment of this inherent duty that the priesthood of believers is to be understood. If justification by faith states the believer's relationship to God, the priesthood of faith states the inescapable obligations of that relationship. The key word for the Reformers (English as well as Continental) is 'faith'. Luther speaks of the priesthood of the faithful, and he regards faith as the true priestly office. We noticed also that Wesley developed the thought that faith was the basis of the priesthood of Christians.

Such continuity as exists in the Church, therefore, is essentially a continuity of faith, for God's justifying activity is a continuous process. If other conceptions of continuity are open to doubt, this surely is indisputable. Succession is of faith, and therefore Luther, Calvin, and Wesley do not hesitate to affirm the apostolic succession of all believers. We have noticed that even for Cranmer the idea of succession has a pragmatic rather than a doctrinal significance. Another Anglican, John Pearson (1659), goes farther still. He says that the Church should, 'by a successive augmentation, be uninterruptedly continued in an actual existence of believing persons and congregations'.[2] This faith-succession is connected with the idea of justification. God's justifying *act* is the Cross; the subsequent justifying *activity* is endless. Now justification means that the primary impact of God's power upon the world is the Cross, the efficacy of which is perpetuated through all believers. There can be no higher conception of priesthood, and it is the privilege of all the followers of Christ.

[2] More and Cross, *Anglicanism*, p. 30.

(6) *The doctrine is intrinsically related to the High Priesthood of Christ.* Any conception of priesthood which is to be of permanent value must be consonant with the priestly character and work of Christ. All the writers we have considered have insisted on this particular truth. Yet this aspect of the doctrine of the priesthood of all believers seems to be the one that is most easily overlooked. The doctrine has often been expounded in complete isolation from its surest anchorage.

Obedience and suffering are the hall-marks of our Lord's priestly action; it cannot be otherwise for His followers. Even for the Son of Man Himself the way to victory was along the pathway of suffering. The followers of Christ cannot too often recall Charles Wesley's lines:

> *Entered the holy place above,*
> *Covered with meritorious scars,*
> *The tokens of His dying love*
> *Our great High-priest in glory bears.*

In the light of such dying love, all thoughts of good works, human effort, pride or self-aggrandizement are seen to be not only futile but shameful. Pride perishes in the flame of pure love. It is then that the humble believer knows where true glory belongs. He does not stand with head lifted high asserting his own rights and dues and claims, and protesting his record of integrity. His righteousness is as filthy rags; his good works as dust and ashes. ' 'Tis mystery all, the Immortal dies!' While he does not understand it, it is nevertheless the tribunal before which man continually stands. Under that judgement he lives. Ever before him is the Pattern of all priesthood. But if his wretched soul can bear any more, he must now realize that implicit in his own priesthood is the necessity of revealing in his own life that which he has seen and known to be true. He realizes that willing obedience and undeserved suffering are now the marks whereby true priesthood will be recognized. His only hope, therefore, of fulfilling his own priesthood is in faith-identification with Christ. So it is in faith, and hope, and love, that he dares to sing:

> *With what rapture*
> *Gaze we on those glorious scars!*

The priesthood of believers should not be interpreted apart

from the category of sacrifice. In the New Testament we found that the phrases 'Royal Priesthood', 'a holy priesthood', and 'priests and kings', are always used in close relation to the Sacrifice of Christ. This is deeply significant, for it means that the priesthood of believers is inseparable from the Priesthood of our Lord. Polycarp has the full support of all the Early Fathers when he says: 'There was now the same High Priest and Mediator for all, *through whom all men*, being once reconciled unto God, *are themselves made a priestly and spiritual race.*' Throughout the long centuries the Church has not always been mindful of this aspect of her teaching, but she has been less sure of her mission, and less able to fulfil it, when this has been neglected. The truth is that the priesthood of all believers means 'the Church under the Cross'.

(7) *The doctrine is significant for an understanding of the word 'ministry'.* Upon this subject our first conclusion is that the 'special priesthood' is of God's ordering. It is given by Christ *to* the Church, to be exercised *in* the Church, and *for* the Church. Each word in italics is significant. The Ministry is a gift of Christ to the Church and is therefore not of human but of divine origin. It is set within the universal priesthood and in no sense *above* it. It is *for* the Church in the sense that all Ministers are called to serve, not to rule. It is their duty to serve in such a way that eventually God may rule in all the world.

The second point we must notice is that this Ministry and all other ministries arise out of the same Gospel. In every ministry Christ is proclaimed. The Ministry, and the various ministries which serve love to one's neighbour, spring from the same source and arise out of the same Gospel. Since the ministries which serve faith, and those which serve love, take their origin in the same source, they possess the same dignity and are different aspects of the same priesthood.

The third point we must notice in this connexion is that every function of the members of Christ's Body is a ministry, and Christ Himself is the primary holder of every ministry. This implies that all Christians are known by one word, 'servant'. God rules through those who serve. There is no other way. Christ continues His Ministry through His people. The Church does not exist for her own purpose but only as the servant of Christ. She serves

God's purpose, but must never control it. She serves the divine Revelation, but must never hide it. She serves the world, but must never forsake it. Servanthood is the key to priesthood. This service, however, is an obligation and no one may contract out of it. It is the priesthood of *all* believers and not merely of some. So having received the benefits of Christ's Passion, the believer goes forth into the life of the world to render to Christ that form of service or that ministry for which God has equipped him. But all are expressions of the same priesthood and one is not more important than the other.

(8) *The doctrine is significant for current Ecumenical studies.*

(a) *The Church exists.* It does not require an adjective or a label. The Church is greater than all churches and transcends them. This supreme fact underlies everything else. It is an irrefutable and unalterable fact. The *Una Sancta* is the People of God. The Covenant was the Word of God pledged to a people. The New Covenant is the Word of God pledged to all people. Only the response of the People of God could make them into a Holy Priesthood. Only the response of the People of God to the Word pledged by the New Covenant constitutes the Church. The Word of God addressed to faith does not make a Church. It is only the Word of God addressed to faith, and the response of individual faith to the Word of God, that makes a Church. When Word and faith meet, there is the Church. Even though only three persons are present, and even if, as Tertullian said, those three are laymen, there is the Church. We must not slip into the fallacy that the Church exists only where there is a Minister. When three persons gather together in the presence of Christ they do so as believers. When they gather in such a way they are exercising the priesthood of believers. They are the Church. All other questions are secondary. Certainly other questions will arise: How will they worship? Where will they worship? and many other questions. The supreme question, however, they will already have answered: Whom will they worship and in whom will they believe? In other words, all questions of structure and organization are secondary. They should be kept in their proper perspective. The response of faith to the Incarnate Word is the sole indispensable qualification for the existence of the Church.

Historical developments will not and cannot alter this fact. The fact that the one Church has been misconceived and misrepresented and, therefore, has never been perfectly manifested on earth, is a regrettable but quite irrelevant consideration. The important question is: Has not the time come when the one Church should be properly understood, and truly represented, and perfectly manifested on earth? And will not a fuller appreciation of the Church as the one indivisible priesthood of all believers serve as a suitable starting-point?

(b) *The Church is universal.* This does not mean that it is a fanciful dream. It is not a creedless ideal, or a *civitas platonica*, or a glorified social Utopia. Nor has it anything to do with the quasi-mystical conception which is associated with Theosophical syncretism. While it is universal in scope, it embraces only believers. It is a fellowship of *believers*. The Church does not become universal; it is universal by nature. Now its nature cannot be altered, but it must eventually be recognized by all men everywhere. This is clearly the divine Will. Jesus prayed that the disciples may be united with Him so that the world might believe. At Pentecost the Holy Spirit was poured out upon all, and He was received by those who believed. The Sacraments of Baptism and the Lord's Supper are the Sacraments of the universal Church. In the one we are incorporated in the universal Priesthood; in the other we become conscious of our oneness in the Body of Christ because we are all partakers of the one Bread (1 Cor 10^{17}). By the prayer of Jesus, by the experience at Pentecost, and by the Sacraments of the Church, the universality of the Church is assumed, but it only becomes a reality to those who believe. It cannot be separated from faith. Moreover, while it cuts across churches, confessions, and sects, it does not cut across religions. This is because the Church is a fellowship of believers.

But the universal Church, now hidden, and not yet fully manifested in the world, will only become a visible reality in the world as each member of the fellowship of believers realizes that his very membership of it imposes a vital mission. By virtue of being a member of it, he shares its priesthood. How can he be expected to fulfil so onerous and responsible a task? At this point Wesley's answer is illuminating: He may do so 'because one Spirit animates all members; because one Lord rules over all those who are partakers of the eternal hope; because faith is the

CONCLUSIONS AND REINTERPRETATION 249

ground of that hope.'³ By these means, therefore, he is able to fulfil his mission: his life is animated by the Holy Ghost, ruled by Christ, and faith is his priestly office. Faith appropriates all. If the Church, already universal by nature, becomes a universal priesthood by mission, the hope of future ecumenical discussion will be bright indeed.

(c) *The Church is continuous.* The continuity of the Church is dependent upon one thing and one thing alone—faithfulness to the apostolic testimony. Failure in this is failure in everything. Successive generations of Christians in all churches and in many nations have been faithful to the apostolic testimony. Their Message is given. It is theirs not to alter it but to proclaim it. All Christians are united to Christ, custodians of the Evangel, and servants of God. Theirs is a high calling, and there is none higher. As 'priests unto God', they have been permitted to 'draw near', also as priests they are sent out to spend and be spent in the service of their Lord so that the vision of the world as His kingdom might be fulfilled. It is to this priesthood that all believers are called.

(9) *The truths inherent in the doctrine should be incorporated in the worshipping life of the Church.*

Worship is faith's active response to the love of God. In the history of Christianity the response has sometimes been interpreted as individualistic, passive, and formal. In fact, it should be none of these. The Early Fathers thought of Christians as a great High Priestly Race, a worshipping community, who sought to glorify God in their every act. Properly understood, worship is the active, corporate, living expression of faith. Far too often this has been forgotten in the history of the Church. No man proclaimed more fervently than Luther the doctrine of the priesthood of all believers, but this did not prevent him from preserving all those liturgical expressions of thanksgiving and worship in the Medieval Order of the Mass, which were free from the concept of Sacrifice. Luther did this because he knew that worship was an act of the corporate priesthood.

Generally speaking Protestantism has forgotten this. The Anglican goes to Church to 'make his Communion' as if it is an entirely secondary matter that in that Service the Eternal

³ *Sermon* LXXIV. 8, 10, 11.

Christ meets and feeds and sanctifies the whole Israel of God. The Nonconformist goes to Church primarily to hear a preacher, as if the rest of the service does not matter and is to be taken on sufferance. Both attitudes are wrong. It is a mistaken idea of worship which allows one man who gives to stand up before a number of people who receive, and which makes one man responsible for all the congregation does. Bishop Newbigin goes so far as to describe this as a false sort of sacerdotalism: 'Does the common life of our churches, the activities of all our members in evangelism and service, really bear the marks of a holy priesthood? Does the kind of worship which leaves the minister to say "Amen" to his own prayers, not constitute a very false sort of sacerdotalism? And does not the demand for lay-celebration as an *indispensable* evidence of adherence to the doctrine of the priesthood of all believers imply the belief that the celebrant is *exclusively* the priest, and thus rest precisely upon the very error which it is sought to resist?'[4]

The first necessity, then, is to reinstate the general active part of the whole congregation in worship so that the members are no longer merely passive onlookers. Some of the Free Churches have proclaimed most fervently the priesthood of all believers but have never troubled to give it expression in the most obvious way—the Responsive Reading. This is an act in which the whole congregation may share and the reintroduction of it on a wide scale would be a salutary thing.

Prejudice must not be allowed to impoverish worship, and Protestants may well have to ask themselves whether some of the symbolical acts of worship which they have rejected may not express the ethos of their Protestantism more adequately than some of the customs which they have retained. What, for instance, is the point of standing while the minister enters the Church, and yet refraining from kneeling for prayer? But the important thing is that those great central acts of worship in the early Church should be restored. One way of doing this is the restoration of the Offertory to its original significance. 'In the Early Church the common priesthood of all believers found active expression in the action of the Offertory, when the people brought to Church their gifts of bread and wine as the symbol of the offering of themselves, and presented these at the altar, that from

[4] *The Reunion of the Church*, pp. 175ff.

them might be taken the bread and wine for the "Sacrament".'[5]
It is important to reintroduce this act for four reasons:

(a) The Offertory links all worshippers with the act of our Lord in the Upper Room.
(b) It emphasizes 'the inseparable connexion which must exist between what the priest does and what the people do'.[6] It is *their* offering, their gift, their bread and their wine which are placed on the altar. It is a corporate and not an individual act.
(c) It signifies the self-offering of the believer in a particular form. Everyone present gives himself to God as God gives Himself to them under the same forms, and by means of these united offerings the Church *becomes* the Body of Christ.
(d) The gifts that are brought, whether offerings in kind (as in the early days), or money or bread or wine, are all the fruit of human labour and therefore signify the offering of the whole range of human life to God.

There is no doubt that the restoration of the Offertory to its true place in worship would be one way of expressing the priesthood of all believers.

Another symbol which emphasized the corporate action of the Church—the Kiss of Peace—has been lost to the Western Church. Yet no symbol indicates more clearly the spiritual unity and fellowship of the whole Church. It is a token of the love for one another which all Christians should regard as a debt (Rom 13⁸). It is also a visible expression of the *koinonia* among all Christians. Yet as a symbol of corporate fellowship it has practically disappeared. It is true that the Roman Church still pronounces '*Pax vobiscum*' but the accompanying symbol has vanished. So it has happened that another expression of the unity and fellowship of the universal priesthood has been lost to the Church. Is there any reason why a form of the Kiss of Peace should not be reintroduced to the worship of the Church? The form practised by the Syrian Church is an appropriate one. The priest touches with both his hands the folded hands of a worshipper who passes it on to his neighbour with the ancient greeting, 'Peace be with thee',

---

[5] *Ways of Worship* (Faith and Order Report).
[6] C. Dunlop, Anglican Public Worship, p. 93. See also Olive Wyon, *The Altar Fire*, pp. 61-3.

and the response is given, 'And with thy spirit'. There are several reasons why this custom should be revived.

(a) It forms a definite link with the Early Church.
(b) This symbol of unity and fellowship which takes place immediately before the receiving of the Bread and the Wine, is a beautiful and appropriate preparation for it.
(c) It is an act in which all may participate, and any such act is a rare thing in the modern practice of worship.
(d) It may well be a means of drawing the churches closer together as they bring into regular use this pledge of piety and love, which is, or should be, common to all.

It is interesting to notice that the theology of the Universal Priesthood has been wedded to liturgical action in the New Liturgy of the Church of South India.[7]

These, then, are some of the ways whereby the priesthood of believers may be expressed in the worship of the Church— Responsive readings, the restoration of the Offertory to its true place, and the revival of the ancient symbol, the Kiss of Peace.[8] There are, of course, other ways in which this may be done. Should not the whole congregation join in the prayer of Humble Access? And will it not transform our attitude to the proclaimed Word if we regard all preaching as, in P. T. Forsyth's phrase, 'the organized hallelujah of the congregation'?

(10) *The doctrine anticipates the full participation of all Christians in the evangelistic action of the Church.*

Important as it is that all Christians should participate in the liturgical actions of the Church, and that they should regard their daily vocation as a medium through which their priesthood may be expressed, it is equally important that they should be identified with, and take an active share in, the evangelistic action of the Church also. It is noteworthy that the Younger Churches on the Mission Field have become vividly conscious of the necessity of such action, and they now regard it as an urgent and imperious command. A statement at the Bangkok Conference says: 'It is when a whole Church with all its members is committed together

---

[7] A. M. Ward, *The Pilgrim Church*, p. 135.
[8] For a full account of recent developments see 'The Liturgical Movement'. J. H. Srawley.

CONCLUSIONS AND REINTERPRETATION

to the task of evangelism that something exists which no force in the modern world can stop. The challenge is to mobilize the entire forces of the Church for evangelism.'[9] Again the International Missionary Council meeting at Whitby, Ontario (1947), points out that evangelism is not primarily the work of theologians and ministers. 'It was not so in the earliest days. They who believed went everywhere preaching the Word. . . . Total evangelism demands the co-operation of every single Christian.'[10] Such teaching is inherent in the doctrine of the priesthood of all believers, and Luther, Spener, Wesley, and the Anglican Evangelicals drew particular attention to this aspect of it. Spener endeavoured to show the Royal Priesthood in action through fellowship, mutual instruction, neighbourly service, vocation and evangelism. All this was to be done 'for the leavening of the whole' so that the Church may become what it was always intended to be—a universal priesthood.

The *collegia pietatis* are not to be regarded as exclusive groups intent only upon their own edification, but rather as a training-ground for the exacting task of evangelization. The same may be said of Zinzendorf's 'Bands'. 'Watchful and careful they viewed all parts of the battle array and endeavoured to fix their field dispositions so as to throw back the enemy.'[11] Wesley adopted similar methods for the same high purpose. The Evangelistic task of the Church became his all-absorbing occupation.

> *'Tis worth living for, this,*
> *To administer bliss*
> *And salvation in Jesus's name.*

Nothing was permitted to impede this urgent, paramount mission of the Church. All Christians were called upon to use their varying gifts for the fulfilment of this purpose. Class Leaders were to teach the Word and equip men for service, and preachers were sent forth to proclaim it, and all were to be 'servants of mankind'. The dominant aim of these men was to harness all the resources of the Church for concerted action in the cause of world evangelization. We have noticed also that Roman Catholics regard Eucharistic action as only truly fulfilled in evangelistic action. 'It is through the laity coming down from the altar to the

---
[9] Quoted in A. M. Ward, *The Pilgrim Church*, p. 90.
[10] H. P. van Dusen, *World Christianity: Yesterday, Today and Tomorrow*, p. 248.
[11] H. G. Addison, *The Renewed Church of the United Brethren*, p. 24.

world and the work of every day that the power and blessing of Christ are to be diffused and the face of the earth to be renewed.'[12] This is the work of the common priesthood. Our studies therefore have shown that the doctrine of the priesthood of all believers cannot be contained with the limits of a doctrinal formula but must be continually expressed in the dynamic action of the whole Church.

Increasing attention has been given to this particular aspect of the doctrine in many parts of the world. In regard to this we may note two interesting factors: first, the attempt to implement the doctrine has cut right across denominational and racial barriers; and secondly, there is a widespread opinion that the doctrine of the priesthood of all believers should not be confined to doctrinal formularies but should be more and more translated into the active life of the Church Militant. Evidence of current interest in the subject is shown in the effective work of the *Kirchentag* (Church Day) in Germany. The whole matter has been thought out with great thoroughness by Bishop Lilje and Dr Reinold von Thadden. In what Bishop Lilje calls 'the actualization of the Church', an attempt is made to use the members of the local Church in such a way that their peculiar gifts will be of the greatest service, and thereby to take the Gospel into places of learning, places of government, and places of industry. Much blessing has attended these efforts. Further evidence of this widespread interest is to be found in the 'worker-priest' experiment in the Catholic Church in France. Under the leadership of Abbé Godin and other priests an attempt has been made to exercise the vocation to the Christian ministry in the very heart of industrial life. Further, the Dutch Reformed Church have a special institution at Utrecht where the laity are trained for the task of militant evangelism, and the Ecumenical Institute at Bossey in Switzerland has shown that the World Council of Churches are alive to the fact that theological training for laymen and lay women is a necessity if the universal priesthood is to be a reality. The Church of South India is 'desirous of implementing the doctrine of the priesthood of the laity expressed in the Constitution'.[13] We see then that if Churches desire to be abreast of theological development in the world Church, they must develop the total ministry of the Church so that it may fulfil its divine vocation.

[12] *The Holy Communion*, ed. H. Martin, p. 44.
[13] A. M. Ward, *The Pilgrim Church*, p. 90.

(11) *The doctrine leads to a fuller understanding of the doctrine of divine vocation.*

John Calvin rendered a singular service to the universal Church when he related the priesthood of believers to the idea of 'Calling' or 'Vocation'. A man is a 'priest' because he finds his calling in God, and he only realizes his place in the Universe as he realizes that he is the 'servant' of God. According to the New Testament all are 'called'. The calling of the individual is not absorbed in the corporate calling of the Church; the one is the complement of the other. The *Evanston Report* includes both: 'In the New Testament ... not only is the Church as the prolongation and restoration of Israel "called" by her Lord, *but every believer is "called"*.' λαός θεου (People of God) transcends distinctions between clergy and laity and includes both. For this reason the words of Dr Paul Tillich that 'Protestantism demands a radical laicism' are somewhat misleading. The opposite would seem to be the case: Protestantism demands a radical priesthood rather than a narrow and exclusive one. The phrase 'People of God' does not refer either to clergy or laity, it embraces both. It presupposes the idea of universal priesthood.

It follows that the People of God are endowed with a single vocation. The term 'secular vocation' is a contradiction in terms. Luther and Calvin are agreed that there is only 'divine vocation', although it may be exercised in various spheres of life. We may recall what was said at the beginning of our study, 'Israel belonged to Jehovah by election, consecration, and mission', and the doctrine of vocation is adequately summed up in those words. It involved response to the divine election, separation to the divine Will, and the fulfilment of the divine mission. Calvin and the Reformed Tradition have continually borne witness to this particular aspect of the universal priesthood, although we found that the interpretation of vocation as the Service of one's Neighbour was prominent in Luther's works also. The distinctiveness of Calvin's teaching, however, is that he connected the doctrine of election with the subject of our study. We may confidently affirm that the doctrine of vocation is the necessary counterpart of the priesthood of all believers, as it is also of the doctrine of election itself. We have also noticed that the Reformers used vocation of everyday tasks as a protest against the use of vocation exclusively as a call to the monastic life. They wished to destroy the 'double standard' and show that God could be glorified in the workaday world. A Christian layman is one who discharges his God-given vocation in the secular calling of life. That is his vocation. He is called to be a 'priest unto God' in the life of 'the world outside.' A realization and actualization of such a priesthood is one of the greatest needs of our time. If this fact was firmly grasped by the whole People of God, it would undoubtedly lead to a Christian Revolution, a new Reformation that would surely transform the life of the contemporary Church. Our circumstances may differ, the sphere in which we are called upon to pursue our daily task may differ, and the gifts which God has bestowed upon us may differ, but our dominant task is the same. It is the task of every Christian to draw men nearer to Christ, to be, in fact, a priest.

(12) *The Eschatological significance of the doctrine.*
The end of all priesthood is to draw near to God and to enable others to draw near. It cannot be that this should always remain simply a hope or an aspiration. There will come a day of final realization and fulfilment. 'We shall be like Him, for we shall see Him as He is.' The Christian Hope anticipates that experience which is the culmination of all priesthood. Here we are permitted to partake of His grace, there we shall see Him. As Charles Wesley sings:

> *Partaker of Thy grace,*
> *I long to see Thy face;*
> *The first I prove below,*
> *The last I die to know.*

The author of the Apocalypse says: 'They shall be priests of God and of Christ, and they shall reign with him' (Rev 20[6]). The believer's triumph will be to be there. The Eternal Priest will then be always present and no clouds will hide His glory. This is the meaning of the glorious hope which inspires every Christian,

> *Till faith itself is lost in sight.*

At every service of Holy Communion the believer is vividly reminded of the End to which he has always aspired. Above

CONCLUSIONS AND REINTERPRETATION

everything else that service is the Eschatological Feast of Joy when, together with the whole Church, he looks forward to the Great Messianic Feast beyond the grave. Even the promise of it beggars description. In those solemn moments when he comes nearest to understanding the sacrificial service of his Lord, he anticipates that day when all the travail of the centuries and the events of the unknowable future will be gathered up in the eternal 'Now'. The 'Now' and the 'For ever' will be the same. This is the goal of all priesthood, as it is the consummation of all things.

Bibliography

GENERAL

Dunkerley, R. (ed.)   *The Ministry and the Sacraments*
Flew, R. N. (ed.)   *The Nature of the Church*
Harnack, A.   *History of Dogma* (Vols 5, 6 and 7)
Henderson, G. D.   *Church and Ministry*
Hodgson, L. (ed.)   *Ways of Worship*
Hughes, P.   *The Reformation in England* (Vols 1, 2 and 3)
McGiffert, A. C.   *History of Christian Thought* (Vols 1 and 2)
Neibuhr, R.   *The Nature and Destiny of Man* (Vol. 2)
Newbigin, J. E. L.   *The Reunion of the Church*
Manson, T. W.   *The Church's Ministry*
Powicke, F. M.   *The Reformation in England*
Sykes, N.   *Old Priest and New Presbyter*
Troeltsch, E.   *Social Teaching of the Churches* (Vol. 2)

CHAPTER 1

Bainton, R. H.   *Here I Stand*
———   *The Reformation of the Sixteenth Century*
Beard, C.   *The Reformation*
Dorner, J. A.   *History of Protestant Theology*
Flew, R. N., and Davies, R. E. (ed.)   *The Catholicity of Protestantism*
Forel, G. W.   *Faith Active in Love*
Hamilton, K.   *The Protestant Way*
Herman, S.   *The Rebirth of the German Church*
Hildebrandt, F.   *From Luther to Wesley*
Kolde, Th.   *Martin Luther* (Vols 1 and 2)
Kooiman, W. J.   *By Faith Alone*
Kramm, H. H.   *The Theology of Martin Luther*
Lindsay, T. M.   *History of the Reformation* (Vols 1 and 2)
Robinson, W.   *Completing the Reformation*

Rupp, G. *Luther's Progress to the Diet of Worms*
——— *The Righteousness of God*
Storck, Hans 'The Concept of General Priesthood in Luther', *Theologische Existenz Heute*, No. 37 (1953)
Tillich, P. *The Protestant Era*
Vatja, V. *The Theology of Divine Service in Luther*
Wace, H. B. *Principles of the Reformation*
Wace and Buchheim *Luther's Primary Works*
Watson, P. S. *Let God be God*
Whitney, J. P. *The History of the Reformation*
Woolf, B. L. *Reformation Writings of Martin Luther* (Vols 1 and 2)
World Lutheranism Today. Essays by various Writers

CHAPTER 2

Ainslie, J. L. *The Doctrines of Ministerial Order in the Reformed Churches of the Sixteenth and Seventeenth Centuries*
Barkley, J. M. *Presbyterianism*
Brunner, E. *The Divine Human Encounter*
——— *The Misunderstanding of the Church*
Calvin, J. *The Institutes of the Christian Religion* (3 vols)
——— *Commentary on Romans*
Curtis, W. A. *Creeds and Confessions of the Sixteenth Century*
Dakin, A. *Calvinism*
Davies, R. E. *The Problem of Authority in the Continental Reformers*
Hooft, V. 't *The Renewal of the Church*
Hunt, R. N. C. *John Calvin*
Mackinnon, J. *Calvin and the Reformation*
McNeill, J. T. *Social Interpretation of the Reformation Tradition*
Milligan, W. *The Ascension and Heavenly Priesthood of Our Lord*
Niesel, W. *The Theology of Calvin*
Schaff, P. *Creeds of the Evangelical Protestant Churches*
Schenck, L. B. *The Presbyterian Doctrine of Children in the Covenant*
Simpson, P. C. *The Evangelical Church Catholic*
Torrance, T. F. *Calvin's Doctrine of Man*
Warfield, B. B. *Calvin and Calvinism*
Whale, J. S. *The Protestant Tradition*
World Presbyterian Alliance Reports (August 1950 and August 1953)

CHAPTER 3

Balleine, G. R.   *A History of the Evangelical Party in the Church of England*
Barry, F. R.   *The Relevance of the Church*
───────   *Ministry and Vocation*
Box, H. S. (ed.)   *Priesthood*
Brilioth, Y.   *The Anglican Revival*
Bromily, G. W.   *Thomas Cranmer, Theologian*
Catholicity (Report)
Dunlop, C.   *Anglican Public Worship*
Harford and Stevenson   *Prayer Book Dictionary*
Hebert, A. G.   *Liturgy and Society*
Hooker, R.   *Works* (Vols 1 and 2)
Hopf, G.   *Martin Bucer and the English Reformation*
Kirk, K. E. (ed.)   *The Apostolic Ministry*
Mason, A. J.   *The Relation of Confirmation to Baptism*
Milner, J.   *The History of the Church of Christ* (Vols 3, 4 and 5)
More, P. E., and Cross, F. L.   *Anglicanism*
Neill, S. (ed.)   *The Ministry of the Church*
Rawlinson, A. E. J.   *Problems of Reunion*
Sanday, W. (ed.)   *Priesthood and Sacrifice*
Smyth, C.   *Charles Simeon and Church Order*
Srawley, J. H.   *The Liturgical Movement*
Swete, H. B. (ed.)   *The Early History of the Church and the Ministry*
Symonds, H. E.   *The Council of Trent and Anglican Formularies*
Woodhouse, H. F.   *The Doctrine of the Church in Anglican Theology*
Wordsworth, J.   *The Ministry of Grace*

CHAPTER 4

Barclay, R.   *Apology for True Christian Divinity*
Barrowe, H.   *A Brief Discourse on the True Church*
Brayshaw, A. N.   *The Quakers*
Browne, R.   *A Treatise on the Reformation Without Tarrying for Anie*
Cartwright, T.   *A Confutation of the Rhemists' Translation of the Bible*
Cocks, H. F. L.   *By Faith Alone*

Dale, R. W.   *History of Congregationalism*
Davies, H. M.   *The English Free Churches*
Fairbairn, A. M.   *Studies in Religion and Theology*
Forsyth, P. T.   *The Church and the Sacraments*
Graham, J. W.   *The Faith of a Quaker*
Grant, J. W.   *Free Churchmanship in England, 1870-1940*
Haller, W.   *The Rise of Puritanism*
Helwys, T.   *The Mystery of Iniquity*
Jones, R. M. (ed.)   *George Fox: An Autobiography*
Manning, B. L.   *Essays in Orthodox Dissent*
Marlowe, J.   *The Puritan Tradition*
McGlothin, W. J.   *Baptist Confessions of Faith*
Micklem, N.   *Congregationalism Today*
Owen, J.   *The True Nature of a Gospel Church*
Payne, E. A.   *The Free Church Tradition in the Life of England*
Townsend, H.   *The Claims of the Free Churches*
Underwood, A. C.   *A History of the English Baptists*
Wakefield, G. S.   *Puritan Devotion*
Whitley, W. T.   *The Works of John Smyth* (Vols 1 and 2)

CHAPTER 5

Addison, W. G.   *The Renewed Church of the United Brethren*
Baker, E.   *The Faith of a Methodist*
Baker, F.   *The Methodist Love-feast*
Bett, H.   *The Spirit of Methodism*
Brash, W. B.   *Methodism*
Bready, J. W.   *England: Before and After Wesley*
Carter, H.   *The Methodist Heritage*
Curnock, N. (ed.)   *Wesley's Journal* (Vols 1, 2, and 3)
Eayrs, G.   *The Letters of John Wesley*
Fitchet, W. H.   *Wesley and His Century*
Harrison, A. W.   *The Evangelical Revival and Christian Reunion*
Hutton, J. E.   *The History of the Moravian Church*
Jackson, T. (ed.)   *Wesley's Works* (Vols 5 and 6)
Lee, U.   *John Wesley and Modern Religion*
Lindström, H.   *Wesley and Sanctification*
Manning, B. L.   *The Hymns of Wesley and Watts*

The Message and Mission of Methodism (Conference Statement)
The Nature of the Church According to the Methodists (Conference Statement)
Piette, M. *John Wesley in the Evolution of Protestantism*
Rattenbury, J. E. *Wesley's Legacy to the World*
——— *Vital Elements of Public Worship*
——— *The Eucharistic Hymns of John and Charles Wesley*
Rigg, J. H. *The Living Wesley*
Stevens, G. *History of Methodism* (Vols 1 and 2)
Thompson, E. W. *The Methodist Principles of Church Order*
Townsend, W. J., and Workman, H. B. *A New History of Methodism* (Vols 1 and 2)
Wedgwood, J. *John Wesley: A Study in the Evangelical Reaction of the Eighteenth Century*
Wesley's *Sermons*

Index of Subjects

Adoption, 73, 74
Anglican, Anglicanism, 24, 44, 45, 105, 112, 126
Anglican Evangelicals, 114-25
Antinomianism, 119, 120
Augsburg Confession, 1, 22, 95
Authority, 4, 217, 218

Baptism, xi, 1, 9, 11, 12, 14-21, 44, 112, 113, 207
Baptist Church, 155, 157-63
Bangkok Conference, 252
Barmen Synod, 53

Call to preach, 220-3
Calling, 41-5, 109
Calvinism, see CALVIN
Caroline divines, 122
Catholicity, 214, 215
Christ, Headship of, 134-6
  Kingship of, 67, 155, 160, 196, 197
  Priesthood of, ix, xi, 67, 69, 70, 101, 115, 116, 134, 195-8, 245, 246
  Sonship of, 74, 197, 207
Church, doctrine of, 2, 3, 247
  government, 143-5
  invisible, 4, 5
  order, 122ff
  under the Cross, 53-6
  Victorious, xi
Clapham Sect, 128
Classes, 226-8, 231
Common Prayer, Book of, 99
Confession, 52, 56
Confirmation, 112-14
Congregational Church, 164-71
Covenant, ix, xi, 137, 155-7
Cross, 1, 53-5, 60, 64, 70, 102, 104

Donatists, 5
Democracy, 144
Duties of Believers, 148, 150

Early Fathers, xi
Ecclesia Abscondita, 5
Ecclesiology, 121-124
Election, ix, 72, 137-40
English Bible, 98, 99
Episcopacy, 82, 198, 199
Erastianism, 105, 106
Ereignis, 2
Eucharist, xii, 14, 23-5, 30, 35, 40, 44, 51, 55, 94, 101

Experience, 183-9, 214-19

Faith, 2, 3, 9, 15, 17, 21, 26-30, 35, 47, 48, 55, 60, 62, 64, 95, 96, 121, 189-95, 256
Fellowship, 229, 230
Friends, Society of, 171-82

German Church, 53, 57, 58
Grace, 3, 95, 168, 188, 189, 195

Hallensian Pietists, 185
Holy Spirit, 2, 3, 6-9, 18, 30-4, 49, 53, 57, 78, 79, 81, 84, 92, 102-4, 107, 112-15, 119, 120, 123, 179, 187, 188, 194, 196
Hymns of Wesleys, 207-16

Inner light, 135, 174, 175

Justification by faith, 3, 9, 10, 15, 20, 21, 50, 59, 60, 67, 71, 72, 81, 88, 91-6, 103, 104, 116-18, 133, 189, 190, 244

Keys, doctrine of, 1, 31-6, 66, 74-8, 90
Kiss of peace, 251, 252

Laity, 12, 106, 170, 171, 229-31, 252, 253, 255
Latitudinarianism, 119
Lutheranism, see LUTHER

Mass, 22-6, 44, 47, 77, 79, 91, 98, 133, 249
Mediator, 69-71, 87
Methodism, 183, 186, 193, 198-201, 205-7, 217-19, 223-5, 227, 229, 231, 234, 236
Ministry, x, 1, 3, 37-41, 59, 60, 66, 78-85, 105-8, 145, 157, 158, 178, 180, 202, 246, 247
Mission, 36, 57, 128, 129, 154, 203-7, 234-7
Montanism, 32
Moravians, 187

Neighbour, doctrine of, 59, 61, 231-4

Offertory, 251, 252
Ordination, 40, 42, 45, 78, 83, 84, 105-7, 111, 161, 162, 199

INDEX OF SUBJECTS

Praise, 50-3, 207
Prayer, 14, 26, 47-9, 200-2
Predestination, 139, 140
Presbyterian, Presbyterianism, 71, 82, 83, 130, 132, 142
Priesthood of Christ, ix, xi, 67, 69, 70, 101, 115, 116, 134, 195-8, 245, 246
Priesthood, corporate, 44, 124, 141, 199
  culmination of, 256
  duties of, 89, 148, 149
  Gospel, 108, 109
  initiation to, 20, 106, 113
  Roman, 9, 118
  royal, 112, 125, 139, 145, 160, 246
  spiritual, 62-4, 84, 87, 132
  universal, xi, 13, 69, 79, 180, 203, 246, 253
Priestly authority, 214
  heritage, 198
  mission, 36, 128, 154, 213, 234
  obligation, 204
  offering, 46, 85, 101, 102, 207, 251
  office, 143, 193, 223
  privilege, 14, 200
  race, xii, 211, 246
  service, 61, 202, 231
  vocation, 60, 71, 255
Private judgement, 80

Proclamation, 168-71
Protestant, Protestantism, 1, 2, 11, 37, 78, 91, 242
Puritan, Puritanism, 130, 131, 135, 137-40, 142, 151-4

Rationalism, 120, 121
Repentance, 52, 58

Sacrifices, spiritual, 46, 50, 51, 85-8, 132, 133, 149, 155
Solidarity, 54-6
South India, Church of, 162, 254
State, 37-9, 53, 105, 158, 159, 163
Stuttgart Declaration, 57
Succession, 82, 111, 146, 198-200

Tractarian Movement, 116, 122
Trent, Council of, 7, 9, 76, 77, 88, 92
Triplex munus, 66, 67, 74
Two Realms, doctrine of, 37

Vocation, 59, 60, 72, 74, 225, 226
Vows, system of, 16
Word, 1-8, 168-71, 219, 225, 243, 247
Worship, 1, 26, 46, 52, 97, 127, 175-8, 249, 252

Index of Names

Adam, T., 123
Addison, W. G., 226, 227, 253
Ainslie, J. L., 73
Aristides, 200
Aristotle, 117
Augustine, St, 4, 5, 11, 76, 105, 136
Aulén, G., 215

Balleine, G. R., 114, 126, 128
Barclay, R., 175, 182
Barker, Sir E., 151
Barkley, J. M., 71, 73, 74, 82, 83
Barrowe, H., 142, 151
Barth, K., 2, 37, 167
Bergendoff, C., 22
Berridge, J., 122-4, 126
Bett, H., 122, 186, 191, 231
Bettenson, H., 17
Bevan, E., 153, 154
Bilson, T., 103
Bora, Catherine von, 220
Bowers, 220
Braithwaite, W. C., 175
Brash, W. B., 230
Brayshaw, A. N., 173, 179
Bready, W., 205, 206
Brenz, John, 94
Bromiley, G. W., 95, 96-7, 102, 105, 106, 107
Browne, Robert, 130, 131, 142-5, 151, 240, 241
Brunner, E., 7, 8
Bucer, Martin, 92, 94, 95, 99-101
Burrage, C., 142
Butler, Bishop J., 189

Calvin, John, 66-81, 84-7, 89-90, 218, 240-1, 254-5
  keys, on the, 74-7
  Mediator, 69-71
  ministry, 78-85
  ordination, 83-5
  sacrifices, 85-7
  threefold Gift, 66, 67
  vocation, 74-1
Cartwright, Thomas, 130, 132-41, 151, 240
Catherine of Aragon, 97
Carver, W. O., 158-9
Chapman, Dom J., 32
Clement of Alexandria, xii
Clement of Rome, xi, xii, 179
Coleridge, S. T., 195

Coomer, D., 157
Cornelius, Bishop, 32
Constantine, 105
Cranmer, Thomas, 91-2, 95-8, 100-3, 105-7
Cross, F. L., see More, P. E.
Cyprian, St, 12, 31, 32, 76, 121

Dakin, A., 72
Dale, R. W., 169-70
Davies, H. M., 145, 153, 154, 169, 174
Denny, J., 21, 70, 74
Dillistone, F. W., 103-4
Donne, John, 56
Dorner, J. A., 71, 193
Dunkerley, R., 16, 44, 77, 78, 81, 82, 168
Dunlop, C., 251
Dusen, H. P. van, 253

Eliot, C., 34
Emissenus, 102
Erasmus, 100-1

Faber, G., 217
Fairbairn, A. M., 164-5, 202-3
Findlay, G. G., 201
Fitchett, W. H., 195
Flew, R. N., 2, 6, 31, 41, 51, 53, 65, 156-7, 165, 208
Forsyth, P. T., 160, 167, 169, 252
Fox, George, 131, 171-82, 240
Franke, A. H., 187, 226
Froude, J. G., 121

Gardiner, Bishop Stephen, 95, 97
Godin, Abbé, 254
Gore, C., 20
Graham, J. W., 178
Grant, C., 128
Grant, J. W., 158, 167-70, 178
Grubb, E., 173, 176

Haller, W., 137, 139
Havergal, F. R., 176
Harnack, A., 11
Hastings, W., 70, 74, 77
Helwys, Thomas, 132, 152
Hemingway, E., 56
Henderson, G. D., 5, 8
Herman, S., 58
Hermelink, H., 43
Hervey, J., 123
Hildebrandt, F., 193, 225

INDEX OF NAMES

Hill, Rowland, 124
Hobbes, T., 135
Hobhouse, S., 176
Hök, Gosta, 40, 43
Holbein, H., 98
Holman, 8
Hooker, R., 108-10
Hooper, Bishop John, 130
Hopf, Constantin, 95, 99, 100
Hort, F. J. A., 14
Horton, W., 163
Howe, R., 175, 177
Hügel, F. Baron von, 203
Hughes, P., 34, 92, 93, 96
Huntingdon, Lady Selina, 126

James I, 112
James, William, 185
Jerome, St, 16
Jones, R. M., 172-3, 174-5, 180-2
Justin Martyr, xii, 179

Kidd, B. J., 1
Kooiman, W. J., 46, 63, 94
Kramm, H. H. W., 109

Laubach, F., 240
Laurentius, S. V., 20
Law, William, 232
Leighton, Archbishop R., 87-9
Lilje, Bishop H., 254
Lindsay, A. D., 135, 136
Lindsay, T. M., 11, 30, 71-2, 134, 193, 232
Lindström, H., 186, 232
Lord, F. Townley, 159-60
Luther, Martin, xii, 1, 3-12, 14-22, 24-31, 34-5, 37-55, 59-64, 66-7, 71, 75-7, 93-4, 105-7, 117-21, 140, 146, 172, 184, 188, 193, 207, 217-18, 220, 225, 240-1, 243-4, 255
   Baptism, on, 18-21
   Cross, 53-7
   faith, 2-3, 5-6, 9-10, 19, 60-2
   Eucharist, 23-31
   keys, the, 31-7
   ministry, 40-6
   neighbour, 59-62
   prayer, 46-50
   Romanism, 10-11
   solidarity, 54-7
   thanksgiving, 50-3
   two Realms, 37-8
   vows, 17
   Word, 2-8

Macaulay, Z., 128
McCrie, C. G., 98
Mackay of Uganda, 57
Maclaren, A., 158
Macleod, John, 80
Manley, T. P., 161-2
Manning, B. L., 166-7, 169
Manson, T. W., 161
Marlowe, J., 151
Marsh, J., 166
Martin, H., 254
Mason, A. J., 112-14
Mather, A., 220-1
Matheson, Annie, 214
Maxfield, T., 220-1
Mede, J., 109
Melanchthon, 118
Micklem, N., 144, 167
Milligan, W., 210
Milner, J. and I., 116-20, 123
Monsell, J. S. B., 213
More, P. E., and Cross, F. L., 108-11, 244

Neibuhr, R., 133, 182
Nelson, John, 220
Newbigin, Bishop L., 2, 4, 250
Northcott, C., 152

Occam, William of, 94
Olivers, T., 220
Oman, J., 166-7
Origen, xi-xii
Owen, John, 142, 145-60, 243

Paris, M., 116
Paul, St, 9, 13, 25, 46, 60, 112
Payne, E., 162-3, 181, 224
Pearson, J., 111, 244
Peter, St, 10, 32-6, 73
Phillips, J. B., 111
Piette, M., 185, 188
Plato, 5
Polycarp, xi, xii, 246
Powicke, F. M., 131

Rattenbury, J. E., 24, 209-10, 230-1
Richardson, C. C., 123
Ridley, Bishop N., 24
Rigg, J. H., 188-9
Robinson, H. Wheeler, 151, 163
Robinson, J. A. T., 56, 219
Robinson, William, 64
Ruler, A. A. van, 79
Rupp, G., 5, 39, 48, 55

Schaff, P., 79
Schleiermacher, F., 185
Schlink, E., 2, 65
Scott, C. A. Anderson, 192
Simeon, C., 122-3, 126
Simon, J. S., 221
Skydsgaard, K. E., 6, 31
Smith, C. Ryder, 210

Smith, K. L. Carrick, 165, 177, 180
Smyth, C., 123, 125
Smyth, John, 132, 155
Spalatin, 117
Spener, P. J., 207, 226, 240-1, 253
Stählin, W., 26
Staupitz, J. von, 11, 184, 226
Steele, Anne, 211
Strahan, R. H., 36
Stephen, J., 128
Sykes, N., 128, 131
Symonds, H. E., 22-4

Tawney, R. H., 151
Taylor, Bishop Jeremy, 23, 113
Taylor, V., 82, 192
Temple, Archbishop F., 215
Tertullian, xii, 33, 247
Thadden, R. von, 254
Thomas, Griffith, 219
Thornton, H., 128
Thornton, R., 128
Tillich, P., 255
Townsend, H., 38, 153-4
Townsend, W. J., and Workman, H. B., 198, 206, 217, 219, 230-1
Troeltsch, E., 122-3

Underhill, E., 156
Underwood, A. C., 158
Usteri and Vogelin, 79

Vassal-Phillips, O. R., 31-2
Vatja, V., 27, 48-50, 52-3, 64
Venn, H., 123
Vidler, A. R., 114

Ward, A. M., 252, 253-4

Warfield, B. B., 71
Warren, Max, 57
Watson, P. S., 28, 47, 96
Wesley, Charles, 26, 184, 188, 190, 198, 202, 205, 207-16, 235
Wesley, John, 122-4, 172, 183-98, 202-3, 206-7, 209, 217, 219-29, 240-1, 244, 253
   classes, on, 226-8, 231
   Christ, Priesthood of, 195-8
   Episcopé, 198
   experience, 183-9
   faith, 184, 189-95, 197
   fellowship, 229-30
   grace, 188-9
   Local Preachers, 220-3
   love, 232-6
   mission, 205
   righteousness, 191-2
   social Religion, 206
   succession, 198-200
Westphal, C., 79
Whale, J. S., 61-2, 123, 168, 201-2, 236
Whitfield, George, 230
Wilberforce, W., 128
Williams, D. D., 64
Wolsey, Cardinal, 92
Woodhouse, H. F., 91, 104
Woolf, B. L., 12-15, 17-21, 25, 29-30, 34-5, 38-9, 41-4, 47, 51-2, 54, 61-3, 236, 241
Workman, H. B., *see* Townsend, W. J.
Wyclif, John, 132, 151, 243
Wyon, O., 251

Zinzendorf, N. L., Graf von, 226-7, 253
Zwingli, U., 70, 79, 218

www.ingramcontent.com/pod-product-compliance
Lightning Source LLC
Chambersburg PA
CBHW071244230426
43668CB00011B/1585